Your Leadership Story

USE YOUR LIFE EXPERIENCE TO INFLUENCE AND INSPIRE

Deborah Henley

Vivacity Publishing
vivacitygroup.co.uk

First published in Great Britain 2018
by Vivacity Publishing (www.vivacitygroup.co.uk/publishing)

Others have had struggles that are greater or lesser than your own. What matters is not what these struggles were but how you faced them and the lessons you drew from them. When you share your story, you change lives. Especially your own.

I hope this book inspires you to do this.

Deborah Henley

'You may tell a tale that takes up residence in someone's soul, becomes their blood and self and purpose. That tale will move them and drive them and who knows what they might do because of it, because of your words. That is your role, your gift.'

Erin Morgenstern, *The Night Circus*

Contents

Stage 2 Uncover: Find your message and story

Stage 3 Craft: Write a compelling story

Stage 4 Deliver: Tell a powerful story

Stage 5 Evolve: Live a greater story every day

Foreword

The power of a well-told story is known to every successful speaker. The power of personal experience is impossible to over-estimate. Combining the two elements into your personal story creates something uniquely persuasive. This book will provide you with everything you need to create stories that will mesmerise, delight and hold spellbound any audience.

I've been telling stories on stage for over forty years. I rarely use a story that is outside my own experience, because I have learned the impact my own stories have. Your audience want to know who you are. Telling your story positions you as a real leader: someone who observes and finds their own insights in the world around them, and story also communicates your message more effectively than any other rhetorical device.

Deborah Henley has a unique talent for drawing such stories out, and helping people to deliver them in an engaging and entertaining way. I have seen her do it on stage many times, and I am delighted to see that she has now distilled her expertise into book form. You will learn the reasons why personal stories work. You will learn how to create stories that will fascinate and educate your audiences. You will learn the secrets of stunning delivery. This book will forever enhance your approach to storytelling and I think you will enjoy the process. Go on, tell your own leadership story. I wish you well, and thank Deborah for writing this superb book.

Alan Stevens *FPSA, PSAE, Global Speaking Fellow and Past President, Global Speakers Federation.*

April 2018

Introduction

MY STORY OF STORYTELLING

Grandmother's Footsteps

'Modern storytellers are the descendants of an immense and ancient community of holy people, troubadours, bards, griots, cantadoras, traveling poets, bums, hags and crazy people.'

Clarissa Pinkola Estés

My grandmother definitely wasn't a crazy person but she was a storyteller extraordinaire. When I was young, she'd come to stay. On golden evenings she would draw the curtains, tuck me in and sit on the edge of my bed to recount tales of Alice in Wonderland and Peter Pan. The strange and wonderful worlds and the characters within enthralled me, but the stories I loved the most were those of her own true adventures and travels.

She and my grandfather had lived in Lesotho, Swaziland and Zambia, where my grandfather was chief factory inspector. In England my grandmother had been a keen actress and had directed some plays; initially she wasn't sure what she would do in her life in Africa. She knew that there was a lot of poverty and many social and health problems related to lack of education but didn't know how she could help.

In the mountain villages of Lesotho she found something that ignited a spark in her. She saw people sharing knowledge and information through their stories. She saw how these stories resonated with the villagers, allowing them to see how they might apply changes to their own lives. Soon my grandmother was eliciting more stories and helping people share their tales and perform plays to help other villagers with their own knowledge and experience. I knew I wanted to do something similar one day; I dreamt of travelling the world helping facilitate stories and plays.

Many years later, I was working in the field of addiction recovery in the London Boroughs of Hounslow and Ealing. My approach, Expressive Therapy, helped my clients through metaphor and image work to understand their own underlying beliefs and values and to discover a renewed purpose and personal identity in order to change their lives. As well as facilitating these groups, I also trained coaches, counsellors and therapists to use my approach. I knew how powerful it was when people expressed their truth and shared their story. I witnessed and helped facilitate some incredible transformations. But, after five years working in the same windowless room, with its indelible stain on the carpet, and always a small group of people, I began to feel confined. When's my own life adventure going to begin? I felt I had people to reach around the world and I wanted to step up onto on a bigger stage. But I didn't know how to start.

Then, on 26 December 2004, the Indian Ocean Tsunami struck, devastating huge swathes of the Thai, Indian and Sri Lankan coastlines. It killed thousands of people and left millions destitute, without homes or a means to make a living. A few weeks later, when the world was still reeling, I was approached by Josep – a counsellor and Tamil leader based in London. He had recently attended a training I had given.

'I'm holding a Tsunami Conference for our community. The participants will be a mix of Tamil lawyers, teachers, cab drivers and shop

owners based in London who want to go out and do what they can to help ease the pain and make sense of things. I want you to explain how they can help their friends and relatives back home,' he said.

Josep explained that even though the world had mobilised quickly to make donations to the Sri Lankan government, much of the foreign aid and government help did not find its way through to the Tamils, because they had been fighting with the Sri Lankans. In fact, many Tamils were left without any help at all. As well as needing practical and financial support there was also a huge amount of restorative help required. People were still in shock – desperately trying to make sense of the disorder and the horrific losses they had faced.

'But Josep, why me? I have no experience of their lives or situation!' I said.

'Because you tell stories and storytelling is the Tamil way. Your stories help others express their deepest truth! Show us how to use these personal stories so we can help each other and heal together,' said Josep.

And so, at the Tsunami Conference in London, I spoke to the Tamil audience who were preparing to go out there, while Josep made a simultaneous translation. They could provide practical aid but were not equipped to help mend broken spirits and injured souls. I gave them some trauma approaches, but mostly I showed them how to elicit stories and metaphors that could transform both the teller and listener.

Some weeks later, when Josep and his group returned to London from Sri Lanka, I was eager to hear of their experience: 'The situation is terrible out there. Our families and friends have lost homes, loved ones and everything else, but, amidst the devastated buildings, smashed-up fishing boats and debris, we created gatherings to hear and share personal stories. People who had been left isolated in their suffering found ways to help one another and there is a sense they are pulling together now to heal and rebuild their lives. The shared stories created a new community spirit, a new energy that has helped people see their world in a new way – restoring a sense of hope that is instigating change.'

Suddenly something clicked for me. Josep's faith in the potential of personal stories and metaphors to effect a transformation made me realise that I had something to offer that was of value beyond the small groups with which I had been working. This was how I could help all kinds of people to connect and share their messages!

That's when I remembered the stories that my grandmother had told me, of the storytelling-people of Lesotho. Her love for stories, her understanding of their power to convey a message, and the way they build communities and create action, had all been carried within me through the years. Now, here I was fulfilling my dream to help others, in a land far from my own, spreading hope and change through the power of storytelling.

Since then, I have travelled all over the world leading workshops and seminars for global businesses such as AmEx, Accenture, Microsoft and PepsiCo. Whenever I share a story, I find people can always relate in some way. Maybe not to my actual experience but to the feelings of my experience, and I am transformed from the stranger in the room to someone people feel they know and are more likely to trust. That impact is universal. Whether those people are Emirati nationals in Abu Dhabi, Chinese workers in Liaoning Province, or an eclectic mix of Europeans at a meeting in mid-town Vienna, we find, through someone's story, how we are more similar than different. We all have our share of struggles, aspirations, disappointments and successes and can relate to others when we hear theirs. When we share our own story, we bring others along for the ride. I came to realise that an authentic leadership story is the wand that every leader needs if they want to create magic at the front of the room and influence, inspire and empower others with their message.

'The role of the storyteller is to awaken the storyteller in others.'
Jack Zipes

The Foundation

GET YOURSELF READY

Your truth and your experience

'Storytelling is the most powerful way to put ideas into the world.'

Robert McKee

When you stand at the front of the room, whether to make a farewell speech or head a boardroom table, you are leading. If you share tips on video or make presentations and pitches within your daily work then you are there to lead people's thoughts and actions and to leave them with a certain impression.

Your greatest asset as a leader, is yourself. Storytelling is how you can convert your experience and insights into something of value to your team, business or company. If you don't tell your story, who will know about the richness of your experience? How will you stand up for what you believe in? And how will you effectively lead others to help your cause or realise your goals?

Leaders do not make their mark by being cardboard cut-outs, following a script and simply going through the motions. In order to connect with people, it is essential that you bring your own personality and perspectives to work. That is why this book is not about just tools or about how to master public speaking or make presentations.

This book will help you to understand yourself as a leader and develop a communication based on your own personal experience, showing you how you can use it to influence and inspire others. You will connect and move your audience by showing your human side, someone who has faced and overcome dilemmas, challenges and setbacks. Instead of giving a wooden, starch-fronted presentation, this book will enable you to tell a human story that is you, that becomes you and that others remember you by.

It will enable you to define and develop your own leadership story and share your message in a way that has real impact, whether on stage, in meetings, pitches or presentations. By revealing more of your heart, and communicating its messages with clarity and presence, you will inspire and influence more people to follow your lead.

Your Leadership Story will help you to:

- connect and engage more quickly with people when you speak;
- develop trust and loyal business relationships;
- establish yourself as a leader with unique perspectives;
- tap into the diverse potential of all your followers;
- develop greater presence and enhance your reputation;
- help you to define your personal philosophy and motivations;
- gain others' support for you and your endeavours and initiatives;

- increase your ability to inspire and influence so you get more done with greater clout.

You can use this whether you are in a presentation to clients and colleagues, or carrying out coaching sessions with your team, because they will learn and engage more when you open up about your own experience.

Suggested way to use this book:

This book provides structured opportunities to reflect, stories to stimulate your thinking and exercises to provoke action. There will also be valuable tips and tools for standing up and delivering your story, so that you can confidently weave stories into your speeches and presentations and convey them with power and presence.

In order to build your Leadership Story, I will take you through a five-stage process that covers all you need to know to use your life experience to influence and inspire. You can dip in and out of each stage or follow it step-by-step to create a leadership story you can use to influence and inspire both others and yourself. These skills will be useful in both your presentations and speeches and your everyday interactions.

Stage 1 is all about understanding the power of storytelling and how to use your life experience for the most impact.

Stage 2 is all you need to know to prepare your story, from defining your message to uncovering your story.

Stage 3 is about how to craft your Leadership Story. You will also have begun to build a stock of powerful everyday stories that you can choose from and use for different situations.

Stage 4 teaches you how to deliver your story with confidence both on the stage and off, to connect with and more quickly and effectively engage your audience.

Stage 5 is about how to live your story day to day in a way that inspires and draws you towards a greater vision, so that you continue to influence and inspire.

Follow the five-stage process and you will have your core message and a leadership story that you will know how to deliver to the people around you in a way that will transform you and your business.

Download your free workbook here so that you can work through the process step by step and I can support you on the way: www.vivacitygroup.co.uk/YLSworkbook

So let's begin your journey ...

Does a personal story work in a professional context?

> *'The most powerful person in the world is the storyteller. The storyteller sets the vision, values and agenda of an entire generation that is to come.'*
>
> Steve Jobs

I have worked with leaders for many years as a speaker, facilitator and coach and have heard a lot of speeches. Some are slick and confident while others are nervous and uncertain. But what I have discovered is that even the most polished deliveries do not always land – while others that are raw and timid may take us by surprise, having a profound effect and leaving a lasting impression.

One of my defining moments as a story coach was at a conference for senior civil servants at the Ministry of Defence. We sat in a huge metallic hangar where arches soared overhead and tanks and other military ephemera were dotted around. It was an army museum but we weren't there to explore the artefacts. My role was to coach this delegation of senior civil servants and decorated military personnel on their own leadership speeches – which they were refining to deliver later to their own cohorts.

Many of the delegates were brilliant public speakers in the technical sense: they spoke with confidence, assurance and eloquence. They gave all the facts, covered what they needed to say. Yet something was missing. Their speeches failed to really convince or rouse any real response. They didn't get you in the gut.

Then James stood up to speak. His role involved resourcing and equipping the troops. Prior to the event, he had felt nervous about speaking to his more senior colleagues so we worked together on his speech:

'Crouching for endless hours in the dust behind the walls of a destroyed fort while the mauves, scarlets and oranges hung in the Afghan sky, our sunset watches had become a sort of meditation. Sometimes, in a quiet lull, there would be birdsong or a sudden crack of a gun. A random shout or the distant thud of a bomb, the hum of a vehicle driving through the dust. But on this evening it was different. Suddenly there was a mad shouting and a staccato of bullets. All hell broke loose and we entered the chaos of theatre. Cries, bloodshed, blind scrambling in the dust as we moved to take cover. Then, the shocking realisation of fatal wounding of a close companion and just as suddenly, silence. As quickly as it started, it was over. All was still and we were left to wrestle quietly with our doubts and fears for the rest of the night.

'Alone with one or two others in an unmarked outpost, that first night became an echo of future nights. All we knew was that we were entirely reliant on each other and our communication and survival equipment. And just one thing pulled me through. Knowing I was part of the finest military establishment in the world. It would hold us. I could trust it

to make the right decisions and to give me the resource that I needed. I trusted it with my life.

'So remember what your day-to-day decisions really mean. Each decision, great and small, is the entire world of each soldier. They are putting their trust in you to equip, resource and support them, and they are putting their lives in your hands. Be sure you are worthy of that trust.'

The audience of James's peers and seniors sat and held their breath for a moment then erupted into loud applause. I took the microphone back from James – 'Wow! Thank you, James!' Then to the audience I said, 'Imagine if James had just said, "Make sure you make good decisions, because you know the ramifications of your actions are huge." What was different about James's speech?'

Then a former general spoke up from the corner: 'James did something that all the rest of us did not. He spoke about his personal experience and in a personal way. We got a glimpse of the human being beneath the words and that was motivating and inspiring.'

It wasn't more polish that was needed in the other speeches. It was rawness and vulnerability. A willingness to show up as the human being he was. James had not just given us a Leadership Speech but his Leadership Story. Without his story, he would have got his point across but it would not have inspired or moved people in the same way.

A fix for nervous speakers

Even the most nervous of speakers can deliver a successful speech that will quickly engage people and move them to action when they know how to share the right information with purpose. Getting personal does not mean sharing all your private experiences, but being open and courageous enough to share what has made you into the person you are today. What is more important is that it is delivered in a natural style with a genuine voice.

That is why, if you lack confidence or experience in public speaking, what I present in this book is a great antidote. You don't have to be a 'great public speaker' in any technical sense to land a great talk. Sure, it helps, but the blood and guts of it – what really connects – is that you are genuine and you share the essential elements. You just need to understand how to craft your own story and know when and how to use it.

The work I did that day at the Ministry of Defence, forms the foundation of this book. We explored how each leader could show more of themselves by using their own stories and anecdotes to get their message across. We looked at how they could do this in a way that was elegant, authentic and in alignment with their objectives as a leader. The transformation was startling. When they spoke again, a little more from the heart and using the power of story to convey their message, it was obvious the audience were more engaged, connected and inspired. I realised this is something I can teach other leaders to do in order to make a huge difference to their work and in their lives.

Why telling your story is a core leadership competency

'Stories are the single most powerful weapon in a leader's arsenal.'

Howard Gardner, Harvard University

It's no longer a secret that stories are the most effective and powerful strategy to get a message across in a way that really gets through to others. It's also the best way to quickly engage your audience and develop a trusting relationship with them.

Leading-edge global organisations like GE, Goldman Sachs and HSBC understand that storytelling is a core leadership capability and so provide their leaders with storytelling skills as a central part of their leadership curricula. Entrepreneurs and millennials also use the power of story in everything they do, from leveraging opportunities and standing up to speak at networking events to creating YouTube empires with millions of followers.

Your Leadership Story explains and demonstrates how you can use story in your own leadership. This book draws upon my work with hundreds of groups in corporate organisations around the world, helping leaders and managers develop their natural presence, their personal brand and their ability to influence and inspire with authenticity.

Stories help to initiate projects, mobilise people, attain far-reaching goals, and achieve many of the other things a leader is called upon to do. Telling stories will help you to motivate, inform, persuade, engage, inspire or even placate the people you hope to influence.

The simple act of sharing an honest story helps you to connect and build trust with your audience because it demonstrates that you:

- Have the courage to tell your story and be visible;
- Possess the strength and conviction to state who you are and what you stand for;
- Have a clear vision to share and inspire;
- Value what it means to be human and imperfect;
- Are willing to admit to mistakes and learn and grow from them.

All of these things are part of what it takes to be a great leader. And it is only by telling your story that your audience can get to grips with what it is that you do differently and uniquely. Richard Branson's success (I know he is often referenced but bear with me, this is worth it) is based on his willingness – from the outset – to just be himself: to do things his way and to tell that story. It worked and has continued to work for him.

When you create a leadership story, you have something powerful in your store that will serve you throughout your leadership and your life: whenever you stand up to make a speech, give a presentation or run a meeting in any context or setting of life and work.

> *'Today everyone, whether they know it or not, is in the emotional transportation business. More and more, success is won by creating compelling stories that have the power to move people to action.'*
>
> Peter Guber

Do I have a Leadership Story?

'"Everyone tells a story about themselves inside their own head. Always. All the time. That story makes you what you are. We build ourselves out of that story.'

Patrick Rothfuss, *The Name of the Wind*

By its very definition, leading is not following. It is about forging your own path and inspiring the loyalty and motivation in others to take them with you somewhere new: a place they may not have arrived at without your leadership.

Whether or not you have some great, dramatic story to tell is not so relevant as the lessons you learned. The story just needs to contain some essential elements for it to swing.

You may not think you have a story but in revealing your personality you will find that you do. The truth is, everyone does. You are built out of your story. Perhaps yours may not appear to be full of swashbuckling high drama. Mine neither. Well, mine has a little bit of swashbuckling, but that's by the by. But what makes a story powerful is, in part, recognising how the experiences you did have shaped you into becoming the unique human being that you are. No two stories are alike because our lives and the lessons we have drawn from them have all been so vastly different. What is humdrum to you might hold something exotic and unique to others, or else something in your experience may be so universal that everyone can relate to it but no-one will have related in quite the way you did. Your story might show them how to relate to their own experience in a new and empowering way. That's leadership.

I will help you to understand what is interesting about you and the journey you have been on, and what it is about your leadership approach that is different. You'll learn how to develop communications based on your own personal experience, and how you can use it to influence and inspire others.

With a well-developed leadership story you will connect and move your audience by showing your human side, that of someone who has faced and overcome dilemmas, challenges and setbacks. It's what you have learnt from these experiences that is so valuable to others. You will define and develop your leadership story and share your message in a way that has real impact. By revealing more of yourself, and learning to communicate your messages with clarity and presence, you will connect more powerfully with others whether on stage, in meetings or at presentations. This will engage people to follow your lead.

As a result, you will develop a strong and engaging leadership story that inspires purpose and self-confidence in you, and it will enable you to inform, engage or inspire your audience. Sharing it will become second nature to you and you will feel good about telling your story as you increase your impact and influence exponentially.

Getting started – the Five Stages of Your Leadership Story

'People think that stories are shaped by people. In fact it's the other way round.'

Terry Pratchett

STAGE 1 ACKNOWLEDGE: RECOGNISE THE POTENTIAL OF YOUR STORY

Stories give colour and life to communications that would otherwise be dull and flat. They connect us as human beings and they have the power to make information more easily understood, and more memorable than bullet points and bare facts alone. When we use our own stories, it takes this a stage further. They instantly enable us to connect with people because we show them something of who we are.

I'll share the latest neuroscience that shows how stories move us in a way that is now proven by scientific evidence, evidence that shows what happens in our brains when we hear a story and how stories enhance communications to more quickly build trust and engagement.

I will ask you to consider your own presentation situations and when and how you can use your stories to best achieve your outcomes. You'll learn about the Seven Cs of leadership storytelling to enhance your connection to your audience, how stories help build your credibility, create context, gain co-operation and collaboration, convince, catalyse action and cultivate a community.

STAGE 2 UNCOVER: FIND YOUR MESSAGE AND STORY

Before moving on to craft your story in Stage 3, Stage 2 is about finding and knowing the message you want to communicate. I will show you how to find your key messages and stories, as well as how to find pivotal moments within these stories, so that you can be equipped and ready to use them before any talk or presentation. We'll also look at the importance of vulnerability, and when personal stories get too personal.

STAGE 3 CRAFT: WRITE A COMPELLING STORY

You might choose to develop just one leadership story as your signature story that you evolve over time. Or you might have a number of leadership stories linked to different messages and audiences. Either way, you can draw out shorter tales to use in your daily working life. Because not every life or business situation requires our whole story, we often need short 'everyday' stories or snippets.

You'll learn the key questions your audience ask themselves before you even open your mouth, and the Essential Elements that your story must contain so that it has the desired impact. And you'll learn how to develop and use this story to entrance and enthrall people on a larger scale.

STAGE 4 DELIVER: TELL A POWERFUL STORY

Stage 4 is about getting on your feet and telling your story, on stage or from the front of the room, and enhancing your delivery style and stagecraft. You'll learn how to read your audience and communicate in response to the real-time feedback you are getting in the room.

Now you have your story, you will discover how to enchant your audience in the telling of it. You will learn what you need to prepare before you share your story, how to connect from the stage, how to navigate through your story, use your voice and body language in the most effective way and how to use the platform to plot out your story to create a living, visceral experience for others.

You will be encouraged to practise so that you build a range of story responses to different scenarios. You will have an opportunity to try out some techniques for using your story as a part of your longer presentations and speeches as well as how you can tell your story 'on the fly' in impromptu encounters. You will also be equipped with how to cope when the unexpected happens and you need to ad lib.

STAGE 5 EVOLVE: LIVE A GREATER STORY EVERY DAY

In Stages 1–4 you will have learnt about the power of story, when and how to use it, how to find and write your leadership story, and how to tell it to others in order to influence and inspire them. Stage 5 looks at the story that you actually live and embody day to day, so that you continue to build the Seven Cs with your audience and live the most powerful version of you.

As you become conscious of the story you tell yourself about who you are, you will be encouraged to give yourself credit for all you have achieved and have the potential to still achieve. There are times when we limit or restrict ourselves through the story we tell about who we are. I conclude the book with a call to liberate yourself from any past limiting stories and develop a greater story that recognises you and the potential of who you can become.

We'll look at how you can continue to share your journey – your successes and your vulnerabilities – with those around you. In doing so and living your story authentically, you will empower others too. Share the value of story with others and invite them to craft and tell their own stories to benefit from the process.

Stage 5 is about living a story that expands your sense of self and increases the impact you make on the lives of others day to day.

Download your free workbook here so that you can work through the process step by step and I can support you on the way: www.vivacitygroup.co.uk/YLSworkbook

STAGE 1

Acknowledge:

Recognise the potential of your story

CHAPTER 1

The power of stories to change minds

'We are, as a species, addicted to story. Even when the body goes to sleep, the mind stays up all night, telling itself stories.'

Jonathan Gottschall, *The Storytelling Animal*

Research* at the University of California shows that a list of bullet-point facts has far less impact than the same information told in story form. Graesser and his colleagues found facts in story form were remembered twice as well despite being read twice as fast as the encyclopaedic ones. Presumably they were read faster because people were more engaged.

---

* 1980 Graesser, A. C., K. Hauft-Smith, A. D. Cohen and L. D. Pyles (1980). 'Advanced outlines, familiarity, text genre, and retention of prose.' Journal of Experimental Education 48: 209–220.

Stories are everywhere

You are about seven years old and the teacher announces: 'Story-time!' You race like a mad thing to plant yourself cross-legged on the floor by the teacher's chair. You sit there, rolling white cotton socks excitedly up and down your leg, waiting for her to get started. Then she begins, all fidgeting stops and you are transfixed. You enter the world of dragons, flying carpets and talking animals.

It's a familiar experience. The people and stories alter but this scene is one that is recognisable all over the world and throughout the ages. Stories are everywhere. The magic of story draws us in, and then transports us to other worlds, keeping its grip on us, even as we grow older. The form might change, maybe into a novel, a film or a drama, or even to gossip at work the morning after an office party. No matter our age or background, colour, creed or religion, as human beings we still find stories irresistible.

Why are stories so irresistible? It is like a compulsion for us to know what happens next, whatever the context. From the cliffhanger in a courtroom drama, to the news item about a missing child, our curiosity is aroused and we are hooked until we find out the ending.

All tribes use stories to share their beliefs, their customs, their history and their knowledge; the Aboriginals of Australia have Dreamtime, which are stories to describe the creation of the world and laws of existence; the Masai of Africa share stories of struggle and victory over animals and other tribes they meet in battle. A Masai boy does not become a man until he lives out his own story by defeating a lion. Only then does he earn the right to tell his story and share his knowledge.

Stories show us how to make meaning of the world from an early age. We think in narratives all day long. Jeremy Hsu, writing in the *Scientific American*, found that 'personal stories and gossip make up 65 per cent of our adult conversations'. They give us a shared context and help us to make sense of ourselves in our environment.

In our society, working in organisations, encountering thousands of people in our lifetime, you might say that a person does not become a real leader until he or she has defined their own message and has the courage to tell their own story.

How stories change our brains

The neuroscience

Narration is as much part of human nature as breath and the circulation of the blood. Modernist literature tried to do away with storytelling, which it thought was vulgar, replacing it with flashbacks, epiphanies, streams of consciousness. But storytelling is intrinsic to biological time, which we cannot escape.

A. S. Byatt

We know that stories are powerful vehicles for conveying information and engaging an audience, but now we have the scientific evidence to back this up.

Not only is there a substantial body of psychological studies that demonstrate the difference storytelling can make, but with the development of brain scanning equipment such as PET (Positron Emission Tomography) scans, we can now actually see and track the difference stories make. These scans show how stories fire up associations and patterns in our brains by creating neural pathways and altering our biochemistry. Stories literally shape our thinking and change our minds.

When we hear information conveyed as bullet points and bare facts alone, the only parts of our brain that light up are Broca's and Wernicke's areas. Two small parts of the brain responsible for language processing. But, when given information within the context of a story, many other parts of the brain are activated. For example, if someone tells us about a delicious meal, our sensory cortex lights up. If they tell us about the physical effort of climbing up a steep rocky path, then the motor cortex, responsible for motion, lights up. The advantage of this is that when we engage more of the brain, the information has more impact and becomes more memorable.

Stories are a whole-brain activity

Our brain is clearly divided into two cortices. There is a big overlap between the functions of the cortices but broadly, the left is connected to the right side of the body and is more associated with rational, logical thought. The right side is connected to the left part of the body and is associated with creativity and free thought. Stories, however, engage our whole brain and so activate both the emotional, spiritual, philosophical hemisphere and the logical, rational, sequence-driven side.

Neuroscientist Jill Bolte Taylor's TED talk is an amazing account of living through a stroke which temporarily disabled the left side of her brain. The way she experienced the world during that time is remarkable. She had no concept of time or of language, but she was lucid and aware of what was happening, though almost as an observer. She sensed the greater power of her consciousness and could see the bigger picture of who she was and what was possible for her on the planet in a far greater way. Now, fully recovered and as a neuroscientist, she is delighted to have had a ringside seat in her own stroke and to have been able to observe it from the inside.

Jill concludes that as humans, we have two cognitive minds, *'And we have the power to choose, moment by moment, who and how we want to be in the world. Right here, right now, I can step into the consciousness of my right hemisphere, where we are. I am the life-force power of the universe. I am the life-force power of the 50 trillion beautiful molecular geniuses that make up my form, at one with all that is. Or, I can choose to step into the consciousness of my left hemisphere, where I become a single individual, a solid. Separate from the flow, separate from you. I am Dr Jill Bolte Taylor: intellectual, neuroanatomist. These are the "we" inside of me. Which would you choose? Which do you choose?'*

Storytelling enables us to choose and access both simultaneously.

Mirror neurons

Although there has been some debate around the validity of the idea of mirror neurons, it is worth mentioning an experiment carried out by Uri Hasson at Princeton. He wired up a speaker and the listeners' brains to track their responses and he found something extraordinary:

> *'When the volunteers heard the woman speaker's story, their brains synchronised with hers. When she had activity in her insula – the emotional brain region – the listeners did too. When the speaker's frontal cortex lit up, so did the listeners'. By simply telling a story, the woman could plant ideas, thoughts and emotions into the listeners' brains.'*

If mirror neurons exist, and it's still early days in the research, we actually get a simulated experience of someone else's story in our own minds. Our neural pathways mirror those of the storyteller so that we get to re-experience something they are experiencing first hand when recounting the story.

Stories help us remember things by creating an emotional response

In his book *Brain Rules*, molecular biologist John Medina explains: 'When the brain detects an emotionally charged event, the amygdala releases dopamine into the system. Because dopamine greatly aids memory and information processing, you could say it creates a Post-it note that reads, "Remember this."'

In fact, stories appear to be the most powerful vehicle for changing people's minds in all senses. As Jonathan Gottschall, author of *The Storytelling Animal*, says:

> 'Until recently we've only been able to speculate about story's persuasive effects. But over the last several decades, psychology has begun a serious study of how story affects the human mind. Results repeatedly show that our attitudes, fears, hopes, and values are strongly influenced by story. In fact, fiction seems to be more effective at changing beliefs than writing that is specifically designed to persuade through argument and evidence.'

Perhaps I should have written this book as a story rather than a non-fiction book!

What are stories for?

We have seen the power of stories to change our minds and, with recent discoveries in neuroscience, such as the discovery of neuroplasticity, we've seen how they can change our actual physical brains too. But why do they have such a profound effect on us? What evolutionary purpose could it serve?

My belief is that stories have a powerful evolutionary purpose – helping us to rapidly learn through experiencing more situations than we would ever have the time and capability to live through in just one lifetime. We can't possibly live through all the variations of human experience. However, by hearing stories and dreaming up different situations, we give ourselves an opportunity to imagine what we would do in multiple situations, so that, when we actually face a new situation, we should be better equipped to deal with it.

The Holodeck in *Star Trek* is used as a training ground for the crew of the Starship Enterprise. It is a place where people can go to have a virtual experience of almost any activity. Experiencing a story, one in which we are truly engaged, is as good as being on the Holodeck. We get the same neurotransmitter release and the same stimulation in our brain not by going through the real experience itself, but just by reading about it, watching a film or hearing a story.

When we know how other people have dealt with a situation, it provides a kind of roadmap for us should we encounter something similar.

It is for this reason that we are such voracious consumers of stories, whether in the form of shared anecdotes, books or films. In whatever way we consume them, stories give us the quickest and easiest way to live many lives and gain the wisdom of many experiences in one short go.

REFLECTION:

In the next chapter, we will look at the role of stories in our everyday lives. Allow yourself to notice just how stories surround you in your daily life. They are, no doubt, having their neuro-chemical effect on your brain! Pay attention to the stories you are hearing and telling – and what their purpose and impact might be.

It certainly makes me pause for thought before I subject myself to too many disheartening or adrenaline-inducing stories such as the repetitive cycle of horrifying news on TV.

CHAPTER 2

How stories are used in our everyday lives

'Stories are memory aids, instruction manuals and moral compasses.'

Aleks Krotoski

Stories are used in a variety of ways in our everyday lives to help us understand the world around us, including:

1. Bringing things to life – and making them more memorable;
2. Giving context to the present and insight into the future;
3. Uniting people and tribes and giving a sense of belonging;
4. Breaking down prejudice and helping us understand others;
5. Showing us how to deal with adversity;
6. Helping us to communicate difficult messages.

1. Stories bring things to life – even the dead – and make them more memorable

'If history were taught in the form of stories, it would never be forgotten.'

Rudyard Kipling

When I was eleven years old, Mr Walsh, my history teacher, gave us a sheet of paper with two columns of dates, and told us to learn them. It seemed an almost impossiblc task: it was a meaningless list of words and numbers. But he told us that by the end of the year, we would know this list inside out. At first, we didn't believe him, but Mr Walsh did something magical. Through stories he brought those events to life and gave them meaning.

We listened to stories about the typical day of a Roman soldier in 44 BC when Julius Caesar was assassinated, the realities of trench warfare in the 1914–18 war and Sir Christopher Wren's bold designs for St Paul's Cathedral in 1666. I still remember its Latin epithet today: 'Si monument requiris, circumspece' – 'If you are looking for his monument, look all around you'. St Paul's was significant as the tallest and most majestic building in London.

The Plague of 1665 was brought to life with a story about Molly, a seamstress, who worked all day on Petticoat Lane. At night, she returned to her dying husband and mopped his brow, not knowing how else to alleviate the dreaded Plague. When he died, she had to draw a big black cross on her draughty little wooden door to await the call of the cart, loaded to the brim with corpses and the famous shout of 'Bring out your dead!'. I could imagine the sordid, cobble-stoned streets, the gutters overflowing with rats and filth. As if that wasn't enough, in the following year, the Great Fire swept through the streets. wreaking devastation and demolishing her home. The more personal the stories, the more compelling they became, and now those dates are etched in my mind.

I still recall that the list started with the first Roman invasion of Britain in 55 BC and took us all the way up to 1979, when Margaret Thatcher became the first British woman Prime Minister. By telling stories about people and places we could imagine, Mr Walsh gave the list context and it was no longer difficult to remember the dates.

The science bears this out. Stanford professors Gordon Bower and Michael Clark* compared how many words are recalled when embedded in stories versus on a random list. Two groups of students were asked to memorise groups of ten words. The group who constructed a story showed six or seven times more recall than the group that did not. A huge difference.

2. Stories give insight into the future

"The narrative impulse is always with us; we couldn't imagine ourselves through a day without it."

Robert Coover

When we are being interviewed for a new role, a common question we are asked is how we dealt with challenges in our past. We tell stories about what we have done, and this demonstrates how we think and how we relate to our fellow workers. We are asked this because our stories of the past allow the interviewer to see more of how we might react to similar situations in the future.

---

* Bower, G. H. and M. C. Clark (1969). 'Narrative stories as mediators for serial learning.' Psychonomic Science 14: 181–182.

We can also tell stories to ourselves in order to create the future we want. We can imagine who we want to become as a leader or how we want to respond to various situations.

I interviewed for a job role once that would required me to do things that I had never done before. I would not have got through the first round had they asked me solely about my past. However, in each of the three interviews, their focus was on how I would solve the problems they already had. I was able to supply ideas and approaches that they had not tried before. I drew on stories from my very different background to validate my experience, but with a focus on how it might apply in their context in the future. I won the role. What they needed was new thinking - they had people to execute in abundance.

Successful leaders, athletes and competitors in all spheres use what you could call 'future' stories to visualise their success. Shaun White, one of the world's greatest snow-boarders, was interviewed after wowing the world on the halfpipe at the Vancouver Olympics. He won gold by showing off some extraordinary new tricks, never seen before, culminating in his dangerous, spiralling Double McTwist 1260 in his victory lap.

'How did you do it?' asked the interviewer.

'Visualisation is a huge part of my game. Nobody can ever do a new move, can ever do anything really, without visualising it first.'

How this works is that when we visualise a scenario, our brain can't distinguish whether the story happened in the past or may yet happen in the future, or indeed if it has happened at all. It feels real to us, which means that a story increases our potential to influence our own future and create our own opportunities. As we have discovered through neuroscience, stories act like a rehearsal for the brain so that we can then follow through in mind and body.

3. Stories unite tribes and show us we belong

'The story is one of the basic tools invented by the human mind, for the purpose of understanding. There have been great societies that did not use the wheel, but there have been no societies that did not tell stories.'

Ursula K. Le Guin

From football fans to ancient groups, stories unite tribes. They provide codes of behaviour, and insight into what matters to that group as well as how to belong to that group. We learn who we are because of the stories our family, society and culture tell us. Our identity is formed through an integration of all the stories around us.

In an environment in which we are overwhelmed by information and choice, our group story can act as a guide. It influences our behaviour and our decision-making processes, from how we structure our day, where we live, who we choose as friends, how we spend our leisure time to what products we buy and consume. A group story shapes our identity.

The power of story is well recognised and used in the advertising industry for brand marketing. Most cars will get you from A to B. So how do you choose? Volvo tells a story of families getting there safely and securely, while Porsche says a 911 will get you there in style. James Bond created an incredibly seductive story around Aston Martin. I defy any man to drive one without feeling that a little bit of James Bond's debonair style has rubbed off on him.

One of my favourite pastimes is sailing. Like all sports, it comes with its own brands that we wear to show we belong. As a teenager, I had a pair of soft red sailing wellies for wet weather but they were getting leaky. I noticed that the best sailors had some very cool leather boots that not only seemed to keep their feet warm and dry but also looked great. These Dubarry boots were way out of my pocket-money price league and I coveted them for a couple of years until my father gave me a left one for my birthday and the right for Christmas. My feet have never felt cold or wet since. But more importantly, wearing them gave me confidence that I truly belonged, a real sailor. I had the story in my mind that the best sailors wear Dubarry boots. And that's how brands and brand stories get us.

4. Stories help us understand one another and increase empathy

'It has been said that next to hunger and thirst, our most basic human need is for storytelling.'

Khalil Gibran

Facing increasing hazards in our daily lives, both social and political, we have more need than ever for stories. To survive and thrive in modern times, we need to learn how to get along with all manner of people as we negotiate our way through our careers. We also need to understand other people and that they might behave differently from us for perfectly good reasons.

We learn from news stories how to think about our world – whose side we are on, who the goodies and the baddies are. But news outlets are selective about the facts they choose to report on and their interpretation of those facts.

Now, in the Trump era of Fake News, we find ourselves in filter bubbles that reinforce our own viewpoint. Social media's algorithms, the people we speak to and the papers we read, all reinforce our narrowing perspectives. It is more important than ever that we tell and hear stories that surprise and expand our viewpoint to pop these filter bubbles.

There are promising examples of a softening of racism and prejudice by encouraging people to identify with each other through story.

Faisal Rashid, former mayor and now the Member of Parliament for Warrington South, in the UK, invites people from the Muslim, Christian and Hindu faiths to share their stories, together with people in the transgender community, 'We won't change the world, we can just bring together our communities in unity,' he says.

When we hear a story, we identify with its characters. People find they can relate to someone they thought was fundamentally different from them.

If you want people to understand a different perspective, tell a human story.

5. Stories show us how to deal with adversity

> *'It is important for all of us to keep feeding ourselves stories of people overcoming obstacles on their way to success, so we realise that – because we're all part of the human family — we can do the same.'*
>
> David Lee

Why are we so fascinated by stories of overcoming adversity? The answer is that they are a dress rehearsal for how to live our own lives in case we are faced with similar devastating experiences ourselves. Stories need a real struggle, not a facile one. Someone unexpectedly succeeds or fails.

An account of a successful guy creating another successful business is not a story. But nor is an account of an unsuccessful one failing. If the adversity is so unrelentingly difficult that there is no resolution, redemption or insight and the struggle continues without end, it can be just as unsatisfactory as an easy story about an obvious success.

It is especially convincing if it is a true story. Danny Boyle's film *127 Hours* is the true story of a climber whose arm becomes trapped by a boulder in a slot canyon in Utah. There is no way out and nobody to help him. He literally gets stuck between a rock and a hard place. As he gradually becomes weaker and more dehydrated, he realises that the only way to escape with his life is to cut his own arm off. We watch fascinated as he evaluates his limited options until he arrives at the almost unthinkable. It's between losing his arm or losing his life. We are gripped because we wonder what we would do in the same situation. Could we bring ourselves to do what he did? How would we cope?

A story is really a metaphor for a piece of human experience. It usually pits someone in a position of challenge or difficulty and then tells us how the situation is resolved or otherwise. Our minds are engaged when there is a problem to be solved. A great story has to demand something of us. We ask ourselves, what would I have done in that situation? We actually learn about ourselves and we learn strategies and approaches that might help us in future.

In the terrible Grenfell Tower inferno in London in June 2017, one story comes to mind that offered some small redemption amongst the greater horror. That of a child who was thrown to safety from a tenth-floor window and survived. It makes us wonder how desperate the parent must have been who threw down that child? What would you do? What would I do?

6. Stories can help us to convey a difficult message

'Think of story as a mnemonic device for complex ideas.'

Annette Simmons

When I practised as a psychotherapist, I was asked by a colleague to help a client, a young boy who refused to go to school. The boy complained of various stomach upsets, nausea or headaches, although numerous tests revealed that he was in good health, and so his GP concluded that something else was going on. The boy wouldn't answer direct questions about what was wrong; perhaps he didn't know the answer. Knowing that I used art, drawing and other expressive forms, therapeutically, to facilitate change in a non-confronting way, my colleague thought I could help.

It emerged through the boy's drawings that he didn't have a fear of going to school, he was not bullied, he liked his teacher, he was happy to do games. In fact, once he got to school he was fine. The problem was leaving his mother behind at home. He felt guilty about leaving her because, as he left for school, she would tell him how much she missed him all day. The boy worried about his mother and so chose to stay at home rather than have to deal with her anxieties every time he went off to school.

One evening, as I was pondering on what to do to help, I happened to see a documentary about a man who had rescued a baby bear cub from the wild. The cub would not have survived alone, and so the man bottle-fed the animal and taught him to play and climb logs and trees. As the bear got bigger, the man built a large enclosure and tried to teach the bear to hunt and catch mice and rabbits. The bear grew up quickly, and the man took the bear out into the wilds and let him explore, climb and forage. As the walks became longer and longer, so the bear travelled further and further afield. Then, one day, the bear did not come back. The man had tears in his eyes.

'I'm so proud, this means that my little cub has finally grown into a bear and has learnt how to fend for himself. This is the day that I have been aiming for all along. I didn't want him to become dependent on me or on other human beings. I'm happy because I have successfully reared him to go back to the wild where he belongs. It's difficult but the greatest gift I can give him is to let him go.'

The next day was my final session with the boy. At the end, I met his mother and I told her the story of the bear. I told her that there was nothing wrong with her son from a psychological perspective. And that his time away at school was the next important stage of his development. Allowing him to discover more of the world outside the home was the best way for him to grow into the man she wanted him to be. Like the man who raised the bear, she could feel proud that she was raising a happy, confident boy.

REFLECTION:

In this chapter, we have looked at the role of stories in our everyday lives, but now let's focus in on stories from a leadership perspective. When and how can you use the power of story and storytelling in a work context in a conscious and well-thought-out way?

This would be a good time to begin thinking about and listing the various presentation situations that you find yourself in, as well as the opportunities you could create to stand at the front of the room. Make a list of all of these scenarios and, in the next chapter, you will discover when and how you can use your own stories in some of these different contexts.

CHAPTER 3

When and how to use your story – the Seven Cs

'Those who tell stories, rule the world.'

Hopi proverb

We have looked at the role stories play in our everyday lives. And considered the power they have to unite, engage and educate people. Now it's your turn. It is time to consider how you can use stories within your own leadership communications to inspire, influence and motivate your audience.

The Seven Cs

The Seven Cs show us when and how you can use stories as a leader. They are incredibly powerful for creating these valuable influencing traits:

1. Connection
2. Credibility
3. Context
4. Conviction
5. Collaboration
6. Catalysation
7. Community

You can either use all the Seven Cs as a step-by-step structure, as I show in the example below, or else focus on just one or two of these Seven Cs and build a story to create that result. It depends on your context and what you aim to achieve within the course of your meeting, pitch or presentation.

Here is an example from a speech made by Adam, a managing director in a large bank. He is speaking at an in-house Diversity and Inclusion (D&I) event.

Adam's Diversity and Inclusion speech

'Good morning, everyone. Are you wondering what a white, middle-aged man is doing talking to you about Diversity and Inclusion? It's a good question worth considering.

Connection

'As some of you may have spotted, I have a slight Welsh lilt to my tone. I am indeed from a small village near Swansea. What they say about Wales is true. There isn't much there other than sheep, rugby players and the chug of smoke from the nearby factory sprawl of Port Talbot. So what could I possibly know about D&I? There isn't much diversity in sheep.

'But I'm stereotyping here. The fact is, there is lots of diversity in sheep although they seem to be indistinguishable from the

flock. Stereotypes are everywhere. Some of them are true and some of them aren't. But D&I isn't about whether or not you fit a stereotype. You may do so or you may not. Be what you are! It's not about making yourself conform or adapt to unreasonable lengths - suppressing and denying yourself. It's about being included for whoever you are. I know about that – both being included and not being included for who I am.

Credibility

'Soon after I graduated, and got my accountancy accreditation, I was interviewed at Hambros – one of the traditional old city banks founded by the Hambro family 150 years earlier and run by Sir Chips Keswick. Here I met a few more stereotypes. The place was staffed by Old Etonians and Harrovians who acquired their roles through the old boy network and treated it like a gentlemen's club. I turned up with my state school education and a Welsh accent – I didn't fit the typical mould but the interviewer saw something within me and I was hired.

Context

'Organisations that are very mono-culture are shown to be more likely to fail because they fall prey to one style of thinking, which becomes imbalanced. It is not agile and able to evolve and respond to the changing environment. Study after study show boards operate more effectively where there is a diverse group of members with diverse personalities, perspectives and styles. Teams collaborate better and cultures are richer as a result.

'I was lucky, the man who hired me was also not typical of the bank. An East End boy who was now in a senior management position, he saw and did things differently. He saw that I had that same hunger and he encouraged me to trust my instinct. I worked hard and my career advanced.

'Like him, I too was different. I laughed along at their Welsh taunts. I didn't really mind if they called me "Taff" or "Sheep-shagger". I just thought, "Is that the best you can do?" I was given a fair opportunity, and I made it work for me.

Conviction

'Where did this hunger in me come from? The village I grew up in was not known for being diverse. All the other children at my school came from backgrounds similar to my own – hard-working people making a decent but modest living. There was no range of ethnic, gender or religious backgrounds.

But I was lucky. There was someone who showed me that beyond our Welsh village, there was a rich and diverse world out there: my godfather, Islwyn, and his long-term partner, Steve, an art dealer. Islwyn grew up a few doors down from my mother. He was 'the only gay in the village' and now he had become a successful antiques dealer.

We would visit his home in London and meet people from all over the world. I sat next to the curator of the Tutankhamun Exhibition at a dinner party once. It opened my eyes and made me realise that there are many ways to live your life. It awoke an ambition in me to live a different life. I also saw the value of diversity to enrich any group, business or community.

Collaboration

'This is also true in the workplace. If we are to benefit as an organisation and individually, we need to include people of all colours, creeds and persuasions.

'I think it is important to be proud of who you are, but a sense of humour might be helpful from time to time. I do fit some stereotypes. I am very proud of being Welsh, I do like rugby ... and I quite like sheep ...

'I am also very much in support of a rich and diverse society. I wouldn't want everyone to be like me!

'I believe that we need to understand and respect the different needs of our colleagues so that we can all benefit from each other as we accommodate physical disabilities, parenting or care obligations or mental health issues.

Catalysation

'Let's allow everyone to be who they are and respect that. Recognise how hugely valuable it is to have that diversity and make everyone feel they belong. Encourage, support and respect your colleagues to be the diverse people they are and ensure that they feel included, even if that means finding other ways to bond: lunches rather than dinners if you have parents that need to get back for childcare, avoiding team drinks if you have non-drinkers; consider community service activities as an alternative. Sure, talk about mutual interests within the team, but be aware of what is alienating and what is inclusive. If everyone is talking football, or fashion or whatever it is, then the one or two people who aren't into it may feel left out. It's about having awareness, curiosity and preparedness to adapt a bit to make others feel comfortable with who you are and with who they are.

'I invite you to have a think about your own story – who you are, where you come from, how and where you fit the 'mould' and where you don't. If you feel comfortable about it, let people know who you are. The more we share our diversity and make it OK to have a range of people, not just OK but positively beneficial, the more it can thrive.

Community

'We are all part of this organisation. We all have a role to play. You can be proud that you were hired because of what you have to offer. Offer it in your own unique way, be proud to be you and be proud to be a vital part of this organisation. Together, as champions of D&I, we can help create a culture that is richer, more effective, more

enjoyable to be part of than it ever was before. As a result, we'll be able to better recruit and retain more people from all kinds of backgrounds, attract a greater range of clients and provide a day-to-day environment in which we can all thrive.'

When and how you can use the Seven Cs

We will now go into the Seven Cs in more detail. For each of the Seven Cs, I offer suggestions and approaches to help you apply it directly to a presentation that is coming up for you. As we go through them, think about what you might say to evoke that C.

Here are some pointers to help you:

- Who is your audience?
- What is your aim for the presentation?
- Will you use all of the Seven Cs or focus on one or two?
- What stories do you have that work with your chosen Cs?
- Do you need to find additional stories?

The First C: Connection

Use a story to show: I am human and vulnerable just like you.

It's important you connect with your audience if you are to influence or inspire them. If your audience relate to you, you will draw them in. Let them get to know you and how you got to where you are today. Your story will inspire trust and empathy.

Introducing your talk with bare facts is all well and good – it may convince the logical mind – but it takes a story or anecdote to build connection.

When I speak on Leadership Influence, I break the ice with a little story:

My first attempt at influencing was a complete disaster; I was about eight years old, sitting at the Formica kitchen table on a small white stool. It was my father's turn to cook.

The problem was that my father had a limited culinary repertoire. In fact, I can only ever remember him cooking one dish – scrambled eggs. While he busied himself getting eggs and milk out of the fridge, all I could think was, 'How am I going to get out of having his scrambled eggs?'

Finally I hit upon an ingenious tactic.

'Dad, is it scrambled eggs again?'

'Yes.'

'Well the thing is ... um ... I don't like yellow food.'

'No problem ...' he replied, without batting an eyelid. A few moments later a plate was put in front of me with a big pile scrambled eggs. Only instead of a fluffy yellow mound, it was bright pink.

'What's this?!'

'Pink scrambled eggs! You said that you don't like yellow food so I added red food-colouring. Eat up!'

This story gets a bit of a laugh at my own expense, which shows me to be real and human. Having connected, I can go on to the content of the talk:

> *So you see, my early attempts at influencing others weren't always that successful, but I have since grown up and researched and discovered some tips and techniques which I have found far more effective, and these I will share with you now.*

Try this:

When you introduce yourself at the beginning of a talk, share a bit of your personal story. Perhaps one that shows the person you were before you became the person you are today. Find a starting point to which others can relate. Perhaps reveal your human vulnerabilities too so that you show yourself to be as human as they are. Everyone has been a child or had their first day at work, so go back to a time before you were the person you are today, showing yourself to be vulnerable.

The Second C: Credibility

Use a story to show: I have relevant knowledge and experience

Having connected with your audience, you can now drop in an anecdote or story that reveals how you learnt something about the topic or message you are communicating. This establishes your credibility far more effectively than reeling off a list of credentials.

I learnt the value of embedding my credentials into a story when leading a workshop at Cisco a few years ago. During the introduction, I put up a slide stating the other big organisations I had worked with, rather than telling a story.

Max had shown himself to be a very intelligent, competent and amiable participant throughout the course. He came up to me at the end and said, 'That was excellent. However, you know, you really didn't need to put that slide up listing your credentials! You established credibility from the moment you walked to the front of the room and started speaking. I knew it was going to be a worthwhile workshop because of how you talked about the outcomes as well as your relaxed manner and connection with the audience. But when you put up that slide, I found myself losing a bit of rapport.' I realised then that I had been 'trying too hard' and it had backfired.

After that I took the approach of gently dropping in anecdotes and stories that show I have the requisite experience rather than just listing my achievements. This was far more effective.

If you are the person who came first in the country in your professional accountancy exams, the youngest sales director in your organisation's history or if you have climbed Mount Kilimanjaro, then far better to lightly slip it into a story than become heavy-handed by saying it outright. Indeed, those kind of explicit attempts to build credibility can actually have the opposite effect, putting people off and reducing your credibility in their eyes.

In the above is an example of a story used both to make the point and to establish my own credibility. I showed that I have led senior groups in blue chip organisations like Cisco by folding details into a story that was making a point. For extra Brownie points, my story also has the Connection factor, when I shared a bit of my human fallibility.

Try this:

Show how you have earned the right to make the point because of your own experience. Embed it in a story or anecdote that supports your message. You can do this by mentioning something, en passant, that makes the point, like how you were part of a winning team, or achieved something significant or helped someone else to success.

The Third C: Context

Use a story to show: how a message or idea fits into the wider picture

So you've made a connection and gained credibility with your audience. Now it is time to position your information in their minds. Information and facts without context lack meaning for your audience.

When Steve Jobs launched the iPad in 2009 there had already been eight tablets since 1993 that had flopped. Undaunted, Jobs put up a slide, not of the iPad, but of an iPhone on the left and a MacBook on the right. There was a gap in the middle. He told his audience that what the world needed was a device that combined the best of both, that was 'more intimate than a laptop, and so much more capable than a smartphone'.

The iPad was revealed as the obvious missing link to Apple customers who had an iPhone but wanted a bigger screen and had a laptop but needed something more portable. Built around multimedia and made with the high level of Apple design style, the iPad became the essential next purchase.

Seth Godin said, 'Invent stuff worth talking about and tell stories about what you've invented.' Steve Jobs was a master at both. If you want your innovation, idea or project to be noticed, position it in people's minds by telling a story about how it came to be, why you thought it was needed or how people can benefit from it.

Stories can also be used to give context to bad news. Don't just give people the bare facts – help them see things from your perspective to understand your motivations. Contrast the following messages about having to lay people off to see how story can help.

The statement: *We at Delish Ice Cream Company are cutting staff due to market conditions. This will mean some employees will be laid off, for which we are sorry.*

The story: *When Hamish and I founded Delish in our farm kitchen twenty years ago, we relied on the local dairy farms for their cream and milk and for local people as our workforce. Some of you have been with us from the start and remember that kitchen table! We grew steadily, thanks to you and the delicious product we produced. Now our biggest local supplier, Meadow Flower Farms, has closed down and we cannot continue as we are. We are in the position of either closing down ourselves or going on with a skeleton crew. This will, regrettably, mean job losses for many of you until we find another supplier. Once we have the need to re-hire people you will be first on the list.*

The first scenario is a bit cold-hearted. The second shows there is genuine care for their workforce. The message is unpalatable either way, but the story shows they are doing the best they can in a difficult situation and their actions are more understandable.

Try this:

Provide context and meaning by showing how and why the information you seek to share is relevant to your audience and where it fits in their world. If you are introducing a new concept, use a story to give people something to which they can relate this new idea. If you are sharing bad news, use a story to help them understand the situation.

The Fourth C: Conviction

Use a story to: convince others why this path is worth taking or a viewpoint worth believing

Conviction can be won through both hearts and minds. People need to understand the motivation behind our message at both a rational and an emotional level. Since story touches both, it is an excellent device for achieving this purpose. Share your own experience. Stories encapsulate our thoughts and actions in a way to which others can relate. They help build belief and trust in who you are and what you stand for. Sir Bob Geldof convinced the top pop stars of his day to perform free at the first Live Aid concert in 1985, after seeing a news story of starving Ethiopian children. The power of his conviction, and the story behind it, led to millions being raised globally and a meaningful change made in Ethiopia. Geldof instigated a worldwide movement of fund raising activities that continue to this day. Once your audience share your conviction, they are more likely to support your cause. We can use stories as proof of our message, to convince people our idea can be done, or is worth doing, in the future.

Stories can be incredibly persuasive. Christopher Vogler, author of *The Writer's Journey*, tells how in a court of law the jury are more likely to believe a witness or a defendant if they follow a story arc in their account. We understand *why* someone has done something, not just *what* they have done, and so we are more likely to view their actions favourably and give them the benefit of the doubt.

A well-told story contains a cohesive narrative. The information slots into place and one fact flows from the next. Stories have cause-and-effect logic that our mind craves. The narrative sits better with us than a bunch of unrelated facts, so we are more likely to believe and be influenced by it.

In contrast, when there's no logical sequence, questions arise in our minds. We try to connect the dots, and if we can't, then we feel dubious about what we are hearing. We wonder what is being hidden. It is not surprising that many liars are great storytellers. They instinctively know that gaps between facts are what make people suspicious.

Try this:

Share case studies and examples to show what others have achieved in similar circumstances. Use stories to provide a precedent or example or tell the story of why something matters so much to you. Don't leave gaps for people to guess at.

When people see things from your perspective, they are more likely to be on side, to share your hopes and dreams and to want to help you to achieve them – whether that is saving the world or adopting a new system to a tight deadline.

Don't be afraid to reveal your own passion or share why and how you are so convinced and energised by an idea. Use the power of your own convictions – along with story examples as evidence.

The Fifth C: Collaboration

Use story to show: We are a team – we are all in this together. The whole is greater than the sum of the parts. Get involved!

Whether you have a mammoth world-changing mission that you want people to join, or you are pitching to sell an idea to a prospective customer, or you're simply aiming to influence team members to work better together, then a story can be your greatest tool to move people from 'you and them' to 'we' and stimulate action.

How? Let them feel they are part of your message and your mission. When your mission becomes a collective mission, people are more likely to co-operate and join your cause. They have walked in your shoes and so are more likely to walk further along the road with you.

The great orators knew this well. With any movement that seeks to recruit people's hearts and minds towards achieving its objective, it helps people to feel that they are part of something greater.

It is no mistake that the American constitution begins, 'We the people ...', a phrase Barack Obama used in his inaugural speech five times. He also peppered the word 'we' throughout the speech no less than 100 times.

And who can forget Churchill's galvanising Second World War speech – which gave the British people a sense of belonging and boosted their resolve to pull together in the fight?

> *'We shall defend our island, whatever the cost may be. We shall fight on the beaches, we shall fight on the landing grounds, we shall fight in the fields and in the streets, we shall fight in the hills; we shall never surrender.'*

People fear collaboration because they fear that there is a smaller and smaller slice of the pie when more get involved, but the reality is that the pie gets bigger and multiplies in size the more people work together to add to the activity.

Try this:

Put people on side with you and with each other. You want them to be motivated towards the same end goals and all feel they belong and that their contribution matters.

Inspire them with an engaging vision of what it will look like when, together, you have achieved that goal. You might include stories of previous things people have accomplished when they have pulled together. Show how everyone will benefit by becoming part of something greater. Let them know that the whole is greater than the sum of the parts. You can do this by instilling pride in what they can potentially achieve together and give ideas on how they can take part. Give your audience a sense of belonging, and of being part of something greater than themselves.

The Sixth C: Catalysation

Use story to: motivate people to act

Stories cause us to act because of their ability to inspire us to think about what's possible. One day, an eight-year-old boy opened up the newspaper and read the story of Jesse Martin, who had just sailed non-stop round the world, becoming the youngest person to do so at age eighteen. It ignited a spark in the young boy, who decided there and then that he was going to do the same thing. For the next ten years, Michael Perham developed his skills and experience as a yachtsman. He campaigned hard to raise the funds he needed and on 16 November 2008, after 244 days at sea, he sailed back into the Hamble, having completed his own single-handed, non-stop circumnavigation. He was just seventeen years old and the world's youngest person to do so.

Why is it that Jamaica produces so many excellent sprinters? After all, there are plenty of people all over the world who are physiologically matched. It's not as if they have superior training environments either. And what about Kenyan and Ethiopian runners winning long-distance races again and again? People talk about the high altitudes, but that does not explain the marked differences in their performance compared to other nations' athletes.

It's because they hear a story of someone just like them, from a similar background and believe: if they can do it so can I!

American footballer Bo Eason has written and performed a one-man play off Broadway. 'Runt of the Litter' tells the story of the pivotal moment when he committed himself to the task of becoming the first person from his school ever to play in the NFL despite his small size. He succeeded against the odds. Although he was the first ever, he was soon joined in the elite ranks by three or four others from his school. It was as if he opened a door. They knew Bo's story, just as the Kenyan and Jamaican athletes knew about their compatriots, people with whom they can identify, and those schoolboys realised what they could achieve.

Deborah Small, a Wharton marketing professor at the University of Pennsylvania, along with two of her colleagues, conducted a study which found that when raising money for a charitable cause, it is far better to appeal using story not statistics. Save the Children's experience bears this out. They released two fundraising apps, one with information and facts and the other with a story about a young girl in need of food and support. Those watching the girl's story gave twice as much as those who had seen facts alone. Story can be a significant catalyst for action. Not just on day-to-day tasks but in how we approach our whole lives. Stories inspire new possibilities for us.

Try this:

Towards the end of your story you may choose either to leave your call to action open and let your story inspire them to respond in whatever way they naturally would, or else to try prompting people to apply it to their own lives with a question such as 'You might not be a sailor but what might you do if you dedicated yourself to your own big goal for the next ten years?' Or let's say you share the story of a workplace disagreement that you managed – you might ask them a direct question that is related, such as, 'I've shared the story of how I managed conflict – what would you do in a similar situation?'

The Seventh C: Community

Use story to: cultivate a community spirit and create a tribe.

A story unites people. It can make us feel we belong, whether we become part of the group because of a shared story that emerges out of a challenge or one built on a shared mission and vision.

It might be that the story of an ill friend leads to a fundraising mission for a group to climb the Five Peaks; or a work group is thrown together for a key project with tight timelines and, through working together, become bonded. Their story can be used to create a new team spirit, enrol others or reinforce their own community.

In the 90s, most people saw themselves as either a Mac or a PC person. It was an identity thing. But in 1997, Apple was losing market share and needed to reverse the downhill spiral, so they launched their new campaign to entice more people to identify with their brand. They showed photos of great thinkers such as Einstein, with the words 'Think Different' underneath. Alongside, they published this ingenious manifesto:

Here's to the crazy ones,
the misfits,
the rebels.
The trouble-makers,
the round pegs in the square holes.
The ones who see things differently.
They're not fond of rules and they have no respect for the status quo.
You can quote them, disagree with them, glorify or vilify them.
About the only thing you can't do is ignore them ...
because they change things, they push the human race forward.
While some may see them as 'the crazy ones',
we see genius.
Because the people who are crazy enough to think they can change the world –
are the ones who do.

Now, all kinds of people identify with Apple because of this clever communication campaign and Apple products can be found in almost everybody's home. Maybe, ironically, most of us are the same in wanting to think differently. Apple have tapped into a latent desire in many of us to be creative, non-conformist and original.

Try this:

Create your manifesto for your people with the qualities to which you aspire. Find stories from your own life that explain why this is so important to you, as well as stories of how you or others have behaved that demonstrate these qualities. Be inclusive in your language: 'Anyone here would have done the same in this situation, it's how we do things.' Highlight what you have in common. Your aim is to create a sense of pride in being part of the group. Give people a story to guide them. One that says 'here's how we think, what we believe, what we value and how we behave.'

If you are someone who likes to think differently, to define your own reality and to make sense of your own experience, if you would like to share your insights in a way that inspires others to a greater experience of life, then welcome to this – the tribe of storytellers.

STAGE 2

Uncover:

Find your message and story

CHAPTER 4

What if I don't have a story?

'A lost coin is found by means of a candle; the deepest truth is found by means of a simple story.'

Anthony de Mello

In Stage 1, you discovered why and how storytelling is so powerful as a leadership tool. You learnt about the various ways stories can be used to have a profound effect on your audience, and the Seven Cs showed you how to use stories within your own context and what to do to amplify your purpose.

In Stage 2, you will prepare and find your own leadership story or stories. In addition to your signature story, from which you can draw or adapt depending on your purpose, it is also a good idea to build up a portfolio of your own anecdotes to meet the different needs and circumstances of your leadership. You may already have identified some stories and anecdotes prompted by the Seven Cs or else you've identified gaps where it would be useful to have a story or two to support your purpose and message.

The aim of this chapter is to help you clarify your purpose further and prepare you to communicate your message most effectively with the life experience that you have.

Get Inspired

Before getting into some practical work, let's consider some well-known people who use their own story to powerful effect. All these people share their fears and vulnerabilities in order to convey a greater message. If you have time now to watch a few of the talks from these speakers, it may help to inspire you in working on your own story.

Sheryl Sandberg is the COO of Facebook and the founder of Leanin.org. She used her story as a mother and worker to give women a message to 'Lean In' and take their place at the boardroom table. She urged them to stand up, speak out and be counted in the workplace. Her aim was to encourage women to take up leadership roles and not let societal and personal barriers stop them. Her story was about how she didn't let motherhood stop her continuing her own career trajectory despite the challenges and doubts that it brought her personally.

What is interesting is that Sandberg's story changed dramatically on 1 May 2015, when her husband, Dave Goldberg, died unexpectedly. She now tells a new story to provide another message about overcoming adversity, which goes with her second book, *Option B*. The message is one of hope and resilience – about how to cope when things don't go the way you expected and planned. What to do when 'Option A' is not available.

The first time she tells her new story is at the UC Berkeley Commencement Address. She talks about how the depths of grief and loss can take your breath away but that what she learns from death is, 'When life sucks you under, you can kick against the bottom and breathe again. I learnt in the face of the void, in the face of any challenge, you can choose joy and meaning.' What gives that message power and resonance is that she prefaces it with her personal story. See it here: https://www.youtube.com/watch?v=iqm-XEqpayc

Dan Pink is an author and speaker on work, management and behavioural science. He was chief speechwriter to Vice-President Al Gore. He uses the story of his background in his speech about motivation and how we run our businesses: 'I need to make a confession at the outset here – a little over twenty years ago I did something I regret. Something I'm not particularly proud of ... in the late 1980s in a moment of youthful indiscretion I went to law school ... I graduated in the part of my class that made the top 90 per cent possible.' This both establishes his Credibility and Connection (two of the Seven Cs) with his audience in a humorous, self-effacing way. See it here: https://www.youtube.com/watch?v=rrkrvAUbU9Y

J.K. Rowling, whose Harry Potter series became the best-selling books in history, has a 'rags to riches' story. She prevailed through her struggle as a single parent who had recently been bereaved of her own mother. In five years she went from living off social benefits to becoming a millionaire. What is most compelling about her, is the transformation of her life. The backstory of struggle alone is not significant until it is contrasted to her later success. In 2007, she was named *Time*'s Woman of the Year, and has received many other accolades, including an OBE. Her past is well known, but what makes it not just a compelling story but a Leadership Story is that it contains a message or gift for others. In her Harvard Commencement Address in

June 2008, she uses it to convey messages of persistence and achievement, along with the fringe benefits of failure. See it here: https://www.youtube.com/watch?v=wHGqp8lz36c

Howard Schultz took on Starbucks as the CEO when it was just a small enterprise. He is now dubbed one of the inventors of coffee in America. His message is about the importance of community and belonging. He grew up in the Projects of Brooklyn in the early 60s. Life was hard in the outside world, but within the Projects there was a deep understanding of community and belonging. As a young man in his first job at Xerox he felt something was missing in the workplace. Later on a trip to Italy he saw how people hung out together in coffee houses. It was an important part of the culture there, and provided the missing link. He saw how he could create a similar culture in the United States, by creating places that foster community and belonging, through coffee. He tells his story at the London Business Forum. See it here: https://www.youtube.com/watch?v=83yInyY1KLs

Elizabeth Gilbert is the bestselling author of *Eat Pray Love*. She uses her story to talk about the challenge of following up after a big success. She calls her book 'a freakish success' and notes how, as a result, anything she does next is likely to be perceived as a failure. She says, 'It's exceedingly likely that my best success is behind me.' Her message is about the vagaries and elusiveness of the creative muse – and how to continue on anyway despite the prevailing notion that artistry has to lead to anguish. She is on a mission to approach creativity differently. Not as the dark path of misery often followed by creative people. Instead she suggests we adopt the ancient idea of a genius that is separate from the self, so that if we fail it is no more our fault than if we are successful. See it here: https://www.youtube.com/watch?v=86x-u-tz0MA

In another TED talk, she uses her own story to give an honest, self-deprecating account of 'how creativity can survive its own success', and the lessons she has drawn from this experience. See it here: https://www.youtube.com/watch?v=_waBFUg_oT8. In both cases she is using the same story of success then failure, but to convey two different messages.

Steve Jobs – the late co-founder and CEO of Apple – used the story of his cancer for his message on 'how to live before you die' in his Stanford University Commencement Address. The outrageous success he has achieved against the humanising challenge of a life-threatening illness gives his message weight and impact. His message is about making the most of life and not being afraid to follow your own passion and 'make your own dent in the Universe'. We need to feel our own vulnerability if we are to be moved and to relate to the storyteller. See it here: https://www.youtube.com/watch?v=UF8uR6Z6KLc

Quick-fire Prep Process: the KFDs and your Key Message

Now it's your turn to prepare for a talk. Here is a quick-fire way you can prepare before any talk or meeting, if you haven't got time to go through the Seven Cs. This should be done before choosing what your story is or how you tell it. Here's how it worked for Alec:

Alec runs the European arm of a global estate management company. He frequently speaks to his two hundred-plus staff members, sometimes off the cuff and sometimes in a prepared presentation. He felt he wasn't making the impact that he wanted and was failing to connect with some key members of his team. He wanted to raise his game. The first tip I gave him was to always find his KFDs first.

'What are they?" he asked. 'How about Kentucky Fried ... uh ... Dromedaries?'

'Good guess, but try: Know Feel Do.

Ask yourself before your speak, what do you want people to:

Know?
Feel?
Do?'

A year later Alec tells me that he still uses his KFDs before every meeting, presentation or impromptu talk. He feels ready for anything. He also has the confidence to know that his focus is on what is most important, that he will stay on track while he is speaking and that he will have the impact he desires by winning both hearts and minds.

Once you have clarity about what you want your audience to Know, Feel and Do, you can easily find your **Key Message** because it is often a summary of all three KFDs.

Your key message will help you and your audience focus on the purpose of the talk. It is the overarching message that you want to communicate, boiled down into a phrase or sentence.

If you don't know why you are telling your story, or what your Key Message or point is, then you may find people will switch off. Ideally, if someone were to ask an audience member, 'What was that talk about?' they would answer with your key message.

It guides you not just in your talk but in selecting the right story and anecdotes to use.

Here is Alec's example:

What is his aim?

His aim was to give his workforce a kick in the behind and improve their working practices. In particular, he wanted them to stop holding and guarding information individually; instead, to share information so as not to embarrass the organisation by approaching the same client another team member had already approached.

K I asked him what he wanted people to **know** as a result of his talk:
'that if they communicate between one another we will all do better.'

F What did he want them to **feel?**:
'engaged by the idea of sharing, feeling a greater sense of teamwork and collaboration.' <indent>

D What did he want them to **do?**:
His first answer was *'to share more'*.

I asked him to get specific and think of examples of what 'share more' looks like in his environment. He recalled a time when, after every client meeting, as soon as they were in a taxi on their way back to the office, his colleagues would send out a quick message to all relevant people with an update on what had been discussed. That meant others approaching that same client would avoid doubling up or being at cross-purposes.

His **Key Message** was:

'When you work together and share information more readily, you will benefit individually and as a team.'

Once he'd defined his key message to himself, Alec was able to immediately find a story from his own experience to communicate his message.

Here's another example of my own:

Before writing this book, I worked out my own KFDs. They are:

Know – I want you to know that stories can be transformational, for both the storyteller and the listener. They elevate communication to something powerful, enabling you to connect and move your audience in a way you cannot with bare facts alone.

Feel – I want you to feel inspired and excited by the idea of telling stories and to feel motivated to use storytelling in your own context.

Do – I want you to excavate your own past for stories and use them to bring your day-to-day communications to life.

The **Key message** is, and I have included part of it in the subtitle:

'As a leader, the most powerful way to influence and inspire is to share your stories from your life experience.'

Try this:

Grab a notepad and think about one of your upcoming presentations. Write down the aim of the talk and then ask yourself:

KNOW
What do I want people to know?
Why do I want them to know that?

In the business world, you might think at first glance that what you want your audience to know is the information you plan to give them. But this is lazy thinking; it is too broad and generic. Would you rather your audience sits there trying to sift through your talk for the point you are trying to make? Or would you prefer them to be clear about your key message because you know what it is and haven't obscured it with extra information? Obviously the latter.

Firstly, if you want your talk to sparkle then you must tell them something that they don't already know, or you must provide a new angle or new way of looking at something that they do know.

Secondly, when sharing a plethora of facts and figures, what is the driving point that you are making with all this information? Ask yourself, 'What would I like them to know that they don't already know? If there was just one thing I wanted them to know, what would it be?'

FEEL

How do I want them to feel as a result of listening to my story – about themselves, about the topic and about the action they might take?

This one often gets scrimped on. It seems unimportant at first glance. Yet the feelings your story evokes are the most important thing. All salespeople know that people buy with their hearts first, then rationalise their decision with their heads. The same goes for a story: people will buy it, be moved by it, feel the magic with their hearts, and then remember the facts of the storyline. The feelings you evoke are both the glue of a story and the magic within it. Your communication will be most successful if it touches people and makes them feel something different after you tell your story; whether that feeling is surprise, anger, excitement, disgust or relief.

DO
Now it's time for action!
What do you want people to do, as a result of listening to your story?

You might want them to do something specific, like, for example, write a letter on behalf of prisoners of war or enrol in a new initiative. Or you might want to them to do something more general, such as feel re-engaged with a long project.

Your KEY MESSAGE
The KFDs can then be summarised as a key message. *What is the distillation of your KFDs in just a sentence or phrase?*

Make this key message your own touchstone. Keep coming back to it, either in your own mind or perhaps as a repeated refrain in your talk. Just as Barack Obama repeatedly used the phrase 'Yes we can!' in his primaries.

How to Find a Story

> *'Do not despise the story. A lost gold coin is found by means of a penny candle; the deepest truth is found by means of a simple story.'*
>
> Anthony de Mello

How do you find a story? The best tip here is to do what all great comedians do: carry a small notebook to record stories and incidents as they occur or as you recall them. Then you will have a ready source from which to draw inspiration. The more you get used to telling stories to convey your message, the more new stories will appear. There are two related approaches you can use to find the right story to use in your leadership.

Approach One: Key Message first

Start with your KFDs and your Key Message, and use this to find the right story to illustrate your point. You will find that you can use the same story or life experience to illustrate a number of different points.

Here are some questions to ask yourself to find a story from your key message:

Why is this message important for me personally?

What specific examples do I have of this working really well?

What experience do I have of this not working, as a counter-example or insight?

Approach Two: Life experience first

Think of an experience you have had that had some kind of impact on you – then draw from it what you learnt or what it made you reflect upon.

It could be a significant moment in your life; an emotional one, a dramatic one or something that surprised or shocked you. What was the pivotal moment in which your view changed or you learnt something new?

It could be the moment you were offered a new role, lost your job, won an accolade, lost a client, made a big mistake, decided on a new lifestyle or had to let someone go.

To make it even more relevant, think about your audience and find a story to which they can relate. Let's say you are speaking to a group of new recruits to your organisation – is there a story from your time as a new recruit that you can use? Or perhaps you could use a more universal experience, such as a story about your travel to work. Most people can relate to commuter stories.

Here are some questions to ask in order to find a key message from your story:

What did this significant moment make me realise or understand?

What did it teach me?

How did this experience change what I do now?

Build your portfolio

You can use these stories and anecdotes, alongside their associated key messages, to enliven all your communications. You will end up with a portfolio of incidents and experiences to draw upon, as well as a list of key messages that you plan to convey. Some stories can apply to a number of different messages, just as some messages apply to a few different stories.

Try this:

In your notebook, record any experiences that have had an emotional impact on you or are remarkable in some way. They might offer up messages later on. When you use your own stories with purpose, you will find they will focus and enliven all your communications, whether ad hoc conversations or prepared presentations and speeches.

CHAPTER 5

Getting Personal and the Power of Vulnerability

'The shortest distance between a human being and truth is a story.'

Anthony de Mello

Tell your *own* personal story

Your Leadership Story is about what your message means to you and how you came to realise it. If, for example, your message is that friends are important, then find a time and an experience in your life that taught you the deep value of friendship.

Your own story is a powerful vehicle for conveying your message. Your Leadership Story is not one that you have lifted from someone else or read in a book. If you want your core message to have real impact then reveal something about your life.

If you are just treading on someone else's tracks and recounting their story, your message is weakened. Alan Stevens, the former president of the Global Speakers Federation, told a story about how he had been working in a family-owned pub in his youth when he served a drink to David Bowie. A few years later, he was travelling in Australia when he heard someone else, another speaker, recounting this very story as if it were his own!

Although it may be tempting to make another's story your own, it lacks integrity. As a leader, you lead the way and show people new pathways to follow. So tell your own stories! They have far more life and spirit to them, because they are connected to you and your heart. And because of this, they will touch other's hearts too. This is the power of vulnerability.

What if your experience feels too personal?

It can be very exposing to tell a personal story and reveal the time when you were lost, afraid, ill equipped or behaved stupidly or badly. Revealing these moments of weakness, doubt or failure can make you feel vulnerable. But, when you share the hard road you have travelled and reveal your struggles, your audience are right with you when it comes to your moment of success. Your story brings your message to life because it enables people to relive your experience and therefore how you came to understand your message.

Often the events in your story start at a time before you understood your core message. Perhaps you were lost and floundering. Then, as the events in the story unfold, you reveal how you gained insights, found your way through and eventually discovered your message.

It takes courage to be visible but if you are prepared to be visible you will engage and inspire others. Show yourself as the human, vulnerable creature you are and they will relate to you.

You may feel that you don't want to expose such personal moments to your audience. Trust this instinct and only share what feels appropriate however you may be surprised at how powerful some personal revelations can be. It can really give your message teeth! At this stage, don't worry too much. You can decide what you actually choose to share later. Just take a look at all the material from which you might draw your story.

If you find that you fail to connect with your audience, something else is going on. You may have become bored by your story or message. It just doesn't inspire you any longer and the passion is no longer palpable. You've grown out of it, and you are now just going through the motions when you speak about it.

The three types of personal stories people tell - and which ones to avoid

In my work, I have heard many leadership stories. They range from the inspirational and life-affirming to the self-pitying and over-emotional to the arrogant and boastful.

Overall, I have realised that personal stories fall into three broad categories:

The 'Open Wound' story

This is a story in which the storyteller exposes their vulnerability. Having said what I did above about the importance of vulnerability, some personal stories are not ready to become inspirational leadership stories. They do not have a resolution.

Perhaps the speaker might talk about being unfairly made redundant and it is evident that the pain or anger still smarts or they might talk about a bereavement that still comes across as too raw. They haven't yet come to terms with it. The Open Wound story needs time to heal before it is ready to be shared in a way that will inspire others.

Although the challenges you have faced and overcome are the grit that can become your pearls of wisdom, they first need you to find and feel congruent about the redemptive message or insight. Exploring an Open Wound story can be a powerful first step, but it is not recommended as a Leadership Story until you are in control of it.

The 'Scratched Record' story

The Scratched Record story is outdated or it might simply not be true for you any more. Perhaps it used to engage your audience but it has been performed so often that it has lost all emotional resonance. I've heard many speakers trot out the same story again and again until it has lost all life and energy.

The Scratched Record story can also be a 'going through the motions' one in which the storyteller is stuck in the past – wishing something were different back then. If you were bullied at school or didn't get that promotion, for example, you can't change that past but you can change the meaning you take from it as your current life evolves. Either stop telling that story altogether or start telling a different story about it from a new angle. Keep it fresh and alive and connected to your present reality through the message you convey. Does the message, if it even contains one, still make you feel passionate and excited?

As soon a story gets boring for you to tell then it's even worse for the listener to hear. If this is the case, it is likely you have a Scratched Record story on your hands.

The 'Inspirational' story

Finally, we have the Inspirational story. This is the type of story you aim to tell as your Leadership Story and what this book is designed to help you achieve. It is told for others' benefit, yet the telling of it also benefits the storyteller. It is told to share the gift of an insight gained through challenge and triumph. The storyteller shares their moments of vulnerability and weakness yet feels empowered by doing so because they see how it was all valuable experience. Most importantly, the story engages and empowers others too.

The events of the past cannot be altered. The story we tell about them can.

Richard McCann is a hugely successful motivational speaker who has spoken to thousands of live audiences around the world. He has had a devastating past and his story could easily be an Open Wound story or a Scratched Record story if it wasn't for the way he delivers it and the message he imparts. The Yorkshire Ripper murdered his mother a week before Richard's sixth birthday. He had a tough start, going into care and getting into drugs before ending up in prison. He could have stayed stuck in the past with his story controlling him but instead he is in control of his story and what it means.

Of course, he had to go through a period of experiencing the story as an Open Wound until it healed. Today, he shares his message of overcoming adversity with humour and joy because that is how he now lives.

Despite telling the same story again and again, he is always present in the moment. Richard told me that what keeps his story alive for him, and engaging for his audience, is that he is there to serve them. He turns his life experiences into messages from which everyone can benefit. And he embellishes his story with connections to what is going on now in his life – the facts of his story don't change but the meaning he derives from them is always evolving and kept alive.

You can see his TEDx SevenOaks talk here:
https://www.youtube.com/watch?v=c7Mvjj8xxPo

How to transform your personal experience into an Inspirational story

'From my perspective as a depth psychologist, I see that those who have a connection with story are in better shape and have a better prognosis than those to whom story must be introduced.'

James Hillman

James Hillman's observation echoed what I found myself in my work as a psychotherapist. I heard many stories in the privacy of my consultation room. Sometimes it was the first time someone had ever told of an experience, perhaps of a traumatic event or about something of which they were ashamed. It was not told for my benefit but for their own. My role was to listen without judgement and help them find their own meaning in it. By shaping it as a story, they seemed to break through to a new understanding.

At other times, people would give an account of their past in an emotionally detached way. It seemed to have been told hundreds of time before, and they had got locked into it as a sort of dogmatic truth about who they were, with underlying convictions such as 'I'll always be a victim' or 'I've never been lucky and never will be – see, here's the proof.' Although they seemed emotionally disconnected from the past, their interpretation of it coloured everything in their present.

Of course, neither the Open Wound nor Scratched Record stories are appropriate or effective as Inspirational Stories. But they can be healed and perhaps transformed into Inspirational Leadership Stories. Here's how:

Transforming your Open Wound story

If you feel your story is possibly still an Open Wound, then do find a way to tell the story to the right person – or write it in a journal – and look for the insights. It can be cathartic to release a story that has been pent up inside you. Get it off your chest, gain perspective and make sense of the experience. It can also remove a lot of shame, blame or guilt. The right listener can help you explore your feelings and thoughts related to the experience, which might one day become incredibly inspirational for others.

If it is unresolved, it may still be seeping out of you in the way you think and behave, so it is worth healing anyway. Find the silver lining to your black cloud. When you can do this, you will find the cloud will lift for you and your story will now serve others to enable their own black clouds to lift. Find the redemptive message in your story. When your Open Wound has healed over, you will have the foundation of an enthralling Leadership Story.

Transforming your Scratched Record story

In a way, this is the opposite to an Open Wound story. The storyteller is almost hiding and detaching rather than exposing anything of their true selves. The story can almost sound boastful; 'I drank three bottles of vodka before breakfast at my worst!' as if it were a badge of honour—proof they've had a difficult time. Sometimes people cover an Open Wound with a Scratched Record story. They become nervous of feeling the real feelings beneath the story because they are still so sensitive. It is difficult to show vulnerability if you are still in pain or feeling anger or bitterness.

If the story sounds hollow, or it fails to touch and move people, it may be because you are not connected and present in the telling of the story because underneath it is still raw or it may be that there is no relevant gift for others. In Stage 3, through examining your story under the lens of the Essential Elements, you will discover where there is still juice and passion in your tale. Explore how the lessons you learnt then and the insights you gained are relevant to your life and your audience today.

CHAPTER 6

Your life experience and its pivotal moments

'Life turns on a dime. Sometimes towards us, but more often it spins away, flirting and flashing as it goes: so long, honey, it was good while it lasted, wasn't it?'

Stephen King

Your Leadership Story might be born out of pivotal moments in your childhood, your home life or in the workplace. Don't neglect these pivotal experiences that made you who you are today. I may not share Stephen King's pessimism but there's no doubt that he knew his craft and how these life shifts and changes are the real stuff of great storytelling.

Leadership stories have, at their heart, a transformation: sometimes of your thoughts, values or beliefs and sometimes of your very identity. A leadership story is not just a story of how you saw something new or experienced a funny incident. That is an anecdote. A leadership story is a more profound one. It is about how you changed as a person: whether going from confusion to clarity, triumph to despair or failure to success. Perhaps you were blind to something and now you are conscious and aware, or you suffered a loss and found some new insight. It may not be obvious at first or seem big or important enough. Dig deep and you'll find something. It may help to discuss this with a trusted colleague or friend because things that you take for granted are often fascinating to others.

Lisa Nichols is an incredibly compelling speaker. The daughter of a Baptist minister, she changes people's lives with the insights conveyed through her stories. She explains the importance of 'The Dip' when telling your stories. First start with a high, maybe a brief intro to the successful person you are today. Next, take people down through a difficult challenge that you faced in your life: the 'dip'. Then bring them back up to the successful result you achieved. After hearing your story, they will relate to you for the vulnerable moments you faced during your struggles and they will understand how far you have climbed back up. This is the most powerful way to convey the gift of your message.

Your audience want to know who you are now, who you were then and what changed you in between. You might start with your message: 'Friends are the greatest asset that a leader can have. I learnt this the hard way ...' Then comes your story about how you neglected a great friend who stuck by you through thick and thin. When you went to thank him, he had moved away and you lost touch. You end by sharing your insight: 'So always look after your friends like gold.'

Some people have one big obvious event that defines them, such as the brilliant Sharon Amesu, who became one of a tiny minority of black women in the UK to be called to the Bar, and is now a Leadership Fellow of St George's House, Windsor Castle. Or it could be a Paralympian's story of devastation, recovery and ultimate success after a crippling accident. These make for compelling leadership stories. However, most people have not just one but a number of incidents and experiences in their lives that together form the basis of their story.

If you have had many ups and downs and a number of big shifts in your life you might draw on a few different moments that create an overall pattern, and demonstrate your multiple attempts to find a new way forward. Or else, you might use just one incident or 'dip' at a time to make a particular point – and therefore you will have a number of leadership stories at your disposal.

My life has given me a number of leadership stories and I draw on different versions depending on what I am aiming to do and who my audience is at the time. The unifying factor is that ultimately they all seem to add up to my one Core Message: 'The best way to serve the world is to be true to yourself.' People feel it when you are faking or are putting on a front. My Leadership Stories are about different ways I discovered this, and so through these, I express different facets of my core message.

Zigzag Exercise

'Let everything happen to you
Beauty and terror
Just keep going
No feeling is final'

Rainer Maria Rilke

This is an exercise to explore pivotal moments and the ups and downs of your story.

Think of the message you want to communicate, perhaps about just one area of your life. It could be about how you became great at sales, or how you discovered your passion for cycle racing. Start right back at the beginning – when you sold cupcakes at school or learnt to ride a bicycle, or the equivalent moment.

Identify the ups and downs along the way. Just get them all out to give you the full picture – the purpose is not to reach a conclusion at this point but to explore. Remember that each moment you uncover does not necessarily have to be included in your final recounted story, although you might be surprised what you draw on eventually.

The way we do this exercise in workshops is to take a walk along each trajectory in pairs so that you can speak your story aloud and practise storytelling. As you walk along one 'zig' you tell your partner of an 'up', then on the 'zag', you tell of a 'down'. At each corner, or turning point, capture the one moment that changed things from a zig to a zag. Can you recall a pivotal event or moment when everything changed? What did you learn from each zigzag?

Here is an example of my coming-of-age story about finding my freedom through boats and the water. The first big line for me was as a happy-go-lucky expat kid in Hong Kong where I sailed on my father's boat and swam competitively, to a zag (down); going to a boarding school in the UK with divorcing parents where I couldn't swim all winter. The next zig (up) was taking up rowing at the age of sixteen, which made me feel strong and empowered. I wanted to take this as far as I could – maybe even the Olympics. Then a zag when an injury destroyed my hopes of realizing my ambitions. I wallowed through a rainy autumn in the UK when I got an invitation to join a friend who was sailing round the world. The next zig was a decision to join him and get on the plane to Fiji and sail to New Zealand then on to Australia for the Sydney Hobart race. Here I also took part in some dinghy sailing regattas and ocean swimming events. This all gave me such joy and wellbeing.

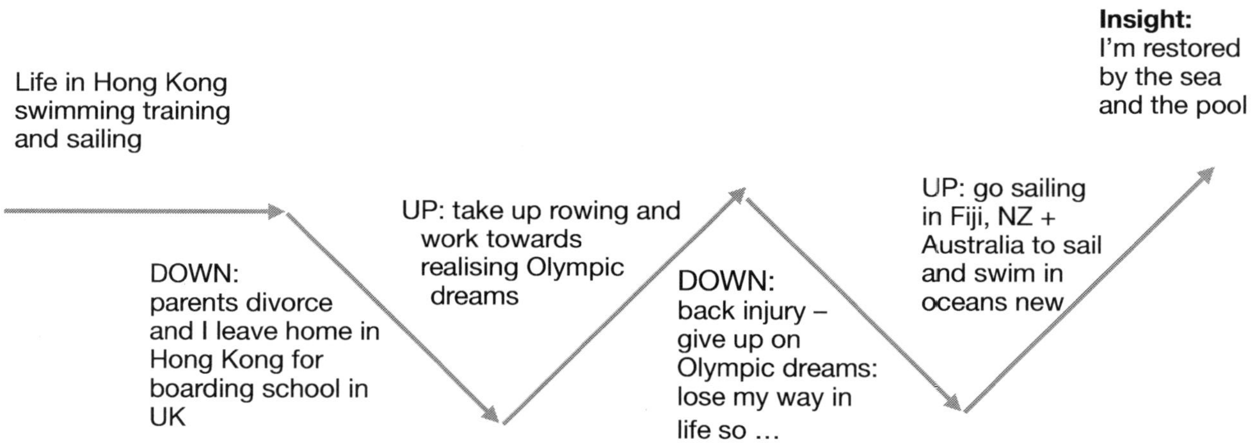

Zig Zag Exercise

STAGE 3

Craft

Write a compelling story

CHAPTER 7

Your Core Message

'The things you are passionate about are not random, they are your calling.'

Fabienne Fredrickson

In Stage Two we discussed how to prepare and find stories for your everyday talks and presentations by defining your KFDs and Key Message. We have also looked at the importance of pivotal moments. Now we are going to construct a greater story. One that you can use to inspire and influence people in a very deep and powerful way: Your Leadership Story, which is a vehicle for your core message.

Why do you need a Leadership Story?

Your Leadership Story is about who you are and the major incidents that have shaped you and therefore the way you lead others. So, as well as everyday anecdotes and stories that you use to deliver your key messages, you will also need to have a story about who you are. Often referred to as a signature story, it is as unique to you as your handwriting or your signature.

It contains the golden thread that runs through your life and is expressed in all your truly authentic communications. The story explains what motivates and gives you purpose: who you are, why you do what you do and how you go about doing those things. This golden thread holds the core message from which your story springs. It encapsulates what drives you and what you consider to be most important, as a leader, for other people.

You might use this as a stand-alone story or draw from it depending on your purpose. If you are intending to build your profile or personal brand, having a Leadership Story is essential. If you don't define it for yourself, others will tell their own stories about who you are and what you are about. Stories will be told about you anyway so it is worth taking control. Define and tell your own Leadership Story and share your message your way.

What is a Core Message?

Before crafting your Leadership Story, you will need to find your Core Message as opposed to your Key Message. As you may recall, the Key Message, along with your KFDs, is an encapsulation of the message you use for each talk. The Core Message is the message that goes with your Leadership Story and, in a way, it is the one that underlies all your key messages. Those various key messages are like little offshoots of your Core Message.

I believe every leader is on a mission, whether they are aware of it or not, to communicate or teach others something. Your Core Message embodies your calling as a leader.

Not everybody knows what their Core Message or calling is, but that's often because it has just been glimpsed but not yet fully recognised. Just like a diamond that has shown different facets to the world which are nonetheless all part of the same diamond, so you may be promoting a slightly different message to different audiences, but these diverse messages are all part of the same Core Message.

Your life experience has led to you developing your own leadership philosophy. Events have happened, people have said things to you over the years, and this has led to you making your own conclusions on how people work or live their lives better. Your Core Message is an encapsulation of this philosophy and it is powerful gift that you have to give people. Your Leadership Story is the best way to share that gift in a way that others can benefit.

Your Leadership Story is all about how you came to learn the importance of your Core Message and the role it plays in your day-to-day life as a leader. It is far more profound, more universal, more human and life-affirming than your key messages. It guides you in your work and your decision-making, whether you are aware of it or not. It encapsulates your philosophy of leadership and indeed of life – it is a message you live by as a deep truth to your existence. And yet, unearthing it is not as difficult as it may appear. In this chapter, you will explore what yours is and what it means for you.

Finding your Core Message

In order to find your Core Message, there are a few approaches you can take. What did your parents, caregivers, teachers or other significant adults say to you that have continued to resonate throughout your life? What are those pieces of advice and words of wisdom that you have continued to tell yourself or pass on to others?

My mother used to say, 'If at first you don't succeed, try, try, try again', and she would tell me the story of Robert the Bruce and the spider. She also said, 'Nothing ventured, nothing gained.' These ideas have become a part of my philosophy and approach to life. When things get difficult or if I am wondering whether to take a new risk, I might echo these words in my head.

Or it could be something that you heard in a film, read in a book or heard in a motivational speech. Perhaps it was something your boss or a senior manager said when you were just starting out in the workplace and have since held you in good stead. What life or leadership truths have struck you as important over the years? Such as 'ultimately you have to have pride in your own achievements, not seek approval from others', or 'in the end, love and human connections are all that matter'.

Or it might be something you heard just once, a piece of advice that really struck a chord at the time and made you stop in your tracks. Perhaps you were going through a tough time and you heard or read something, even in a song, that helped you get through it. 'Love is all there is', 'the best things in life are free', 'I am beautiful, no matter what they say, words can't bring me down'.

Try This:

Make a list:

Give yourself ten minutes to note down as many of these wise insights as you can. List any messages which struck a chord through your life. Think of different stages of development in your life and its pivotal moments. Make a note of insights gained at these significant times. You can continue to add to this list as you go.

Notice the associated stories that they bring to mind. You might see themes emerging. Also reflect upon how they have guided you. I have a story for each of the following because of how they changed the direction of my life:

'An idea is worth nothing in your head – make something out of it.'

'Be yourself, everybody else is already taken.'

'Today is the first day of the rest of your life.'

What did someone say to you that made you sit up and take note? What did someone say that helped you change the course of your life?

A phrase I heard recently, which I have now adopted is: 'A day without laughter is a day wasted.'

How does the advice you heard still play out in your life today?

Add to the list:

Try going deeper into your story and ask yourself this:

'If there was one piece of advice I was able to give the younger me, about how to live and lead my own life, what would it be?'

You could think about this question and the advice you would give yourself for different stages of your life and career.

Define your Core Message

Now it's time to define your Core Message.

Take a moment now to reflect on what themes you see emerging from your list. What do you want to be known for and stand for? What is it that you believe is important for your team, colleagues or future leaders to know?

Ultimately, I believe that we are always trying to communicate our own Core Message whenever we have a 'deep and meaningful' conversation about life and leadership. I asked the former president of the Global Speakers Federation and media expert Alan Stevens about his Core Message. Without hesitation, he said 'to keep it simple'. As a leader, he helps people simplify the complexity of their lives and their communications.

My Core Message is certainly what I am expressing again and again in many forms. It is 'to ignite the spark of true self-expression'. I seek to help people have the courage to express their true selves. Can you see how this can be used in many different ways? It can be applied in managing conflict, speaking on stage or finding your way through a professional or personal dilemma. My Leadership Story shows why and how I believe this Core Message to be important.

Here are some questions to ponder:

- What is an important life truth for you?
- What is the one piece of wisdom or knowledge you would like to impart to others?
- What is it that you wish you had known earlier in your profession?
- What are you seeking to communicate when you help others through challenges?

- What is a guiding principle for all your leadership work?

Now attempt to summarise this in one phrase or sentence.

What if my Core Message doesn't feel original?

They say that there is nothing new under the sun. That applies to messages. There may be many other leaders conveying the same message as you:

'We're better as a team', 'Always do your best', 'Play to your strengths', or whatever it is, so don't worry if your message does not feel too original. What is original is your take on it, why you believe it and how you learnt the truth of it. When it is told in the context of your own unique personal history the message is given wings.

In motivational speaking, many speakers are ultimately talking about the same thing – 'be yourself', 'trust yourself', 'you can do it', 'never give up', 'your potential is amazing'. However, what differentiates these messages, and makes a message really land, is that the speaker owns it and communicates it by telling their own story – why it matters to them as a message and how they came to learn it. This is what your Leadership Story must do.

Live your Core Message

When Gandhi said, 'Be the change you want to see in the world' he was talking about being an authentic example, of practising what you preach. Your core message is a central motivating idea that defines what you think is most important for people to know, feel and do (KFD) in their lives. Once you have your core message clear in a way that makes sense in your mind, it will permeate all your communications and actions, even if you never have a chance to tell the whole story in one go.

CHAPTER 8

The Essential Elements of Your Leadership Story

'A coherent life experience is not simply given.
The thing must be made, a story-like production.'

Stephen Crites

Now that you have a sense of your Core Message, it's time to craft your Leadership Story. In this chapter, you will discover the Essential Elements that your Leadership Story must contain and how to write it up so that it is ready for presentation.

The questions in the minds of your audience

But before you start, you must think, not of your own life experience but of the people for whom your message and story is meant. Your audience. From the moment you stand at the front of the room, your audience will immediately start asking themselves some questions about you:

1. **Who are you?** Who are you now and who you were before and after the experience?

2. **Where are you going – what is your aim?** What set you on a new path? What was your mission?

3. **How will you get there?** They want to know you faced and overcame struggles and the sense you made of the experiences by what you learnt along the way. They also want to know if you achieved your aims. What was the result of your efforts?

4. **Where will you end up?** Have you achieved something that they admire or is a result that they want for themselves?

5. **How does it relate to me?** The insights gained through hard-won experience, which you now can impart to others.

The Essential Elements

I have identified five essential elements that your Leadership Story must contain if it is to be powerful and persuasive. Each Essential Element relates to a question that is likely to be in the minds of your audience as you speak. So if you really want to unleash the full power of your story, make sure you answer the following questions by including the Essential Elements.

Through my research into the work of Joseph Campbell and others, I discovered that these Essential Elements are contained in all kinds of narratives, from myths, plays and religious rituals to personal accounts. As I mentioned earlier, it has been shown that in a court of law, if these elements are present in either prosecution or defence, the story related is more likely to be believed.

These Essential Elements each relate to key moments within what is known as 'The Hero's Journey'. In the Hero's Journey, the protagonist starts out as the 'ordinary hero' but then is called to adventure. Through facing various struggles and challenges, the hero learns lessons and gains deep insights. The story is not complete until the hero brings home these insights as gifts for others who were once like him (see appendix).

The Essential Elements are: Identity, Inciting Incident, Struggle, Breakthrough, and Insight. Sometimes we unconsciously include these essential elements because if they are not there, something seems to be missing. But if you want your story to be truly believable, and for it to touch and inspire people, run every story you tell through this checklist.

The Essential Elements

1. **IDENTITY: BEFORE everything changed** Who were you before learning the insight or message of your story? It will connect with the audience more powerfully if you begin your story as an ordinary person coming from your ordinary world than if your starting point is you already successful. People want to know who you were when your story started and how you developed through the story. Paint a picture of the world you lived in, its frustrations and limitations, before things changed. This provides a context for the ensuing action. In my zigzag example, I am an expat kid swimming and sailing and enjoying life.

2. **INCITING INCIDENT: MISSION moment** This is where you cross the threshold from doing what you'd always done and living in your ordinary world to doing things differently or going somewhere new. You may have a number of pivotal moments – as I did in the zigzag story above – but focus on the one that instigated the first significant change. In my case going to boarding school. At that point of change, what did you set out to do? I set out to find a way to live happily in my new surroundings. You may or may not succeed, but you will gain something that will be even more valuable by the end of the story. Sometimes you choose your mission and at other times it is thrust upon you as a 'Call to Action' by circumstances outside your control.

3. **STRUGGLE: ATTEMPTS to solve the problem** The bulk of the story is here, with obstacles faced, challenges met and conflicts to be resolved. This is where you find out what you are made of as you attempt to solve your problem. I took up rowing and that worked well for a number of years but then I had a back injury. I had to find a new way to do things. You learn lessons, either from others or through your own experience, that are put to the test as you go through your struggles. Sometimes you prevail and sometimes you don't, but what is important is that you learn, grow and change through these experiences.

4. **BREAKTHROUGH: RESULT or REDEMPTION** Here you need some kind of resolution or punch line that provides a denouement of the story. You get some kind of redemption or reward either in material form or in the form of wisdom. You might understand yourself or the world better or you might have met with great success. It should be some kind of result to which your audience can relate and to which they aspire.

5. **INSIGHT** Your Breakthrough is linked to your core message and encapsulates many of the lessons you learnt upon the way. After telling your story, it is often worth articulating the insight you gained and how it is relevant to you nowadays and also how it is relevant for your audience.

Here is an example of a leadership story:

John Stapleton is the co-founder of the New Covent Garden Soup Company. In 1998 John moved from the UK to California, where he introduced the chilled soup in a carton concept to the USA. He then co-founded another market-disrupting brand: Little Dish, the first chilled food brand for children. I spoke with John to uncover his Leadership Story. This is what he told me. Notice how it contains the Essential Elements.

A Fresh Approach

'At New Covent Garden Soup Company (NCGSC) we were a bunch of happy amateurs really!' he laughs, yet he, with his friend Andrew Palmer, pioneered a whole new category within supermarkets and changed the way many people shop and eat. Now, ready-made fresh food has a significant amount of shelf space but back then, all liquid soup was sold in cans. In fact, in 1987, there was very little fresh convenience food at all. And absolutely nothing in the fresh ready meal category.

Identity

'A young boy stands in short trousers in the middle of a cow field in the West of Ireland. Calves are dying all around him. Nobody knows why. They had been let out to pasture and now they are sick. John feels like his world is caving in. What has caused this? Who is to blame? As he watches how his father deals with this catastrophe, he learns a gritty lesson that stands him in good stead throughout his life: 'You can do all the preparation you like, but shit happens so you just have to get on with it.'

In his teens, John became a good athlete, representing Ireland in the Triple Jump. He won a scholarship to University College, Dublin, which he accepted in order to pursue his sporting ambitions. His microbiology studies were really an afterthought. John aspired to get into the Irish Olympic team. In 1984, he was training with the national squad when injury struck. As he watched his comrades go off to Los Angeles to compete at the Olympic Games, John felt cheated. 'In hindsight,' he says, 'maybe I wasn't quite good enough but at the time it felt so unfair.' However, he never forgot his coach's advice: 'It's a bitter pill to swallow so, of course, you can wallow all summer long, but where will that get you? Either feel sorry for yourself or get back on track and start training again.'

'I learnt then that it's easy to be the victim, and say, "It's not fair", but actually if it feels too easy you are probably not putting yourself out there enough. If the road you are taking is tricky and difficult, then keep at it! It probably shows it is worthwhile. If you are doing stuff that's challenging you're going to get more than your fair share of resistance and adversity, but persevere.'

Inciting incident

In 1987, John had just completed his MSc in Food Science at Reading University, when he met his future business partner Andrew Palmer. One afternoon, in a local supermarket, looking for a spot of lunch, they asked themselves why all the soup came canned.

Why didn't anyone sell fresh soup from fresh ingredients?

It was in that moment that John and Andrew decided to try creating it themselves. This meant educating people in the difference in taste between fresh and canned soup. Tinned tomato soup, for example, tastes very different from fresh tomato soup. Fresh tomatoes have a slightly bitter taste but canned tomato soup has a caramelised taste because a lot of sugar has been added and then it has been subjected to the high temperatures of sterilisation that give canned soups their long shelf life.

Everyone said it couldn't be done. 'There is no shelf space for fresh soup. It's too risky. We'll end up throwing stock away,' said the supermarkets.

'How can we distribute soup with an eighteen-day shelf life rather than an eighteen-month one?" said the distributors.

'If it's such a good idea, someone else would have done it by now! Consumers are fine with the canned soup,' said the marketing experts.

'You'll poison someone!' said the academics and food scientists. 'There's a reason why soup comes in a can. It has to be sterilised.'

But John and Andrew looked at the size of the canned soup market, which was some £350 million per annum in the UK. Despite all the naysayers they thought, 'All we need is a 1 or 2 per cent market share. If we can design a product that's so much better than the canned soups, and design a brand that communicates what the consumer has been missing all this time – the market is so big that it has got to be worth a chance.'

Struggle

Their path was tricky. 'We could have fallen at any one of the hurdles along the way and that would have been it, but our belief did not waver.'

First, they had to ensure the safety of their product and avoid poisoning anyone. Next they had to ensure they had a brand that communicated the benefits of a fresh soup, then convince the supermarkets to stock it, and finally build market share with loyal customers before competitors realised this was an emerging market.

'If we had known how big the mountain was that we were about to climb, we might have given up before we started. But by the time we realised it we were halfway up and thought, "Well, we might as well keep climbing to the top."'

Competition came in the form mainly of supermarket's own brands. Baxters and Campbell's had a play at fresh soups, but left within one or two seasons. They were used to long-life canned products and could not make the logistics of a short shelf life work. By the time New Covent Garden Soup Co sold the business to the

Hain Daniels Group in 1998, they still held over 60 per cent share of the (rapidly growing) market.

Breakthrough

'In the early days, I felt, at times, like a fish out of water. I almost felt I was a fake. I'd sit in meetings and think, "Who's responsible for this particular decision?" To my horror, I realised it was me! I thought, "I can't make these decisions when I'm not an expert in any of the topics!" As a scientist I followed a logical and analytical approach: build on first principles and make informed decisions as an expert. Then I realised that now I was a successful entrepreneur!

I am not meant to be an expert in anything. I need to be creative, make judgements and do it all very quickly! You don't have the luxury of being an expert. You have to provide the vision of the business and inspire everyone involved.

Insight

'I learnt that it's OK to wing it. As a scientist, winging it was an anathema but as an entrepreneur, it's a question of who wings things best. Seek advice (and maybe take it), but trust yourself.

'Don't make the mistake of thinking that all that matters is your business acumen. Everything you have experienced as a person has shaped you. Recognise who you were as a kid and be happy to live that out in a professional environment. Your personality goes a long way. If you don't try to leverage your personality in life you can't really be an effective leader. As a business leader, you need to be inspirational in order to secure investment; to convince retailers and consumers to list and buy your products; to convince people to come to work for you (without the big salaries!) and the many other times you need to be able to influence people in business.

'You can't be inspirational by trying to be someone else. Inspiration comes from a place of authenticity. In any event, there's no point in putting yourself under so much stress by constantly trying to be someone else. There's enough to deal with, without trying to impose another layer that's not natural for you. If you can understand what has shaped you, it can give you the confidence to find things in your professional life that make you comfortable and that will guide you to make the right decisions.'

If you had one Core Message as a leader, what would it be?

'Keep calm and trust yourself. Leadership, motivation and, ultimately, success is rooted in authenticity. Without it, you won't be successful – and you'll break your heart trying.'

CHAPTER 9

Writing your Leadership Story

'People don't want more information. They are up to their eyeballs in information. They want faith – faith in you, your goals, your success, in the story you tell.'

Annette Simmons

Write your story step by step

Now it's time to write your own story in full. First, have in mind your *Core Leadership Message* from Stage 2, and identify that *Pivotal Moment* when it became important to you. Recall the scenario that set you on your journey to where you are now.

When it comes to telling your story, you can either dive right into your story or you can introduce your message first. If doing the latter you might say something like this: 'I believe that it is important for people working in our industry to make decisions quickly and to trust their intuition,' then say, 'and here is the story of how I learnt the importance of quick decision-making.'

Let's delve deeper into the Five Essential Elements so that you can use them as a structure for your story. As a reminder, here they are:

Identity: Who were you at the start?
Inciting incident: What set you on a path of change?
Struggle: How did you face your challenges?
Breakthrough: What did you finally achieve?
Insight: How can your audience relate to your experience?

1 IDENTITY

'If a story is not about the hearer he will not listen. And here I made a rule – a great and interesting story is about everyone or it will not last.'

John Steinbeck

Who were you at the start?

Lay the foundations of what your life was like before you set out on the adventure that led you to find the gift or message that you now share. As Steinbeck's quote reminds us, your story is about everyone, and anyone should be able to relate to it – at least at the start. Be vulnerable and show your ordinary world before you launched on your adventure. John's identity is established as a farmer's son and athletic student. The two significant moments in his early life, the cows in the field and his failure to get to the Olympics, show something about who he was before he set out on his path to create a fresh soup company.

Who were YOU before everything changed?

'When I was a new recruit to this organisation ...', 'When I led my first deal ...', 'When I was a novice golfer ...' or whatever is your starting point.

Batman's story starts with him being orphaned as the young Bruce Wayne, Dorothy started in Kansas before her adventures in Oz, Richard Branson was a dyslexic who struggled at school. It may be that what was ordinary for you is extraordinary for your audience. For instance, my early stories start with my childhood in Hong Kong, which may be extraordinary to some. However, people can relate to it because they have all been children. The key is that enough must be ordinary that people can relate to you.

Remember to be vulnerable

Even superheroes have their flaws and weaknesses. Superman may have super-strength and the ability to fly but he has that very human desire to be accepted and loved. He lives as a normal boy adopted by a farming family to hide the fact that he is different. We can all relate to wanting to be accepted by others. And of course, he has his vulnerabilities and struggles too: kryptonite can weaken him – and he has enemies who want to undermine him. We can relate to that kind of unfairness in life too.

In her book *Daring Greatly*, Brené Brown talks about how it takes greater courage to show our vulnerabilities than it does to have a hard exterior. In a Leadership Story, it is paramount. Our audience need to connect with who we are. They will connect with a real, vulnerable human being who shares their fears – they won't connect with someone who just strides through life without a moment of self-doubt.

Begin by describing a vignette of your early life. It may feel exposing but it will pay off. Share what confused, frustrated, bored, concerned or inhibited you at that time so that later your audience understand your motivations to act the way you did.

2. INCITING INCIDENT

'Happy are those who dream dreams and are ready to pay the price to make them come true.'

Leon J. Suenes

What set you on the path of change?

The next Essential Element is the moment of change and the reason for you moving from your known 'ordinary' world and into the unknown. The Inciting Incident for John was that he was unable to buy fresh soup at the supermarket. This led to him asking, 'Why not?'

The 'hero' either chooses to go on an adventure or it is thrust upon him. Some want to expand their world or chase a dream as John did, others are forced onto a new path. It may be because of a redundancy, an accident or a tragedy that everything changes for that person – or it could be an enormous lottery win.

How did the dream begin?

What made you cross the threshold? What was the turning point for you?

It's not enough to tell us you always had a dream (although it worked for Martin Luther King). If you can, boil it down to one or two significant moments that set you on this path.

Instead of saying, 'Oh, I just always wanted to be a vet', seek out that moment that prompted your interest. For example:

'One day I was walking down the street on my way to school, when a dog scampered into the road, in front of an oncoming car. There was an unholy yelp and a crunch as the dog's rear legs got caught by the wheel. The driver stopped and got out, and both of us looked

down at the dog, unsure of what to do. The dog was bleeding heavily and whimpering in pain. We had to help but I had no idea where to start. Just then a woman came round the corner; she calmly knelt by the dog and gently but firmly placed her hands around the dog's muzzle so it wouldn't bite while she dealt with the injuries. She staunched the bleeding with a tourniquet made from her cardigan. Her quick actions saved the life of the dog. But I was horrified by my own hesitation and confusion. If she hadn't been there the dog would have died. I love animals and didn't want to see another animal suffer unnecessarily just because of my own lack of knowledge – so I decided right then and there that I'd become a vet.'

Your motivation

The secret to making this element a success is to make your motivation clear. Your motivation is what sustains you in the story later, as you tell of the challenges you encountered on your way to realising your dream.

There are two kinds of motivation: 'away from' or 'towards'. Like a donkey on a beach we go towards the carrot (pleasure and reward) and move away from the stick (pain).

One of the critical parts of a storytelling is to explain why you set out on your journey and took action. The 'away from' or 'towards' motivations need to be evident, whether it is because of a change in circumstance, an encounter with a certain person or coming across an object like a long-lost photo that prompts action.

Is your motivation that you never ever want to re-experience a certain embarrassing, painful or shameful event again or is your motivation encapsulated in an appealing vision of future success? Or both? Remember it's not your vision alone that makes a story compelling, it's your reasons for having that vision. Make sure your audience understand directly how your vision is the answer to your prayers and how there is a direct link between this vision and the action you take. Your vision motivates and drives the action in your story.

Making it happen

You would think that in life we would follow this simple formula to make all our decisions in this way: constantly moving towards our desires, wishes or yearnings and away from unpleasant, painful or uncomfortable ones. The fact is, though, that we will often stay put. Unless things get bad enough or the allure of a dream is strong enough we will not embark upon our adventure.

The expression 'better the devil you know' is an attitude that keeps people stuck in an unwanted situation, sometimes for years. The comfort zone has to become extremely uncomfortable before we leave it. Change is something people often avoid until the motivation gets great enough. Your story begins when you break out of a comfort zone.

A lot of dramatic tension can be created when the audience knows the hero should get out of their predicament and move on, but he hesitates and things get worse and worse. When writing your own story, you might want to ramp up your indecision, before you accept your call to adventure.

Sometimes the hero doubts his dream or loses motivation en route. In your story, something needs to happen to renew it. You encounter some new success, somebody gives you some encouragement or you find a new way through.

The Inciting Incident element of your story is about the pivotal moment when the vision becomes great enough or the pain becomes bad enough that you do something differently and make a change.

3. STRUGGLE

'The philosophers have only interpreted the world in various ways.

The point, however, is to change it.'

Karl Marx

How did you face your challenges?

Next comes the struggle and conflict, which is the blood and guts of your story. The struggle element is about facing and often overcoming adversity. This may come in all kinds of forms, from internal, personal struggles of self-doubt to external physical blocks that may be entirely beyond your control.

Joe Simpson's book, *Touching the Void,* which has since been made into a film, is about how he and Simon Yates, both experienced mountaineers, attempt to ascend the unclimbed West Face of Siula Grande in Peru. After reaching the summit, a ferocious storm ensues and Joe falls and breaks his leg badly. As the storm rages on around them, Simon tries to lower him down on a rope but Joe drops over the edge of a cliff and is left dangling in mid-air. Simon can neither see nor hear the predicament that Joe is in amidst the howling storm. Unable to pull him up and losing traction in the snow, he believes there's little chance of recovery from the situation as they are, so he cuts the rope between them. Joe falls into a crevasse but survives. Over the next few days, in sub-zero temperatures, he crawls on his hands and knees despite his broken leg, frostbite and dehydration. Unbelievably, he arrives back at the Base Camp just hours before Simon had planned to evacuate.

Your own psychological struggle may be more prosaic. Did you need to face up to and overcome a mental block of your own making? Or perhaps you faced up to a difficult boss or awkward client. Often the most compelling stories are the ones where we discovered that something within ourselves had to change in order for us to get through, around or over the impasse. It's not that something outside of us needs to change. The struggle is the tension between holding on to who we once were, and who we now need to become, in order to survive and succeed.

In John Stapleton's story, he faced both external struggles to get his soup on the shelves against an army of naysayers, and his own internal struggle in the form of self-doubt. He asked himself, 'Who am I to be sitting in these board meetings making these decisions?'

Your success needs to be in jeopardy to make the story truly gripping. How have you faced failure and difficulty? What made it a challenge to overcome? What different things did you try in order to get through? What attempts did you make? Why not echo struggles that your audience might be familiar with in their own life? Let them see themselves in your story.

4. BREAKTHROUGH

What did you finally achieve?

In John's story, his breakthrough comes when he realises that he is an entrepreneur and it is up to him to believe in his product and to make it happen. No one else could or would do it for him.

After the tension of your struggles and challenges, it's a relief for your audience to hear of some final success. Sometimes that comes in the form of actual success, or it could come in the form of lessons learnt through failure. It could be a story of how a loved one finally died after a long struggle with illness, and the insights you gained from that experience. It could be about what you gained through being made redundant or something similar that led to new doors being opened for you. Sometimes walking away from a situation or realising it's time to quit can also create a huge sense of relief.

What was your breakthrough moment? This should be uplifting in some way so that there is a sense of resolution – a shift has taken place within you.

The identity shift – connecting with your audience

Your Leadership Story is ultimately about the identity shift that you made from the person you once were to the leader you are today. It is about embracing this new identity, and how you discovered the leader within you.

By sharing your challenges and setbacks you show yourself to be vulnerable and therefore human and relatable. By voicing the same concerns and insecurities, that your audience may now face, you show empathy and understanding. This will also establish a deeper connection and rapport with your audience.

Then, by sharing how you met with those setbacks and challenges – what you learnt from them and how you attempted to resolve them – you show that you have what it takes and why you can be trusted as a leader. Your character traits as well as your demonstration of relevant experience will strengthen the audience's perception of you as a leader who is prepared to learn, grow and respond to a variety of situations. Whether or not you successfully overcame your challenges is sometimes less important than how you faced them and what you learnt along the way.

As Rebecca Solnit wrote in *The Faraway Nearby*, 'In the strongest stories we see ourselves, connected to each other, woven into the pattern, see that we are ourselves stories, telling and being told. Stories like yours and worse than yours are all around, and your suffering won't mark you out as special, though your response to it might.'

What was your response? What have you learnt from whatever has gone wrong in your life?

5. INSIGHT

How can your audience relate to your experience?

You leverage the power of the story when you offer up lessons to those who identify with who you once were. Your character, in the story, has been on a journey and learnt something valuable that you did not know at the start – so share that message at the end clearly.

It has been hard won through your experience.

John's story ended with this message for others:

'Keep calm and trust yourself. Leadership, motivation and, ultimately, success is rooted in authenticity. Without it, you won't be successful – and you'll break your heart trying.'

Whether you make your insight explicit, or allow it to stand for itself, the message must be there in some form. Let it be conveyed through the action of the character in your story (you) and what you realised and applied along the way. An implicit insight might be more subtle, but beware that it may be more open to misunderstanding.

Your Leadership Story is an intentional story, so at least articulate for yourself what it is you hope for people to get from it. Stories act as metaphors in people's minds. As you tell your story, you will naturally focus in on those aspects that underscore your message. Your story does not have to have exactly the same features as those your audience experiences, it just has to have themes to which they can relate, and of course a message that is relevant to them.

As you end your story, emphasise your message or give your audience something to ponder, a question to consider or an action to take.

Nicholas McCarthy and the Essential Elements

In 2013, I attended a TEDx event at the Royal Albert Hall. The stage was in the dark with just a spotlight on a grand piano.

Then a speaker took to the stage and sat at the piano. Without saying a word, he played the most beautiful composition and when he stood up to take a bow we saw that he had only one arm.

His name was Nicholas McCarthy, and he had recently graduated from the Royal College of Music, he told us. One day, he sat at a piano and found he had a natural talent. Despite his missing limb, he decided he wanted to be a concert pianist, but in order to get there he had had to overcome a trail of obstacles – from the doubts of his first piano teacher, to the cynicism of his high school peer group. Now he is proud to be the only one-armed pianist ever to have graduated from the one of the world's most illustrious music schools. A few months later he played at the Paralympic Closing Ceremony in London, alongside Coldplay.

He took his seat again and played a Bach piece. It was exquisite and when he came to the end he turned to us and said, 'Thank you so much. I hope you enjoyed it. But more importantly, I'd like you to know that if there is something you have a burning ambition to do, then ignore the naysayers, believe in yourself and just get on and do it.' That was his call to action, his gift to us the audience. He also provided an interesting twist on what I've been relating to you. He took to the stage and started with what looked like straight-out success, and then demonstrated to us that it hadn't all been smooth sailing. Without having to say a word he told us his story by demonstrating the undoubted Struggles and Breakthrough when he stood up and revealed his true Identity as a one-armed pianist who was evidently extremely accomplished. When he spoke he gave an even fuller account of all the Essential Elements. The Inciting Incident, the realities of his Struggle, the incredible Breakthrough and the culminating Insight.

TRY THIS:

Now it's your turn:

Think about what your own life experiences mean to you.

What stories of your life could be a gift to others?

When have you overcome challenge?

When have you succeeded in your ambitions?

What have you learnt along the way?

Excavate bravely and honestly then go out and share your stories. They are your gifts to others and will become gifts to you too when you share them. Tell your stories because it might just be that the words you have to say are exactly the ones that somebody needs to hear. That is my call to action for you.

Pixar's Story Formula

Pixar Animation Studios, a subsidiary of Disney, make the highest-grossing animated films worldwide. They use a simple story formula in all their animations, from *Toy Story* to *Monsters, Inc.*

Here it is in all its simplicity:

Once there was ...
Every day ...
One day ...
Because of that ...

Because of that ...
Because of that ...
Because of that ...
Until finally ...

Here is an example of it with a story:

Once there was ... a fish called Nemo who wanted adventure.

Every day ... he swam to the edges of his known world.

One day ... he crossed the threshold.

Because of that ... he got lost and couldn't find his way back.

Because of that ... he was swept into a strong current.

Because of that ... he was caught and put in a dentist's aquarium.

Because of that ... his father went on an adventure, searching high and low for him.

Until finally ... he was found and brought home, now knowing that there was a world out there full of adventure, new friends to be made, experiences to be had and sights to see, but all not without risk.

Now it's your turn. Try it out on a story in your own life where you struggled and eventually found an answer or a way forward.

STAGE 4

Deliver:

Tell a powerful story

CHAPTER 10

On your feet – transport your audience

'There's always room for a story that can transport people to another place.'

J.K. Rowling

When you tell a story well, it's as if you cast a spell. The listener forgets that they are sitting in an air-conditioned meeting room or conference centre and finds him- or herself transported to other worlds and other situations. Instead of seeing what is in the room around them, they are there, with you, wherever your story is set, visualising, feeling and imagining your experience alongside you.

A well-told story is a form of hypnosis; it's a trance which, as neuroscience has shown, activates parts of the brain relevant to what is being described. When you talk about the salty sharp taste of chips covered in vinegar, the parts of the brain associated with taste become activated. Even though your listeners are not tasting the chips right now, as far as their brains are concerned, they are able to simulate the experience.

If you do it well, then when you talk about the pain of heartbreak, the pride of an unexpected promotion or the joy of holding your firstborn, it will resonate with your listeners, producing a similar emotional response in them – reminding them of their own experiences.

Equally, provided you have already connected with your audience, they will also delight in your good fortune and have empathy for your struggles as you recount your story. Merely telling a tale of woe and hardship it is not enough if your audience cannot relate to you. If you establish your identity (the first Essential Element) first and make a good connection with the audience they will take the journey with you.

This chapter will show you how to hook them and evoke the responses and emotions that transform the storytelling experience into one that transports the listener.

I will give you three ways to do it:

1. **Show not tell** – bring it to life so it can be re-experienced.
2. **Chart the course** – have a storyboard and know where you are.
3. **Navigate well** – links and drivers.

1. Show not Tell

'Don't tell us that the old lady screamed. Bring her on and let her scream.'

Samuel Clemens

When you use the 'Show not Tell' approach, you let your listeners re-live the scene with you. Let them hear the words you heard and let them see a scene unfold just as it did for you. Don't 'tell' them about what happened, 'show' them what happened.

Telling: 'I really wanted to go there but I didn't get into the music college.'

Showing: 'For the previous three months I had practised from dawn until dusk. My fingers were red and raw. The day arrived that had been starred in my calendar for months: the Audition. I sat on the stool and began. My fingers moved nervously, skipping notes. Finally, the examiner said, "I'm sorry, we cannot offer you a place."'

In the second version, we live through the experience. Rather than saying, 'I really wanted to go', it is shown by the dedicated practice sessions. Instead of saying, 'I didn't get in', we re-live the experience as the storyteller did. It is more immediate and alive.

A master storyteller conveys the bare facts, without interpretation yet in such a way that the listener comes to the same conclusion and emotional response as the teller. It is far more powerful to be moved to tears by the events in the story because you are re-living them alongside the storyteller than to simply be told someone was upset.

The aim is to re-create each scene so that your listeners get to re-experience it for themselves. Play out your story scene by scene, like a film, only better. Reference all the senses. Films don't tell the viewer things. Everything is shown. How do you know someone is upset, angry, happy, sad, frustrated? Through their facial expressions, movements, actions and gestures, not because you are told.

Here's another example of 'telling': John discovered that his wife was having an affair with his best friend. He had never been more angry than he was that night.

While 'showing' would be like this: John walked into his local for an after-work pint and was surprised to see his wife with his best friend at the other side of the bar. They were laughing, and as he made his way towards them he noticed that their hands were tightly clasped under the table. And then they leant in, their mouths touching in passionate kiss.

John roared, pushing chairs out of the way to get to them faster. 'What the hell are you doing?!' Grabbing his friend by the collar he pulled him away from his wife, swung his other arm back and socked him in the jaw.

The second example may be less economical with words but it does have more 'punch' – if you'll excuse the pun! It does not interpret or describe John's feelings – it just shows you exactly what he saw as it unfolded, and how he acted in the situation. Rather than tell you that 'He had never been more angry' it shows you his level of rage by his actions.

TRY THIS:

Think of a time you felt something powerfully.

Now, how would how show it, instead of telling it?

For example, instead of saying, *'being in the dark forest was scary'*, you might show it by saying;

'I was surrounded by a tangle of trees so thick that it made it impossible for the sun's rays to penetrate. There was an eerie silence. No birdsong, not a breath of wind. Suddenly there was an ear-splitting crack. Something or someone was there in the forest. A chill ran down my spine.'

2. Chart the course

'No pessimist ever discovered the secret of the stars, or sailed to an uncharted land, or opened a new doorway for the human spirit.'

Helen Keller

Be optimistic. When sailors navigate across the oceans, the first thing they do is to chart the course they intend to sail – and they expect to get there. They don't just head out into the blue. And instead of heading directly to where they want to go, they might have to take a more circuitous course in order to avoid landmass, rocks or poor weather conditions. They plot out the 'waypoints'. A short journey may have only one or two waypoints, while a longer one may be composed of hundreds, which are re-evaluated and assessed along the way.

In the same way, before launching into a story a storyteller must have some waypoints to the story. Waypoints, or plot points, give the story a structure and make it easier to follow. They also act as markers in your mind. You aim for each one, thus keeping yourself on track. Without these, the story will just be a jumble. It will confuse you and the audience if you ramble on formlessly.

How to set your waypoints

Plan your story out with one headline per waypoint and use these prompts as you tell your story. These might relate to each of the five Essential Elements but you will probably have some additional ones related to each struggle or zigzag of your story. Take a moment to ensure each waypoint links to an image in your mind, like a snapshot of time, so that you can 'Show not Tell' each important part of your story.

Here are the waypoints of my story on how I become a clinical hypnotherapist:

a. 'Sorry, it's over.'
b. My heart is in pieces.
c. Bookshop: 'find peace in your heart.'
d. Reading on floor of bookshop.
e. Yellow Pages to book appointment with hypnotherapist.
f. Hypnotherapist saying, 'You could train in this.'
g. Front row at college with happy face and a happy heart.

Here's the story:

I was in my mid-twenties; my boyfriend of five years looked at me over the chicken dinner I'd just cooked for him and said, 'I've something to tell you. I'm sorry but it's over. I've met someone else.'

'Agh!' The shock was like a deep punch in my gut, followed by almost physical pain in my chest. My heart was in pieces. In the weeks that followed, I became numb. I walked through life like a zombie until one day, walking into a bookshop, I spotted the title of a book that transformed my mindset: Find Peace in your Heart. *'Wow! Imagine that! That's just what I'm looking for – peace in my heart.' Right there, in the corner of the bookshop, I sat down and read it.*

The author was a hypnotherapist who revealed a whole new way of thinking about and understanding the mind and how we work as human beings.

I had studied psychology at university but what I read had a different quality to it. I discovered we all have both a conscious mind, that makes our everyday decisions, and a subconscious one, in which our greater wisdom, our hopes and dreams and memories are held. It is the subconscious mind that is really running the show and it was why I couldn't think my way out of being heartbroken just by rationalising it away.

The next day, I looked in the Yellow Pages and booked an appointment with a hypnotherapist. I wanted to tap into the deeper wisdom of my own subconscious mind and find a way forward. Perhaps even find peace in my heart.

After the first session, the hypnotherapist said, 'You're a natural!', and suggested I might like to train as a hypnotherapist myself. A few months later I found myself sitting on the front row at Birkbeck College embarking on a two-year course. I knew I was where I needed to be. I sat in the front row, ready to absorb all I could about the workings of this powerful part of our being, our subconscious mind. And my heart? Utterly transformed and soon as good as new, ready to love again!

TRY THIS:

Think of your own career path and how you became whatever you are today. Write a list of each waypoint in your story. Now, to bring the story to life, applying the Magic Postcard technique below.

The Magic Postcard technique

'The great speakers do not just tell and re-tell stories on stage, but live and re-live stories.'

Lou Heckler

This is an approach I have devised for re-living your story on stage and for having access to each waypoint to help you deliver it. It will help you map out the bare bones and enable you to immerse yourself in each moment. You'll then be able to stand in front of people and bring your story to life with just a few prompt words or images in mind or written on some postcards.

Here's what to do:

a. Create one postcard per scene or waypoint. Use a blank postcard, prompt card or Post-it note and sketch an image that goes with that scene. Sketch it out as a stick figure drawing and then write your headline, and prompt words, to describe what's in the shot.

b. Now for the magic bit: bring your scene to life with a few seconds of action just before and after the moment snapped in the postcard. What can you see through your eyes? What can you hear? Remember, this is a magic postcard, which means you might also be able to feel, smell or taste things in the scene too. Feel the texture of the wind blowing against your cheek. Smell the aroma of newly ground coffee beans. Hear the sound of the traffic or someone's voice.

c. Now lay out all the postcards and you have a storyboard from which you can speak. When you have this before you, you may choose to change the order. Stories don't have to be told chronologically. Play with the end scene coming first and then leap back in time and show how you got to the end point.

d. Before speaking, review all your magic postcards. Doing this will make it much easier to memorise your story because it's easier to remember a few images and key headlines than a long chain of words. But you might also choose to lay them all out on the stage in front of you so that your postcards jog your memory. I sometimes do this when I have limited time to prepare a story and so need a memory-prompt.

3. Navigate Well

'It's all in the telling. Stories are compasses and architecture; we navigate by them, we build our sanctuaries and our prisons out of them, and to be without a story is to be lost in the vastness of a world ... like arctic tundra or sea ice.'

Rebecca Solnit

When you use story, it needs to be within the context of your presentation and with the purpose of conveying a message that is relevant to your audience.

There are three phases to your talk when using a story

a. The Opening – context-setting for your story.
b. The Main Body – your story is told here.
c. The Close – summarise your message and reiterate your call to action.

Here are the secrets to ensuring each phase lands successfully:

a. The Opening

When you stand before an audience, they have a lot to take in. They need to get used to who you are, tune into your voice, accent and style. They may be trying to decide, 'Is this a funny talk, a heartbreaking one, a serious one?' Are you giving a performance or having an interactive conversation? Ensure you connect with your audience either way.

While they are orientating themselves to you and your style, they may be distracted and miss the first couple of lines, so don't plunge in immediately. Start from a point of stillness and silence – just be you, standing at the front of the room. Take a breath, then, if they don't know who you are, introduce yourself and the name or purpose of the talk.

Before taking people back to the start point of your story, you might set the present context: 'Now I'm an experienced salesman but it wasn't always this way. I remember my first sale ...' However, if your current identity is already established with the audience or you have been introduced, you might choose to dive straight into your story.

As your story begins, have a good powerful starting phrase that orientates the listener to a time and place, such as, 'When I lived in the Australian Outback in my twenties ...' or 'There's nothing like waking up to the lapping of the waves and the clink of halyards on the mast. That sound always brings me back to my time spent sailing around the Fijian Islands ...' Let the listener know where they have to imagine themselves to be and when – set the context and describe the surroundings. Let your words paint the picture, in the way that a television drama or a film can show a location and people in the opening sequence.

Don't be tempted to make your opening phrase or first few sentences extra-dramatic. A common mistake is to open with direct speech (the actual words somebody spoke at the time). The problem with doing this is that the audience don't know who is speaking. Is it you, the storyteller, or another character in the story? If they haven't met you yet, they don't know your voice. For example, instead of starting with, '*We've forgotten the presentation pack,' my colleague said to me.* Try: *We were at the office of one of our biggest clients ... about to pitch the biggest deal we had ever done ... The lift doors opened and my colleague gasped, 'We've forgotten the presentation pack!'*

In written form, you may be able to get away with a story that starts with direct speech because there are indicators, such as quotation marks, to show somebody is speaking and that it is not the narrator's voice.

b. The Main Body

This is where you include the main story, composed of the next three Essential Elements, the **Instigation, Struggle** and **Breakthrough**, as well as all the waypoints that got you there. Be particularly clear on the motivation throughout the story. For this to work, you need to link each piece of action with a phrase that shows how that scene drives to the next waypoint.

If it doesn't drive through the Essential Elements then it probably doesn't fit in the story except as an embellishment. If the reason for including an action or waypoint is not self-evident then you might want to qualify it with the phrase 'This means that ...' or 'I'm telling you this because ...', or else drop it.

Ideally, the motivation needs to be there throughout the telling of your story.

In *The Lord of the Rings*, why does the hobbit, Bilbo Baggins, put himself through hell and high water? Because he is looking for the Ring. You never lose sight of that fact, and there is always a clear motivation for his actions. Keep clear on why are you taking each step so that your story continues to make sense and retains dramatic tension.

For example, you might use linking phrases that remind the audience that you are having repeated attempts to achieve your end. 'First I tried talking about the problem to my colleague ... but that made it worse, so then I tried speaking to their line manager about it ... but that was a disaster ... so finally I tried writing an email about how I saw the issue ... and then we had a breakthrough. It made me realise ...'

c. The Close

When you get to the end of your story, and the final Essential Element, the **Insight**, it's like closing a book. You transition from the end of the story back to speaking directly to the audience. Turn to them, look people in the eye – you may even change your tone of voice and link the Insight back to their reality.

You might do this by giving your story context in their world. How does it relate to them?

'Perhaps you have never abseiled down a rock face but I'm sure you have faced your own fears and taken the plunge anyway' or 'It may not be your boss who is giving you a hard time, but we have all met challenging people in the workplace.'

Or you might summarise your key message and insight and create a call to action for them. Make sure your talk ends with some kind of resolution, moral or message for your audience or, if not, a surprise.

Here are my favourite ways to close with a bang:

i. Title close: Give your story an intriguing title and close with the title, which will now make sense because of your story.

ii. Top and Tail close: Open and close your story with the same phrase or question.
iii. Question close: 'What would you do if you found yourself in my shoes?'
iv. Moral of the Story close: 'So remember, when things get tough, dig deeper' or 'Sometimes your worst enemy can become your best friend.'

Signposts

Signposts will let your audience know where you are, and help you navigate too.

They are the visual, verbal, vocal and visceral signals, both within your story and throughout your presentation.

Use them to highlight, emphasise and indicate what is going on in your talk. When you speak, you cannot underline, embolden or put words in italics for emphasis as you can when writing, so the words you use and the way you speak and move have to perform these functions.

It's better to make your signposts overly clear and obvious to your audience than to have no signposts at all and leave them confused. Make a conscious effort to use them until they become a natural part of your speaking repertoire, just like remembering to deliberately mirror, signal and manoeuvre when driving so there is no doubt in other road users' minds about where you are going, what you are doing and what your intentions are. Examples of signposts include:

a. Pauses and changes of voice intonation

Use these just before a big reveal. Such as, 'He turned to me and said ... (voice change) ... "You're fired!"' or 'Perched thirty feet up in the air, poised at the end of the diving board, was ... (pause) ... my boss in bright yellow polka dot trunks.'

b. The Rule of Three

'Three is the Magic Number' rapped De La Soul, an Eighties hip hop trio. There is something that delights people when speakers and storytellers group things in three. Such as, 'There are three things you should know about John: one, he was always looking for food; two, he never stopped chewing and nibbling; three, he was a squirrel', or it could be a repeated phrase or word, for example, 'As I looked out of the window, I could see nothing but rain, rain and more rain.' It gives your talk a rhythm that is pleasing to the ear and mind.

Comedians know and use this device because the funny moment always comes on the third repeat of a certain line. People wait to hear you repeat something three times. They almost hold out for it and are relieved when the triumvirate is complete.

c. Touch phrases

One way of keeping the thread, and providing emphasis to your waypoints, is to use a repeated touch phrase. This could be your key message or insight – 'it never rains but it pours' – a refrain you might repeat after every part of your story that shows this. It becomes reassuring for your audience and they stay in touch with the overarching message all the way through. It's a tricky balance – you want your listeners to feel you are reinforcing your point rather than becoming repetitive.

d. Physical gestures

'There were three reasons why I did not want to go parachuting ...' as you hold up three fingers. 'One, it was raining ...' said as you hold up one finger. 'Two, I looked silly in the bright pink jumpsuit ...' as you hold up two fingers. 'Three, I was absolutely terrified!' and you hold up three fingers. This helps people to keep track of where you are in your story, and which point you are on.

e. Presentation slides

Slides can be useful signposts if they are simple, with just a few words, a number, a phrase or an image that supports and adds to your content. You can use devices like bullet points and headlines to highlight a point, and images to make things clear. The problem is, slides can all too easily dominate, trampling roughshod over the magic you are weaving with your storytelling. If the aim is to move and entrance your audience then practise without presentation slides before doing so with slides – and then only use them sparingly if they really enhance the story. There is a very good reason for the much-touted phrase 'Death by PowerPoint'. I am not against presentation slides but, if they are not used well, they can interfere with the transporting experience you are creating.

CHAPTER 11

Bring your story to life – the Four Vs

'Great stories happen to those who can tell them.'

Ira Glass

In the last chapter we looked at how to structure your delivery – and what devices you can use to drive it forward in a compelling way. Now we will look at how to bring your story to life. Instead of flatly narrating it, you want to elicit powerful emotional responses and create images in people's minds. The Four Vs will help you do this.

1. Visual

Your appearance is the first thing people notice, and first impressions count. The first thirty seconds are particularly crucial. It is worth thinking about how you want to appear as the teller of this story. There are six things that create a powerful visual impression. It seems a lot to think about but they will all become second nature as you practise them:

i. **Stance** – Make sure you stand comfortably, in a relaxed but poised posture. Start with both feet planted on the floor and your arms loose and hands relaxed by your sides. Don't fiddle with your PowerPoint clicker, pace around or rustle your notes. The more relaxed you are, or at least give the impression of being, the more relaxing it is for your audience to watch and listen to you.

ii. **Breathing** – Take a few slow breaths before you start speaking, to collect yourself, relax your body and clear your mind. Don't forget to breathe in the middle of your talk too! It's OK to take a moment to do so, while you pause for dramatic effect!

iii. **Eye contact** – Look one or two people in the eye before you start speaking, in order to make a connection. Then, as you deliver each part, maintain a connection for a few sentences or so with one or other individual in the audience. Many inexperienced speakers don't stop to look anyone in the eye but continuously move their head from left to right like a lighthouse. Try to make contact with people at both sides of the room and the front and back. By connecting with one person you connect with all.

   However, when you are in the midst of a performance element in your story, perhaps recounting dialogue or a particularly emotional experience, it may work better not to look anyone directly in the eye because you are in your own world.

iv. **Smile** – The more you enjoy your story, the more your audience will too, so it doesn't hurt to smile at appropriate times. If you are tense you may find that a smile relaxes you, because a smile releases endorphins that make you feel good. It's a chicken-and-egg situation: you smile, you feel good, you feel good, you smile. And everyone else feels good too because smiling creates a small spark of connection between you and others.

v. **Gestures** – If you have a big audience or a big stage you need to make your gestures grow accordingly and use more of the space. Don't feel the need to constrain yourself to one spot with your arms held tightly down – let your gestures be natural and expressive.

vi. **Props and slides** – As you speak and move, your story will produce images in the mind's eye of your audience. They make pictures in their own heads, drawn from their own memories and imagination, seeing, hearing, feeling, smelling and tasting your experiences. Especially when you describe things in full sensory detail. Storytelling is at its most compelling when it engages and entrances, but sometimes a small prop such as a hat, a special object, a photo or something that is relevant can add an extra frisson to your story.

2. Verbal

The next way to bring your story to life is through the words and phrases that you use. Your foundation should be language that is clear, precise and grammatically correct. As well as following form and structure, it should also sound compelling and exciting. To add to that, you may want to enrich your speech with words that are interesting – using a rich and varied vocabulary

Instead of using tired clichés and descriptions like 'the woman was as old as the hills' or 'white fluffy clouds' – be more inventive. Try weaving in the following rhetorical devices:

alliteration – words beginning with the same sound, such as 'a particularly powerful protest' and 'keep cooking cakes'.

onomatopoeia – words that sound like the concept you are describing, such as 'the train whooshed past' or 'Bang! The firecracker exploded!'

simile – a simile is *like* something else: 'the snow lay across the hills like a soft white eiderdown', and

metaphor – is something that *is* something else: 'the moon was a slither of a silver fish suspended mid-leap in the sky'.

Add in detail. Instead of saying, 'he took out his pen', you might say, 'he plucked out his Parker'. Although that could sound a little like a euphemism, so only use a humorous detail if you are happy to break the ice with a laugh and if appropriate.

You can even invent your own words! 'Supercalifragilistic-expialidocious' wasn't a word until the Sherman Brothers, the songwriters for Disney's *Mary Poppins*, made it up. Not that it's used much for anything, but you might say, 'there was a bam-bam-bam coming from the engine.

Fellow professional speaker and media coach, Penny Haslam, explains how people launch into long 'Titanicdotes' and to avoide this you must develop 'brevitas.'

Of course, your own need not be as flamboyant but if you can pepper your talk with the occasional unusual word it does add colour to what you say. Instead of saying 'car' you might say 'a battered old banger'.

3. Vocal

What is the difference between the 'verbal' and 'vocal'? The vocal is the way you use your voice, which, like a musical instrument, has a pitch, a tone, a rhythm and a volume. 'It ain't what you say, it's the way that you say it', while the verbal is the words you use.

Tone conveys the emotional content; it might be warm, happy and upbeat or cold and dull, for example. Pitch is the frequency of sound. A shrill voice is pitched at a high frequency and a deep, bass one at a low frequency.

We use different voices for different purposes. Newsreaders pause, speak clearly and deliberately, and keep their pitch fairly deep with a reassuring downward inflection. They add gravitas to their tone in this way because often they are speaking about serious, grave or even tragic issues. Children's television presenters, on the other hand, tend to speak quickly, in a lively animated way, with their voices going up into the higher registers.

How is this relevant to you? A flat narration will bore people and you will lose their attention. Use variety in your voice. Otherwise your story might sound like a monotonous, funereal lament. *As well as being dull, it is very difficult to follow a speech or a talk that is given all at one volume, with the same tone, pace and pitch and no any kind of vocal variety. And if you give everything you say equal emphasis it is like reading something set on 'Caps Lock'.

Just as with jokes, so it is with stories – it's how you tell 'em. A brilliant story, poorly told, has far less impact than an average story, well told. Imagine that your voice could paint a picture for the listener even if he or she did not speak your language. You would do this by speeding up and slowing down, adding emotion to your voice and perhaps adopting different speech patterns for different characters. You can weave an experience with your voice alone.

A well-written story will only get you so far. The real way to breathe life into your storytelling is through the use of your voice. Think of how a baby will be afraid of a gruff or angry voice yet soothed by a calm, loving voice, even if they can't understand the words. You can provoke emotion and transport your listener with your pitch and tone.

---

* Research at the University of Glasgow's Institute of Neuroscience and Psychology found that if quotes are given in a dull voice, our brains drown them out with our own inner dialogue.

4. Visceral

The visceral quality is what brings the magic to your story. It is difficult to evaluate.

People can visualise and feel things that they can't quantify with their usual sensory system. This occurs both with objects described on stage and the person who is speaking:

Spatial anchoring – When you tell your story well, the space becomes psychoactive. It's as if your audience is hallucinating. They visualise or imagine people and objects in the space around you as you describe them. Of course you must visualise them yourself first. If you imagine a throne and then indicate towards a wooden chair, saying, 'I approached the majestic bejewelled throne before me', they will start to see a throne for themselves. This is called, in drama terms, 'suspension of disbelief'.

Use your gestures and movements to place imaginary things on the stage around you, but be careful – you must honour the space you create. Like a mime artist who places the flats of his hands in the air to trace an invisible wall, stay true to what you are creating out of thin air. If you've just closed a door with your actions, don't walk through it without opening it again!

Spatial anchoring can also be used to separate out time, so that you stand on different parts of the platform when talking about the past, the present and the future. Or use it to separate parts of your story: happy times and sad times, the East and the West. Create zones on the stage so when you speak about different scenes, topics, times or people they are not cluttered into one space.

Presence – Some people effortlessly create a visceral experience in others because they have powerful natural presence. They are the sort of people that you notice the moment they walk into the room. Apparently you can sense Bill Clinton from 200 metres away, and meeting him in the flesh really is a visceral experience.

Your presence is something you can develop. In the next chapter I will give you some more tips for holding the space. The good news is, you do have an immediate head start when you step up on stage. At the front of the room, all eyes are upon you. There is no hiding. It's as if the cameras are rolling and the director has shouted 'Action!' and here you are in the full glare of the audience's gaze as they wait expectantly for you to utter the next word or make the next move.

You are in the privileged position of being able to lead your audience's thoughts and emotions. Whatever you feel and do up there can be sensed by others, so you need to be able to master your emotions and master the moment.

Feel it! – Strong emotions can connect people and be felt in an almost tangible way. Emotions such as anger, fear and sadness are often palpable. Don't be afraid to use them and show them. A talk is brought to life when it is fuelled by emotion rather than by cool reason alone.

Positive emotions like passion, determination and laughter can also be contagious. According to Professor Robert Provine, author of 'Laughter,' you are thirty times more likely to laugh if you are with someone else, and even more likely to laugh if you know, like or trust someone. Neuroscientist Sophie Scott researched the contagious nature of laughter and found evidence of two types of laughter: voluntary social, appreciative laughter that we use to show acceptance or that we like someone, and the involuntary guffaws that happen when we really are tickled. Let your natural passion, enthusiasm and energy show. This will light a spark in others.

CHAPTER 12

Stagecraft – own the space and master the moment

'Sometimes your only available transportation is a leap of faith to another place.'

Margaret Shepherd

The journey is often different from the plan. Just as sailors have to find their way according to the wind and sea conditions, rather than just sail a pre-determined path, your talk is also subject to the vagaries of your environment and your audience.

If and when this happens, don't be a slave to your plan. Be in the moment: present and attentive to your audience, rather than in your head, desperately trying to adhere to your intended journey.

Remember earlier I mentioned how sailors use waypoints to know where they are in the moment, as well as where they are going. You need to know where you are even if the current position may not be where you intended to be. Once you are under way, you may find that you are not where you had hoped to be. This is not uncommon and is not necessarily a problem – sometimes you go off track deliberately and sometimes better things or alternative things occur in the moment.

When you speak, be aware of the moment while also keeping an eye on where you need to be and what you are driving towards. How do you know you are on track? By sensing the audience's response, trusting your own judgement and by knowing the material really well because it has been rehearsed so many times before. Rehearsed? Something I haven't yet mentioned, but in order to 'master the moment' you need to be prepared and practised before the moment arises.

This reminds me of a line I once heard: 'Amateurs practise and practise until they get it right; professionals practise and practise and practise and practise and practise until they can't get it wrong.'

Which does not mean to say that you can't ad lib and improvise. These things show real mastery of the moment – more on them later.

The main thing is to be able to think on your feet and do a quick check whenever you are able. Of course I don't expect you to do all of this in the midst of your talk, but do keep these things in mind, and the more you practise the more likely these things will start coming naturally to you.

- How is the story going down with the audience? Are they smiling, making eye contact, nodding, following?
- Are they responding as expected? Are they amused by the funny bits and moved by the emotional bits or do they appear bored and uninterested?
- What about the time and the structure? Has the story hit the waypoints as planned or is it changing shape in the telling?

- Do you feel engaged and connected to the material? Is it flowing naturally or is it stilted and halting in the delivery?
- Are you enjoying yourself? If you find a way to do so you will soon get back in flow.

Seven Secrets to Stagecraft

1. Manage introductions

Establish from the start that you are in charge. As I've mentioned, first impressions count, and this includes how you are introduced, or how you introduce yourself. You might not have control over how you are introduced, but if this sets you off on the wrong foot, it is essential that you take back control.

I was once introduced to a team of managers who had just been told that there would soon be hundreds of redundancies made throughout their business, and that they would be expected to deliver these redundancy messages to their own staff members 'and Deborah is here to ensure that all these conversations go well, and people are OK with the outcome.'

I felt I'd been set up to work miracles. I'm sure my audience felt it was unrealistic too, so I had to reset people's expectations right from the start to show that I was in tune with them and was there to help as much as I could. 'Ouch! I'm not sure I can guarantee that. We all have to give and receive negative news as leaders, and that I can't change, but what I can do is to provide you with some approaches to reduce the negative impact. I can also suggest effective approaches to manage people's reactions so that you feel more equipped to have these conversations in a respectful way.'

At other times you can make a quick lighthearted comment as you are being introduced in order to gain some rapport and show you are confident and in control. For example, I was about to speak at an insurance company and their team leader introduced me with: 'I have brought Deborah in so that you don't have to listen to me boring you all day.'

'He wants me to bore you instead,' I quipped as I took the stage.

2. Manage the environment

One thing that can be a distraction, unless you embrace it, is the physical environment.

If people are uncomfortable, they won't be ready to listen to you. As much as possible, take care of all of the basics of the environment such as seating, noise, temperature and lighting, so that your audience can tune in, be attentive and participate properly in the presentation or conversation you have planned. If there is something you can't resolve, at least acknowledge it to let them know you are aware of it – and if you can, turn it into a benefit – so that they can move on from that situation.

I was leading a workshop on team bonding. The small room was filled with a large boardroom table and as the delegates settled around it, they found that there wasn't enough room and that they were having to cram themselves in. Rather than ignore the crowding and have people feel irritated by conditions that were beyond my control, I made light of it: 'Make yourselves comfortable, cosy up next to one another or find a nice knee to sit on. This is all part of the plan, as a way for you to get to know one another better and do a bit of team bonding.'

Another time, I was about to start a seminar in a particularly cold room. A few people wrapped themselves more tightly into their clothes and began muttering. So I began: 'I would say "A very warm welcome to you all" but it is rather cold in here. Feel free to don a coat and mittens while we find someone to sort out the temperature.'

I could have just ignored it but the temperature would only become a greater distraction as time went on, preventing the participants from concentrating. As the speaker you own the space. You might have to get a volunteer to speak to the facilities management or to sort out problems – but take charge. Even if you can't change it, acknowledge it.

3. Endow the audience

Janie is a RADA-trained actor and stage performance coach. She gave me this useful tip: 'Most people endow their audience with all kinds of things. They make unhelpful interpretations of what the audience could be thinking while they are on stage. Things like, "They hate me, they think this is a pointless waste of time, and so forth."'

Instead of endowing your audience with negative thoughts – do the opposite. Assume what they feel towards you is kindness, fascination and interest, for example. Think of the audience as receptive rather than hostile and you will probably find it becomes a self-fulfilling prophecy.

Relax and enjoy your talk. On the whole, people are not out to get you and it certainly doesn't help to imagine that they are. Richard Bandler, one of the co-founders of Neuro-Linguistic Programming (NLP), says it best: 'Develop pro-noia instead of paranoia.'

Tell yourself, 'They are loving this, they think this stuff is great.' Who cares if it is true? The point is that you are going to give a much better performance if you think that your listeners are interested and that they want you to succeed. Be calm, relaxed and friendly and you will have more presence.

And even if it isn't true and you are facing a hostile audience, it is far better to believe the opposite. Although, I must add here as a note of caution, it doesn't pay to be cocky or crack jokes unless you know you can pull it off.

When you endow the audience with a positive reaction, it almost becomes a *fait accompli* – it pulls out a better performance in you and puts you in a better physical and emotional state.

4. Hold the space

When speaking, expand your awareness and gestures to include everybody. It is important to make everyone in the audience feel part of the same experience. Embrace the whole room. Imagine you have an invisible lasso that you throw out to encompass everyone, so that they each feel as if your attention, eye contact, questions and so forth are personally aimed at them.

You can see how this works with comedians. Most people know that if you sit on the front row at a stand-up comedy gig you are likely to receive the attention of the comedian, but some real masters like Peter Kay will work the entire room and have back-and-forth conversations with people from all parts of the theatre.

Many speakers have a lasso that only goes out to the front few rows, so that people at the back become mere observers rather than participants in the experience. Others have a tendency to lasso just the left-hand side of the room, ignoring the people on the right. Or vice versa.

Most of us have a default lasso size that reflects the number of people we are comfortable to speak to and are able to embrace. We need to expand our energy and presence as we work with more people, just as we must increase the size of our gestures and slow down our pace the more people that there are in the room.

It may be that you are perfectly at ease with a small group but as soon as it gets beyond double figures, you find it unnerving. Or you find 25 people fine but with 50 or 100 you feel less connected. Perhaps you are more comfortable with large numbers and you are unfazed by audiences of 300, though you have to work hard to consciously include everyone in your embrace.

Action:

What is your current default size? Set an intention to expand this by speaking with larger groups. Ensure you include everyone around all the perimeters of your room. There does come a tipping point, where you start to do this naturally and automatically.

5. Be responsive

Knowing where you are, determining your position in relation to your surroundings, is only part of navigation. The other part is knowing what to do about it. A good sailor needs to respond to the conditions in the moment. Unexpected things could happen – a squall might suddenly blow up or the wind might die down to nothing and all momentum be lost.

When you are telling a story, you may notice that people are not responding as expected. Perhaps they missed a joke or a reference. It may be that you need to really hit that waypoint and so you need to re-emphasise it. Or maybe the waypoint can be skipped, if it's not of interest to the audience, and so you need to change direction. Should this happen, stay calm, breathe, focus and check in with your audience.

The issue might be that they don't understand something. I was once telling a story in the Middle East that involved peanut butter. As I was speaking, I noticed a bit of confusion in the eyes of my audience. I was losing them somewhere but didn't know why.

I asked, 'Is something not clear in this story?'

A young man spoke up: 'What's peanut butter?'

'Oh! It's like humous but it's made with peanuts,' I replied. Everyone smiled and nodded – and we were back on track.

I was more careful after that to use references that audiences could relate to from their own world rather than ones that I could relate to from mine. A well-told story is successful if it transports the listener. What breaks the trance is confusion or the audience having to constantly search their memory banks to remember what things mean in order to make sense of the story. A well-told story needs to be clear, to wash around them so that they can easily imagine being there, looking through your eyes, seeing what you see, hearing what you hear and feeling what you feel.

6. Manage interruptions

Unexpected occurrences are unavoidable, but you can be prepared for them. There are many things that might happen that are beyond your control – a fire alarm might go off or your time might be shortened. Outside, a passing ambulance siren may drown out your voice, or the catering staff rattle the tea trolley while chatting, or someone in your audience might laugh at the wrong parts, have a coughing fit or walk out of the room for all kinds of reasons.

You can't let any of these things put you off your stride. 'Mastering the moment' is about preparing for and responding to these occurrences, whether they be technical, environmental, or audience-related. Even if your audience is unresponsive, disruptive or downright sceptical, see it as an opportunity to find out what they really think and feel.

You can either ignore the interruption and hope it goes away or acknowledge it by reassuring the audience that all is fine: 'Oh that's just the catering staff bringing the coffees in.' Or you can go one stage further – make interruptions a meaningful part of your story: 'As I was saying, we all need a moment to reflect in life. We can't just keep going and going, and it sounds like the teas and coffees have arrived at the perfect time to remind us of the importance of a break.'

When training to be a clinical hypnotherapist I was given a great tip for what to do if I had somebody in a lovely, drowsy state of trance when suddenly a loud noise interrupted the calm. Perhaps a drilling sound from outside the window. I wouldn't want my subject to be jolted wide awake on high alert for danger, so instead I'd use the noise, as if it were part of the narrative.

I'd reassure the subject that they are feeling very relaxed: 'You are able to tune into my voice so successfully that all other noise is simply a reminder of how comfortable and calm you are now. Isn't it good to know the world can go about its business outside while you are safe, warm, comfortable and relaxed inside? In fact, as you hear that noise it can relax you still further.'

Or I might tie the interruption into my narrative: 'The sound of the aeroplane reminds you that you too are going on a journey – a journey of the mind – and you can imagine what it is like to be up in the sky moving smoothly past clouds and feeling the sun shining on the side of your face, looking forward to arriving somewhere new, exploring new thoughts, ideas and ways of doing things.'

7. Stay connected to your audience

When you tell your Leadership Story, you may be the only one speaking but in reality the communication is still a two-way process. The other party, your audience, may not be saying anything but if they are engaged with your story, then their brains are busy processing and relating your story to their own experiences. Allow them feel their response to your story – make it easy for them to smell, taste and fully experience the journey.

Stay connected to your audience. They need time to consider what you are saying, they need it brought to life for them, and they need to feel that you are a human being responding to them as much as they are responding to you. I know a standup comic who bases his entire set around audience input. He doesn't worry about being heckled. Quite the opposite, he sees that as a positive thing. His act is dependent on audience interaction.

How? Here are five ways to connect:

1. Questions

Ask the audience questions. These might be rhetorical: 'I wonder what you would do if you found yourself locked out of your house in the middle of a rainy night with no keys and no way to contact anybody? Here's what I did ...' You might notice people nodding their heads or smiling in agreement.

Or they might be direct questions, where you expect and wait for an answer: 'Who here has ever found themselves locked out of their house?' If you want people to raise their arm rather than shout out, simply raise your own arm to indicate how you expect them to respond.

2. Conversation

You might actually speak directly to or about an audience member – for example you might say, 'I spoke to Ned here earlier, and he was telling me about when he got locked out of his house. He has a great tip to avoid it. Ned, what was it you said about how you avoid getting locked out of your house? I wish I had known this when I got locked out of my house. Here's what happened to me.'

3. Pause

Allow your story to breathe. Give your audience time to reflect on what you are saying. For example:

'I stood at the top of the rock face ... staring ... thirty feet below, the water shimmered back at me ... beckoning, daring me to jump. Just one more step ... one more step. The others had already jumped. They were already swimming round the corner, out of sight. It was now or never. [Pause.] I will go on the count of three! One ... two ... thr— and then there was a strong hand on my back!'

Now pause again – let three or four beats go by. Was it pulling or pushing? This is a kind of mini-'cliffhanger'. Literally, in this case.

It doesn't just have to be about scary situations. It might be the moment a stranger's eyes met yours across a crowded room and you shared a smile. Give the audience time to soak it in, to recall a moment similar in their own life or to feel the moment as if it were happening to them now.

4. Participation

Get the audience to take part in some way. I once told a story about a trip around South America. I decided to bring it to life by getting them to imagine they were actually on this tour with me, taking a whizz around the continent in a rocket. I said that we could not begin until everyone had put on their safety helmet. I got them to reach under their seat and pick up the imaginary helmet and put it on their head and then each turn to their neighbour to help them tighten the strap. Although the audience were a group of professional adults they all got into the spirit and had some fun doing this. It's a bit like getting the audience at a pantomime to take part by yelling out, 'He's behind you!'

5. Apply the story

Stories can evoke strong feelings and resonances in people. At the end of your story you might like to help your audience digest what they have heard and think about what it means for them. You could let them verbalise their own responses by recounting similar experiences to one another. Of course, in a large group you can't listen to what it provoked in each person, so better to get people into pairs or threes. Give people a chance to express how the story applies to them and what thoughts or ideas it has stimulated.

Let's say you are speaking to a group of salespeople and you have told them a story about an experience in your life that led to you learning a powerful sales technique. You might ask people to share their own experiences of effective sales techniques. Carefully manage how you ask them to share. Some may feel too inhibited to discuss their thoughts and others can get into their own in-depth stories and go too far off your piste. To manage this, give a time limit or set a specific content limit such as: 'Just turn to your neighbour and give them one or two lines about your own sales experience.'

STAGE 5

Evolve

Live a greater story every day

CHAPTER 13

Master the past to keep your story alive today

'The real difference between telling what happened and telling a story about what happened is that instead of being a victim of our past, we become master of it.'

Donald Davis

By this stage, you have honed, crafted and told your story, but now the challenge is to keep that story fresh and alive. Stage 5 is about how you evolve your story and keep it rich and exciting as you share it with others. When you do this, it will bring all kinds of new opportunities and possibilities. It's time for a new level of mastery.

We have already established that your story can limit or empower you and the people around you. Crucially, though, it does so whether this story remains unspoken (even unconscious) or is something you consciously share. You may not even be aware that it leaks out, through your actions and perspectives on things. So, whether you tell your story or not, it still has a bearing on you as a leader.

In this chapter, then, we will look at how you can keep your story alive and relevant. We will explore how you can master the narrative of your past, to take control rather than being a product of it and how you can continue to connect with your audience despite present emotional challenges. Then, in the final chapter, we will address your vision for your future as a leader, and how to go out and live a greater story. You will stretch the concept of who you are, and who you can become. This will enhance your presence and natural ability to influence and inspire. In this way, you and your story will continue to grow and evolve.

Here are three ways to keep your story alive

1. Continue telling your story to keep your skills honed – in other words, weave your story into your daily narrative;
2. Keep your core message front of mind, so that it becomes a seamless part of how you portray yourself, and naturally comes out in your everyday conversations;
3. Keep evolving your story as you, your audience and the situation around you change.

Story-weaving

Real mastery of storytelling takes practice. Try weaving stories into everyday conversations so that this practice becomes familiar and natural to you. If somebody asks, 'What led you to start this business?' or 'Why did you become an aerospace engineer?' and you have a compelling story to tell – tell it. It will bring the conversation alive. Get used to opening up, and you will not only become adept at storytelling, you will more quickly engage people with your message.

The caveat is, of course, to ensure you aren't pulling out a shaggy-dog tale at every turn! Conversation has more of a call-and-response rhythm than a stage presentation. You share just the parts of your story that are relevant in that moment, and others might share their own stories too.

In formal presentations, don't shy away from telling parts of your story either. If you are uncomfortable public speaking, you're not alone. (Remember that statistic about people fearing public speaking more than the idea of death?) Having your Leadership Story on hand will help you feel more confident.

If you are already comfortable with formal public speaking but not so self-assured when it comes to revealing yourself, sharing your own crafted Leadership Story is a fantastic way to start opening up. Let people get to know what's behind that polished exterior. It's tempting not to reveal anything personal, but when you express your own vulnerabilities it's easier for people to connect with you and your passion.

Become a 'Rough Water Specialist'

> *'We think we tell stories, but stories often tell us, tell us to love or to hate, to see or to be blind. Often, too often, stories saddle us, ride us, whip us onward, tell us what to do, and we do it without questioning. The task of learning to be free requires learning to hear them, to question them ... and then to become the storyteller.'*
>
> Rebecca Solnit, *The Faraway Nearby*

My challenge to you is to actively seek out and accept opportunities to use and expand your repertoire of stories and anecdotes. Of course, the more you do this, the more comfortable, confident and experienced you will get, which, most importantly, will dramatically increase your presence and the visceral experience that you create for others.

When I was training in my sculling boat, I would relish the beautiful days when the water was like a mirror – absolutely flat with not a gust of wind on it. I would get to the river at dawn, place my boat on the water, and with one foot on the pontoon, one in the boat, I'd push off and settle into the seat.

The boat carved a wake, like a knife-slice, through the surface of the river. In flat water, it was far easier to be technically proficient and to let the boat run smoothly, without wind or waves to knock me off balance. All my competitors felt the same way. We all loved training when conditions were still and calm, but when they were rough and choppy we might choose, instead, to train indoors.

One day something happened that fundamentally changed the way I thought about this. I was listening to a radio interview with a rock climber who had suffered from vertigo. He took up climbing as a way to face and overcome his fear. Now he excelled at the very thing he had most dreaded.

I decided then and there to become a 'rough water specialist'. On windy, choppy training days, my competitors would be hiding inside, while now I was out on the river. Not only was I getting more practice in rough water but I actually started to enjoy it.

The next race came around. Conditions were grim. Some people put their boats reluctantly onto the water while others scratched completely. I sculled the whole way with a smile on my face, beating two of my closest rivals as they struggled in the chop.

Most of us avoid what we find unpleasant. When we become consciously aware of that avoidance, and decide to embrace it, we can turn it on its head and become a specialist in that area. In the same way, it is possible to become an excellent storyteller – whatever challenge you might have now, be it public speaking, being more vulnerable, crafting your story better, involving your audience, using more stagecraft, commanding the space or using more dialogue. My greatest challenge is putting humour into my talks, so I enrolled myself onto a comedy course that culminated in delivering a five-minute stand-up session in a rowdy pub. The scariest thing I've ever done. That's my new rough water. What's yours?

Tell your OWN story

'Speaking your truth is the most valuable tool there is.'

Oprah Winfrey

Your Leadership Story is the story you tell others about who you are, but it evolves out of the story you tell yourself about who you are. Some people are putting on a front. This may be because they don't believe the story they tell themselves about who they are or it may be because they are telling a story which they have inherited. For example, it might be the story a teacher or parent told about them. They may be unaware that there is something disjointed about the way they portray themselves. But others sense this inauthenticity.

In any event, if you want to be truly compelling, these inner and the outer stories must be aligned. What you say to others on stage needs to be what you say, live and breathe within yourself. If you don't believe it, the story you tell will be thin and unconvincing. If, for example, at one level you believe yourself to be inept in technology and yet you purport to be a tech whizz then, despite your bravado, your lack of inner confidence will come across. It is critical to be self-aware and know who you are.

Your inner story, how you feel about yourself, will directly influence the words you use as you go about your daily life. Even if you are trying to convey something different on the outside, people will see through it. Your inner story is reflected in the way you live, breathe, move and speak, like 'tells' in poker. An astute player can spot if someone is bluffing.

That said, it can be a bit chicken-and-egg. Which comes first: aligning yourself to your story or aligning your story to you? The process happens simultaneously and can often take some personal soul-searching and a commitment to understanding the insights you have gained through your own struggles. Once you do this, and you live those truths with authentic presence day-to-day, then you will have mastery over your past, and the power to inspire and move others in extraordinary ways.

Ultimately, your story is not just told for others' benefit, it really is an expression of who you are and how you interpret your past experience: what shaped you and now guides you in your work and life. If you want to inspire and influence others, you need to understand your inner story and ensure it is empowering. With a strong, life-affirming internal narrative, and the courage to voice your own truth, you will achieve this.

Other people's stories of you

'The most important question anyone can ask is: What myth am I living?'

Carl Jung

We all have a defined idea of who we are, and that is a reflection of who we were in the past and how we dealt with the challenges thrown at us. But your past story may no longer reflect who you are now, nor who you could be.

Is your internal narrative actually someone else's story of who they think you should be? Dana was an accomplished solicitor who had been to Oxford University and worked in a big law firm. She had convinced herself that this was what she wanted until one day she gave it all up and enrolled in dance school to become a teacher.

'I realised that I had been living out my father's story of me since I can remember! He wanted me to go to Oxford and become a lawyer but deep down I had always longed to become a dancer – and no matter how much I ignored it, that passion never left me. It was time to tell a new story about who I am and the life I want to lead.'

Personal development guru Tony Robbins worked with a woman in marital difficulty. She tells the story of herself as the princess that her father, the king, loved unconditionally. Then she married and had children and her husband, who had loved her, began to be aggressive and abusive towards her. Tony made her realise that she had played a part in the deterioration of her marriage too. She was angry with her husband for not loving her in the way she'd been brought up to believe she deserved – as a princess – and so she punished him by withholding her affection. This made her husband feel bereft. She would manipulate him in the way she gave, then withdrew, her love. Her story of being a princess painted her and her father in such a glowing light that she was subconsciously angry with her husband for not measuring up to her father and for not tolerating her spoilt behaviour. She needed to tell herself a new story: not of herself as a little princess who deserved to be loved no matter what, but of herself as a mother and a wife who was both as flawed and as precious as anyone else. And to accept that her husband was human too, with his own frailties and qualities. There's footage of an interview with this couple shot a few years later with Tony Robbins, which shows that they now enjoy a happy marriage.

Many of us see ourselves through the eyes of our parents and continue to define ourselves in that way even after we've grown up, instead of recognising ourselves as the accomplished adults we are today. Until I realised that it was time to live a new narrative myself, I too underestimated my own capabilities. I saw myself through the eyes of my parents, as the little girl I once was rather than the empowered woman I am today.

Do you recognise who you are now and all you have achieved? Do you recognise what you are capable of? Is it time to tell yourself a new story about the person you are and the person you can be today?

How to reinterpret the past: same facts, different story

'If you want to change the world, change your story.'

Joseph Campbell

We could all tell a different story of the same bare facts and events of our lives. When it rains, some people state: 'It's a terrible day – I'll get cold and wet! It is miserable outside', and others say, 'It's a great day because at last the gardens will get watered and the flowers will spring into life.' The fact that it is raining is incontestable but the story you make of it is entirely your interpretation.

The meaning you give to an experience is how you bring a story to life. How you interpret the facts in your life will affect everything you do and how you behave. If someone is friendly, are you suspicious – or do you take it as a confirmation that you live in a friendly world?

It reminds me of the tale of the blind men describing an elephant. The first feels the trunk and declares that an elephant is just like a snake. A second feels a leg and says that an elephant is like a tree. The third feels the side of the body and says, 'No! An elephant is like the side of a leather-clad wall.' Still another feels the tail and is convinced that an elephant is like a rope.

The danger is that we can get so entrenched in our old story that it becomes hard to divorce our story from reality itself and all its different possible interpretations.

For example, I remember when I was five my father came home from work one evening and told us we were moving to Hong Kong.

'It's only for eighteen months,' he said, as if to reassure us, but when we arrived in Hong Kong we immediately loved it. I quickly settled into a new school and when the teachers asked me how long we would be there, I sadly said, 'It's only for eighteen months!' The same words, but this time said with disappointment. The facts remained the same but the meaning changed. It went from a hardship to be endured to an exciting but regrettably short time span. Fortunately, as it turned out, we ended up staying for most of the rest of my childhood – but that's another story.

Be present in the present

'Those who do not have the power over the story that dominates their lives, the power to retell it, rethink it, deconstruct it, joke about it, and change it as times change, truly are powerless, because they cannot think new thoughts.'

Salman Rushdie

Don't let your leadership story get stale. Could it be time for a refresh of your story? If so, you can go through the earlier stages of this book again, taking a fresh look at the facts of your life. Is there a more relevant insight or lesson you can draw from your past to create an even more powerful story that is right for your current situation?

Your presence – or stage presence – is your ability to be relaxed, to be in the moment and to be responsive to your audience, while also maintaining your ownership of the room and the stage. It is the single most important factor in communicating your Leadership Story successfully, in a way that connects with your audience and gives your story and you credibility. Once you are conscious of the story you are choosing to live, and it is aligned to the one you actually tell, your power and presence will occur naturally both on and off the stage.

Of course, being human; all of us encounter emotional ups and downs in life, that may not be compatible with your story, yet you still have to put on a brave face and continue to present or speak to your audience. Sometimes doing so may be the last thing you want to do and it can be tempting to glide over your real emotions, put on an act. But rather than doing this, there may be a way to use them to connect even more powerfully with your audience.

Matt Weinstein, a speaker on the value of humour and levity in the workplace, found himself dealing with profound grief after the death of his wife. He felt at odds with himself when he had to go on stage and talk about having fun. One day he decided that, instead of presenting a façade, he would talk about what was affecting him so deeply: the loss of his wife. His message became about seeing the role of fun and play even during the difficult times. He realised he still felt her loss keenly but, in no longer hiding something that was so important for him, he could be present for his audience. It gave his talks a new quality and depth. He also realised there were probably people in his audience who were also suffering from loss and grief with whom he would now connect far more profoundly.

One way to explore your past with fresh eyes and make it relevant to your present message is to ask family or friends who know you well how they perceive or interpret your reactions to your life events. This could give you a new angle but, of course, in the end, you must adopt your own interpretation.

> *'Use the truth of your own experience to help draw a map into the unknown for the members of your audience ... You will not be "present" for your presentation if you do not speak from your present-time reality.'*
>
> Matt Weinstein

CHAPTER 14

Into the future – live a greater story

'If you can dream—and not make dreams your master;
If you can think—and not make thoughts your aim;
If you can meet with Triumph and Disaster
And treat those two impostors just the same...'

Rudyard Kipling's 'If—'

How your Leadership Story affects your future

Whatever story you tell yourself about your past, and who you are, it will have an immediate effect on how you live your life in the present and interpret events that will have their impact on your future. Instead of letting the past define or limit you, use your story as a springboard for your future. When you bounce down, you bounce back up and beyond (remember 'The Dip'?). Learn and grow from failures and mishaps rather than becoming diminished by them, so you can create a greater story in the future.

Finding and defining meaning in challenge and adversity will enable you to lead people through thick and thin, because it gives both the good and bad times a greater sense and meaning. It is the foundational mindset for a leader – and it comes out in the stories you tell others and the story you are living today.

The America's Cup is one of the world's longest-running races, and started at the Royal Yacht Squadron in 1851 when fifteen of its boats raced and lost to a US yacht called America, *from which the cup eventually got its name. Britain has still not won the trophy back. For the 2017 event, Ben Ainslie led a monumental battle to get the funding for a British boat. His campaign slogan was 'bring the cup home'. #bringthecuphome*

But before he had a chance to contest the Auld Mug (as it is known), he and his team suffered a devastating blow. They were knocked out of the final qualifying races by the eventual winners, Team New Zealand. It had all been for nothing.

As he stepped off the water, the press asked him for his thoughts on what had just happened. What response would he give them after such a catastrophic setback? After all, he had shown such confidence in his chances of success, which had gained him the support he had needed to design and build a competitive race boat and team. Now it was all over.

'Yeah, I'm just so proud of the team to put on the performance that we have ... coming into the event we were on the back foot ... but the whole team turned it around ... and did an incredible job. Hats off to Team NZ. They sailed very well, they've obviously got a fast boat, and they were just too quick for us in the end. But we're a brand-new team. We will be continuing the America's Cup and we will be stronger next time. Already the work starts for next time. There's a reason why the America's Cup hasn't been won [by Brit-

ain] since 1851. This is the start of something special for us, we've got a great team ... and the way we've responded to some difficult times gives me great heart for the future.' He didn't pretend that they hadn't fallen short of their goal to bring back the Cup on this occasion, but his focus was instantly on how valuable lessons had been learnt and that they were now in even better shape to be successful next time round.

In a matter of minutes he turned it all around. He led his team, the press and his supporters into a new way of thinking about the situation – from devastation to hope and strength. As a result, instead of walking away, his key sponsors quickly announced they would continue to back Ainslie's cause into the next campaign.

What could have been perceived as a devastating failure was now reframed as a challenging step on the way to success. The greater story Ben Ainslie was telling himself and others, his compelling vision for the future, enabled him to contextualise those setbacks in the present as the stepping stones to the ultimate goal.

Creating and living a greater story

'Throw your heart out in front of you then run ahead to catch it.'

Ancient Arab proverb

Creating a greater story for yourself is like putting a plant in a slightly bigger pot so it can grow to fill it. The story that you've just created, your Leadership Story, needs to be able to expand. Let it become a greater story.

That greater story is an aspirational vision of your future: one you can grow into, yet it is still aligned with who you are today. It stretches, challenges and allows you to expand. It's uplifting and stimulating, driving you and others onward.

Four steps to create and live a greater story:

1. You need a dream

Just as a vision statement for an organisation should be compelling, so should the greater story you have for yourself. What's yours? Now think bigger.

What do you dream of creating, doing, becoming? Jack Welch, former chief executive of GE, said, 'Good business leaders create a vision, articulate the vision, passionately own the vision and relentlessly drive it to completion.'

What do you dream of for yourself and for those you potentially influence? What would you like to make happen? What vision for your leadership or life really fires you up?

Think of it as a legacy that you would like to leave after you've gone. What contribution would you like to make to humankind? What would you like your obituary to say about you? How do you intend to make other people's lives better?

2. Flesh it out

When you've identified your dream, it's time to put some meat on the bones. Imagine a time when this dream is coming true: what do you see, what do you hear, what do you experience day-to-day? How about the people within your organisation and how about the people your organisation serves? Write this all down in the present tense, as if you were writing a series of 'Magic Postcards' to yourself or your loved ones from this future time. When you do this, things seem to fall into place to provide a pathway there.

3. Build motivation and momentum

Remember, people need a strong impetus to change. Watch out for what's sometimes described as 'The Fur-Lined Rut'. This refers to the fact that, often, things have to get very uncomfortable before we get out of our comfort zone. In Gay Hendrick's *The Big Leap*, he says the most dangerous place to be in is 'The Zone of Excellence'. When you are there, why would you risk changing or losing anything to make a leap into your 'Zone of Genius' and fully manifest your potential?

So, in order to realise your vision, you must know why it matters so much for you. Understand both the 'towards' and 'away from' motivating factors.

If, for example, your dream is ... *to create workplaces where severe anxiety and stress is eradicated;*

First, find an 'away from' scene – perhaps an experience in your own life when ... *the pain or cost to yourself and others of having too much stress at work was immense.*

Next, find a 'towards' – what would it look like if there had been a different response in place? What might workplaces look like in your new vision and what are the advantages and payoffs? Why is it so appealing? Why does it matter to you?

Create vignettes, by writing about them or finding images or video clips of what you would like to see – drawn from your own previous experience or two or three scenarios from others' experience.

4. Commit – mobilise events around you by beginning

Once you have your antennae up, the world seems to mobilise around you, presenting opportunities, people and events that help make your vision a reality. You must do your part by taking the small and big actions that are in front of you – but don't worry about what is beyond your current scope. Don't hesitate in taking action just because everything isn't yet in place. Just begin and keep putting one foot in front of the other.

William Hutchison Murray, in his 1951 book *The Scottish Himalayan Expedition*, explains:

'Until one is committed there is hesitancy, the chance to draw back, always ineffectiveness. Concerning all acts of initiative (and creation), there is one elementary truth, the ignorance of which kills countless ideas and splendid plans: that the moment one definitely commits oneself, then Providence moves too.

All sorts of things occur to help one that would never otherwise have occurred. A whole stream of events issues from the decision, raising in one's favour all manner of unforeseen incidents and meetings and material assistance, which no man could have dreamt would have come his way.'

Maybe all these opportunities were already there or maybe you'll have had a hand in creating them. Either way you now notice and take advantage of them, because you have a clear vision in mind. Keep stoking the fire to keep that vision alive – by speaking about, visualising or imagining yourself in the future – and take whatever steps you can to get there. A path will emerge and all the support, guidance and resources that you need as well.

How to begin

'What you can do, or dream you can, begin it,
Boldness has genius, power, and magic in it,
When you engage, the mind grows heated,
Begin! And the work will be completed!'

Johann Wolfgang von Goethe

Instead of starting from where you are, start by imagining where you would like to be. Many people make the mistake of defining a vision statement in an incremental way. In other words, they think about where they are now and then look a couple of steps ahead. For the moment, don't worry about whether it is possible, but think entirely about how things could be if you were to wave a magic wand.

As Stephen Covey said in *The 7 Habits of Highly Effective People*: 'begin with the end in mind'. Indeed, this is the first habit. So start with a vision that inspires you. This is a dream, not a plan. Martin Luther King did not say, 'I have a plan ...'. That would not have inspired anyone. He had a dream, one that outlived him and is still alive today, inspiring people and giving them direction. This is what a leader does.

Disney Creativity Strategy

At the Disney Corporation they developed an approach that led to all kinds of successful creations, from the inception of Disneyland itself to many of their films and new approaches in animation. Their Creativity Strategy had three parts:

1. **Visioning** – here people worked together to imagine what they might do if money, resources and practicalities were no issue. When John F. Kennedy had the dream

of 'landing a man on the Moon and returning him safely to Earth', nobody really knew whether this was possible. But it inspired NASA and a whole generation, and led to many young people wanting to become astronauts and to a leap in aerospace engineering. It all started as a vision.

2. **Planning** – their brief was to take the vision and make it happen. 'How can you land a man on the Moon?' Their only rule was to not criticise the vision or dream. Their only role was to create a plan for making it happen.

3. **Constructive Criticism** – again, the critics do not criticise the dream, only the plan. They are looking for potential issues and assessing risks, which they can pass back to the creative vision team to solve.

So where would you like to be? It's time to create your dream, flesh out the vision, build motivation and commit to action to make it happen. Here is your first step:

A letter to the future

Write an account of a day in the future, at a time when you have already achieved your vision or are on track to doing so. Write it as if it has already happened and you are making the impact you want to make in the world. So, you write it from the future but in the past tense. Don't over-think it. Just let the pen flow – and (although it is up to you) I do recommend pen and paper over a keypad for this exercise as it frees up the creative flow when you use your own handwriting.

Here's mine:

This morning, I awoke to the sound of my children splashing in the pool outside and looked out of the window at the azure seas across the bay. After breakfast by the pool and an energising swim, I strolled to my office with its seascape views and joined my team for a pow-wow about the international seminar programme, books and events that we had coming up.

The news came in that my latest book had reached New York Times *bestseller status, leading to numerous PR opportunities on radio, television and in the press. Our products and services formed a cohesive, sleekly designed and colourful range of material, which looked fantastic and was full of original ideas and really useful contents, but what was really great was how they seemed to ignite the spark of true self-expression and authentic presence in our customers all over the world.*

That afternoon I would welcome senior global leaders to my five-day REAL Leadership retreat before flying to Cape Town to lead much larger seminars in a stunning waterside hotel.

Perhaps by the time you read this, my Vision Story will be true. I am getting closer to it every day.

Now it's your turn.
Write an account of a day in your life when you are living your dream. Fill it with details and sensory experience.

The Vision Story: a future story told in the present tense

In your future letter, you'll be describing a future situation to yourself as if it has already happened. Now, how do you use this principle of a future story to convey a compelling vision to others? Here, a future-oriented story is a bit tricky. It hasn't already happened. The thing about stories is that they are generally told in the past tense. Here we put your Vision Story of the future into the past by using the device of pseudo-orientation in time.

For example, when I worked at a large management consultancy, I was asked to lead the annual flagship event. It ran over three nights and involved a huge investment by the partnership, so it was important that they were sold into my vision in order to agree to the investment. Also, it would be up to them to invite their key clients and prospects, some of whom were very high-powered City movers and shakers.

My success hung on not only the conception and delivery of a great event but in getting all the right people into the room in a way that they could enjoy the company of their hosts and feel impressed by the firm. The partnership, as hosts and investors, had to be excited by the concept and be able to convince their clients that it would be worth attending. To do that, they had to be convinced and enthused themselves.

I used the Vision Story approach. Having conceived of the idea and developed the vision, and after weeks of research into venues and exploring various concepts, I booked meetings with all the key people, the heads of each business area, and said,

'Imagine if, a year from now, your clients said, "Remember that event that we went to last year – the 'Palace of Genius'? Now that was a memorable event. It was completely different from all the normal corporate events we go to. Not only was it in a beautiful venue full of amazing art, but in each room there was a genius from the world of arts and literature, including television personalities, talking about the relevant work on display. From the start, our invitation was unusual. It was a simple embossed piece of gold leaf, and when we arrived we were presented with a beautiful gold book all about our surroundings ..." '

I continued to describe what would happen through the event – the chocolate stiletto shoes in the Marie Antoinette room, Andrew Graham-Dixon, the well-known art historian, discussing the portrait of The Laughing Cavalier, and so forth. I used a future situation to describe the event through the eyes of the client – the people they were most keen to impress, get to know, and ultimately do more business with – in order to give them confidence and convince them that this would be a great night.

Once I saw that I had enthusiasm and engagement in the eyes of my audience, I then made use of the moment to ask if they'd like to be involved.

Sure enough, this created a huge buzz and the event lived up to expectations and became a self-fulfilling prophecy. After we ran the event, both clients and people from the firm said that it was the best event they had ever been to. The Vision Story created the reality and everyone touched by the story became part of making it the success that it was. So what was it that made this story work?

How to make a Vision Story work for you

Here are the key components to tell your own story as a compelling vision for the future:

1. Define what actions you would like your audience to take in response to your story.

2. Begin your story at a time after the vision has been accomplished or is coming to fruition.

3. Use the phrase 'Imagine looking back from a future time at this vision ...' It helps to put in a definite date such as 'a year from now'.

4. Involve the audience. Put them inside the story: 'Think about how you and your clients reflect on this achievement ...'

5. Bring it to life using sensory detail as well as what people would actually say about it. Voice the conversation they might have and the specific experiences they might comment on.

6. When you see the light in their eyes and some engagement, ask them if they would like to be part of making this happen (or whatever your desired response is from them).

Now you have the insights into how to lead change in the world around you through your vision story, you can lead a change in yourself.

Don't be afraid of failure

Arianna Huffington, co-founder of the *Huffington Post*, tells the story of how she failed many times. 'One failure that I always remember was when my second book was rejected by thirty-six publishers. Many years later, I watched *HuffPost* come alive to mixed reviews, including some very negative ones. But my mother used to tell me, "Failure is not the opposite of success, it's a stepping stone to success." So at some point, I learned not to dread failure. I strongly believe that we are not put on this Earth just to accumulate victories and trophies and avoid failures; but rather to be whittled and sandpapered down until what's left is who we truly are.'

Find out who you truly arc and tell the story of the failures that made you that way. Then keep moving forward, learning and growing and evolving your story as you discover more about who you are becoming. It is an ongoing process – we never arrive – we are always 'becoming', so stay present, aware and fresh.

As poet, Wallace Stevens said, 'Each of us is continually writing and rewriting the text of our life, revising our memories and hopes, proposing plans, filtering disappointments through our defences and rationalisations, making adjustments in the way we present ourselves to ourselves and others. To the degree that we are self-conscious, we live in our narratives – our discourse – about our actions, thoughts and feelings.'

Stay conscious of your own narrative and aware of how this drives your actions thoughts and feeling day to day.

Future voyages

So let me wish you bon voyage. May you transport those whom you touch with your story – show them the star-spangled heavens, the glorious sunsets and the beautiful frothing, rolling waves and let them know the struggle you had to get there, but most of all share the gift of your insight.

You can't change your past but you can change the way you tell the story of what happened, what it means to you and who you are today. As you share your story, you will build your storytelling muscle and it will become more aligned with who you are becoming. Speak the truth in your heart, because it might just be that the words you have to share are the very words someone else needs to hear.

Your story has the power not just to change other people's lives – but to change your own.

I wish you the greatest success.

'Don't cry because it's over, smile because it happened.'

Dr. Seuss

Appendix

THE TWELVE-PART STRUCTURE

Christopher Vogler's twelve-part structure of The Hero's Journey is a synthesis of Joseph Campbell's work, and can be applied to many films, stories, myths and legends, and to your own personal story.

1. THE ORDINARY WORLD: The hero, uneasy, uncomfortable or unaware, is introduced sympathetically so the audience can identify with the situation or dilemma. The hero is shown against a background of environment, heredity, and personal history. Some kind of polarity in the hero's life is pulling him or her in different directions and causing stress.
2. THE CALL TO ADVENTURE: Something shakes up the situation, either from external pressures or something rising up from deep within, so the hero must face the beginnings of change.
3. REFUSAL OF THE CALL: The hero feels the fear of the unknown and tries to turn away from the adventure, however briefly. Alternatively, another character may express the uncertainty and danger ahead.
4. MEETING WITH THE MENTOR: The hero comes across a seasoned traveller of the worlds who gives him or her training, equipment or advice that will help on the jour-

ney. Or the hero reaches within to a source of courage and wisdom.

5. CROSSING THE THRESHOLD: At the end of Act One, the hero commits to leaving the Ordinary World and entering a new region or condition with unfamiliar rules and values.
6. TESTS, ALLIES AND ENEMIES: The hero is tested and sorts out allegiances in the Special World.
7. APPROACH: The hero and newfound allies prepare for the major challenge in the Special World.
8. THE ORDEAL: Near the middle of the story, the hero enters a central space in the Special World and confronts death or faces his or her greatest fear. Out of the moment of death comes a new life.
9. THE REWARD: The hero takes possession of the treasure won by facing death. There may be celebration, but there is also danger of losing the treasure again.
10. THE ROAD BACK: About three-fourths of the way through the story, the hero is driven to complete the adventure, leaving the Special World to be sure the treasure is brought home. Often a chase scene signals the urgency and danger of the mission.
11. THE RESURRECTION: At the climax, the hero is severely tested once more on the threshold of home. He or she is purified by a last sacrifice, another moment of death and rebirth, but on a higher and more complete level. By the hero's action, the polarities that were in conflict at the beginning are finally resolved.
12. RETURN WITH THE ELIXIR: The hero returns home or continues the journey, bearing some element of the treasure that has the power to transform the world as the hero has been transformed.

Resources

CONTINUE THE JOURNEY

There are several resources to support you in influencing and inspiring with Your Leadership Story:

Your Leadership Story: The Workbook
To accompany the book I've designed this tool to enable you to work through this material and develop your leadership story.

Download it at: www.vivacitygroup.co.uk/YLSworkbook

Leadership Story Events
These events give you a live experience of leaders sharing their own Leadership Story to engage and connect with their audience and convey their message. Hear how they have used their story to shape their experience in the workplace and leave a legacy.

Visit: www.vivacitygroup.co.uk/events

Your Story, Your Message
Book Deborah for a keynote or a live half-day session on the magic of finding and using your story and discovering your message. Explore how you can use your story to engage others live and in person! www.vivacitygroup.co.uk/contact

Get Social

Visit facebook.com/yourleadershipstory and like the page for ongoing updates and bonuses.

Watch case studies and talks on:
YouTube.com/yourleadershipstory

The REAL Leadership Programme

Our flagship programme is ideal for senior leaders who believe in the value of authentic presence and want to shape the way they lead to empower their team and engage their clients most powerfully. Find out more, visit: www.vivacitygroup.co.uk/realleadership

Further Reading

A.S. Byatt, *On Histories and Stories*, Vintage ed. 2001

John Grinder & Richard Bandler, *Trance-formations: Neuro-linguistic Programming and the Structure of Hypnosis*, Real People Press, 1981

Brené Brown, *Daring Greatly*, Penguin, 2013

Joseph Campbell, ed. Diane Osbon, *Reflections on the Art of Living*, HarperCollins 1991

Philip Collins, *When They Go Low, We Go High: Speeches that Shape the World - and Why We Need Them*, 4th Estate, 2017

Stephen Denning, *The Leader's Guide to Storytelling*, Wiley, 2011

Gavin Esler, *Lessons from the Top: How Successful Leaders Tell Stories to Get Ahead - and Stay There*, Profile Books, 2012

Klaus Fog, Blanchette, Budtz and Munch, *Storytelling: Branding in Practice*, Springer, 2010

Seth Godin, *All Marketers Are Liars/Tell Stories*, Portfolio/Penguin, 2012

Jonathan Gottschall, *The Storytelling Animal*, Mariner Books, 2013

Gay Hendriks, *The Big Leap*, HarperOne, 2010

Carl Jung, *The Archetypes and the Collective Unconscious*, Routledge, 1969

Lakoff & Johnson, *Metaphors We Live By*, Chicago, 1980

Ursula K. Le Guin, *The Wave in the Mind*, 2012

Robert McKee, *Story: Substance, Structure, Style and the Principles of Screenwriting*, Methuen Film, 1999

John Medina, *Brain Rules*, Pear Press, 2014

Nick Owen, *More Magic of Metaphor, Stories for Leaders, Influencers and Motivators*, Crown House, 2004

Rebecca Solnit, *The Faraway Nearby*, Granta, 2014

Christopher Vogler, *The Writer's Journey: Mythic Structure for Writers*, Michael Wiese, 2007

Acknowledgements

Many people have supported and helped me to bring this book into being but, in particular, I'd like to thank the following: -

Dan Priestley for the initial focus and book title. *Joe Gregory* for reading through the first draft — and telling me it was a book worth writing. *John Stapleton* for your leadership story. *Alan Stevens* for encouraging me to become an author and professional speaker — and holding me to account by believing in this book. *Jacq Burns* for an amazing edit and, with *John Williams*, for great guidance and advice. *Ed Peppitt* for your huge generosity in sharing your knowledge and help in so many ways.

Leah Blackburn for your quiet wisdom, insight, humour and friendship. *Sylvia Baldock* who shines bright and inspires me to shine my own light too and to the other members of our group; *Marissa* and *Nicky*. *Julie Van Breda* for a supportive, restorative environment in Cape Town. *Russell-Olivia Brooklands* for incredibly generous contribution, encouragement and input.

Helen Pisano for your kindness and attention to detail in the final copy edit. *Tanja Prokop* for all your wonderful cover designs - you got it right first time! And to *Andrea Reider* for a beautiful interior layout - and for deciphering my scrawl.

Also to the many outstanding and wonderful individuals at the *PSA*, my *Speaker MasterMind* and *JFWI* (*Just Flippin' Write It*) groups whose example, wisdom and support have transformed my own business as a speaker, author and leadership development expert.

Finally, a very big thank-you to my mother, *Celia Wesley*, for going through it page by page with me — especially during Wimbledon week. And to my husband, *Adam*, for all your love and support.

47003530R00116

Printed in Poland
by Amazon Fulfillment
Poland Sp. z o.o., Wrocław

El juego del hater

Raúl Álvarez
AuronPlay

El juego del hater

mr

Ediciones Martínez Roca es un sello editorial de Editorial Planeta, S. A.
Avenida Diagonal 662-664
08034 Barcelona (España)
www.planetadelibros.com

Diseño de la cubierta: Planeta Arte & Diseño
Imagen de cubierta: © José María Carrillo (fotografía) / © Wenyuri (muñeco)
Fotografía del autor: Sara Moledo Mato

Edición y fijación del texto: Ramón Tarrés

Primera edición: octubre, 2017
Segunda edición: noviembre, 2017

Preimpresión: MT Color & Diseño, S. L.

Depósito legal: B. 19.581-2017
ISBN: 978-84-270-4391-6

www.espasa.com
www.planetadelibros.com

Impreso en España / *Printed in Spain*
Impresión: Unigraf, S. L.

Editorial Espasa Libros, S.L.U.
Avda. Diagonal, 662-664
08034 Barcelona

El papel utilizado para la impresión de este libro es cien por cien libre de cloro
y está calificado como papel ecológico.

—Pero, ¡¿qué cojones es esto?!

Estaba acostumbrado a ir al videoclub de Silvestre y, a pesar del ambiente tétrico propio del local, nunca me había llevado un susto como ese. En mis manos sujetaba un *flyer* que había descolgado del tablón que mi amigo tenía junto a la puerta de entrada y donde cualquiera podía anunciar lo que quisiera: representaciones de teatro, conciertos, cursos para hacer cupcakes, clases particulares de inglés o... lo que me tenía absorbido desde que acababa de entrar: un pequeño papel con forma rectangular cuyo reclamo era un gran titular escrito en Comic Sans: «venta de muñecos hechos a mano».

Vender muñecos en sí mismo no tenía nada de particular; no era el único artesano que anunciaba sus productos ahí. Lo que casi provoca que se me desprendieran las retinas de los ojos fue el resto del anuncio:

> *Se venden muñecos realizados con mucho mimo, cariño y de manera totalmente artesanal. Muñecos de gran calidad inspirados en personajes famosos e inventados por mí. Como pueden observar tienen un gran parecido y*

están perfectamente realizados, hasta el más mínimo detalle. Se aceptan encargos a partir de 350 €.

Sin duda, lo que tenía delante, o era una broma o estaba escrito por un invidente, ya que la imagen que ilustraba el texto era una foto de uno de esos muñecos de «gran parecido y perfectamente realizados» que ofrecía el anuncio: una reproducción de Cristiano Ronaldo o, mejor dicho, algo que pretendía serlo. Ni después de la peor borrachera de cumpleaños del futbolista portugués, lo que aparecía en la foto llegaba a asemejarse a él.

—Tío, que aún quedan meses para Halloween. Un poco exagerado vender esto ya, ¿no crees? —insistí.

—Bah, esto es como la primavera, que no empieza hasta que lo dice El Corte Inglés —respondió Connor de espaldas, mientras repasaba con la mirada los lomos de los DVD de cine coreano.

Ahí solo trabajaba Silvestre, pero desde siempre había sido nuestro punto de encuentro. Era un cuchitril oscuro y con olor a humedad. Las estanterías repletas de pelis iban desde el suelo hasta el techo que, por suerte para los bajitos, apenas superaba los dos metros.

—¿Yo qué sé, Joel? —se defendió Silvestre mientras colocaba carátulas en las estanterías. Era prodigioso ver cómo sabía dónde iba cada, aunque a veces sospechaba que las ponía al tuntún—. Para eso está el tablón, para que la peña cuelgue lo que quiera.

—Pero hay que filtrar, Sil, esto ahuyenta a la clientela.

—¿Más aún? —dijo Connor, que ya había pasado a la sección de cine taiwanés.

—Es un país libre, ¡déjame en paz! —protestó de nuevo Silvestre. De profesión era dependiente, pero de vocación, cascarrabias. Un abuelo prematuro.

—Pero, ¿lo habéis visto bien?

Connor ni se inmutó. Movía la cabeza de izquierda a derecha como un autómata por cada una de las estanterías. Siempre hacía lo mismo, como si buscara el santo grial entre las decenas de películas de títulos impronunciables que se alquilaban en el videoclub. Era el único que quedaba en la ciudad y si aún no había cerrado era porque tenía lo más raro de lo más raro. Y, lógicamente, su clientela no le iba a la zaga. Bien pensado, un anuncio como ese solo podía estar ahí.

—¡Qué pesado! —dijo Silvestre acercándose a mí y mirando por encima de mi hombro el *flyer* que sujetaba entre mis manos—. ¡Hostia!

—Te lo dije —afirmé triunfante—. Filtrar, Sil. Esa es la idea.

—¡Por fin! —exclamó Connor con un DVD entre sus manos—. Llevaba meses buscándola.

—¿Y no podías haber preguntado al dependiente? —pregunté asombrado.

—Me gusta conseguir las cosas por mí mismo, ¿algún problema? —respondió Connor al tiempo que dejaba la película en su sitio. No tenía interés en verla, solo en encontrarla. ¿Absurdo? Conociéndole, no.

—¿Qué coño es esto? —Silvestre seguía mirando el *flyer*.

—Es lo que os llevo preguntando desde hace media hora.

Connor se acercó y se unió al corrillo. Fiel a su estilo, ni se inmutó.

—Prodigioso —sentenció—. Una auténtica payasada.

—Si esto es lo que hace inspirándose en personajes famosos, no quiero ni pensar cómo serán los inventados por él —dije con sorna.

—Mejor no preguntar. El cerebro de este tío tiene pinta de ser complejo. Muy complejo —añadió Connor.

—Y que lo digas. ¡A la basura! —respondió Silvestre mientras me arrancaba el *flyer* de las manos.

—¿Qué haces? —grité alarmado.

—Filtrar, ¿no? —dijo Silvestre confundido.

—Esto es una joya, amigos —dije recuperando el *flyer*.

—¿Te va el rollo freak, ahora? —dijo Connor—. En mi casa tengo un auténtico museo sobre el tema, si estás interesado.

—No, no... —respondí—. Es que esto merece...

—No, Joel, no estarás pensando... —interrumpió Silvestre.

—No me digáis que no —dije afilando la sonrisa.

—¿Iba a servir de algo? —preguntó Connor sabiendo la respuesta.

—No, la verdad —se rindió Silvestre.

—Chicos, esto está pidiendo a gritos una llamada para mi canal.

—Obvio —resumió Connor.

Me guardé el *flyer* en un bolsillo y me dirigí a la salida. En la puerta me crucé con Jan y Flavia, que acababan de entrar.

—¡Hey, Joel! ¿Se te quema la comida o qué? —preguntó Jan bromeando por mi urgencia.

—Si no tiene ni idea de cocinar, ¿qué dices? —preguntó Flavia descolocada. No tenía una gran habilidad para pillar los dobles sentidos. Por eso tardaba en llegar; aunque al final siempre llegaba—. Ah... Vale, que es por las prisas.

No me detuve a responder. Solo sonreí y salí corriendo de ahí.

—¡Os veo, chicos! —me despedí.

—¿Qué le pasa? —insistió Jan.

—Los cerebros creativos, que sufren de incontinencia —dijo Silvestre meneando la cabeza.

—O de maldad —resumió Connor con una sonrisa.

—¿Cómo, va a hacer algo malo? Pero si Joel es un trozo de pan —Flavia miró a Connor asustada. Los otros tres, incluido su novio, Jan, la miraron expectantes. Sabían que en dos segundos iba a aterrizar en el planeta de los humanos—. Ah... Sí, ya. Que va a hacer uno de sus vídeos.

—Bravo —sentenció Connor camino a la estantería de cine filipino.

1.

Mi cabeza no había parado ni un segundo desde que salí de la tienda de Silvestre. Sentía el anuncio en el bolsillo trasero de mi pantalón como si llevara un billete de lotería premiado. Era lo que me sucedía siempre que sabía que tenía una gran idea para mi canal. Aunque... ahora que lo pienso, tal vez debería presentarme. Me llamo Joel Graham y soy *youtuber*. Mi canal lo siguen miles de personas. En realidad, unos cuantos miles. Lo digo así para ser modesto, decir millones suena prepotente. Y levanta ampollas, para qué nos vamos a engañar. Pero, ¡qué narices! Mi canal tiene... algún que otro millón de seguidores. Vaya, no puedo evitar ser modesto otra vez.

Si dijera que ser *youtuber* es duro, volvería a sonar prepotente. Pero a veces lo es. No porque todo el mundo conozca tu cara y casi no puedas salir ni a comprar el pan. Eso, en cierto modo, es una ventaja: siempre tengo una excusa para pedirle a otro que lo haga por mí. Es duro porque, por mucho que parezca lo contrario, ser *youtuber* es un trabajo. A ver, que no soy el único que trabaja en el mundo, lo sé. No me quejo. Es solo que, detrás de los vídeos que aparecen en mi canal hay un montón de horas dedicadas a pensar, a preparar, a ensayar, a repetir, a probar. Por eso, cuando encuentro algo que sé que va a funcionar, no puedo más que dar saltos de alegría: sé que tengo una buena idea y, sobre todo, que no voy a tener que dedicar unas cuantas horas a esperar a que se me ocurra. El anuncio de los muñecos era mi idea. Un diamante en bruto. Un auténtico bombazo para mi canal. Hacía algunas semanas que no acababa de sentirme cómodo con mis vídeos. Estaban bien, me gustaban y a mis seguidores también. Pero tenía la sensación de que necesitaba un vídeo que se saliera de lo habitual. Un pelotazo, vamos. Y la llamada al fabricante de muñecos iba a serlo. Seguro.

Al llegar a mi casa, me dirigí directo al estudio. Me salté la clásica parada en la nevera, parada inútil la mayor parte de las veces, ya que mi nevera no era lo que se dice un «mundo de posibilidades». De hecho, mis amigos la llamaban «Sahara» por estar siempre desierta. Esta vez tenía prisa. Quería prepararlo todo para hacer la llamada cuanto antes. Una vez sentado frente a la cámara, respiré hondo y miré al frente. No quería darle muchas vueltas a lo que iba a hacer, prefería que todo saliera de forma espontánea. Improvisación pura y dura. Marqué y esperé. Tras varios tonos, que se me hicieron interminables, alguien descolgó.

—Buenas tardes —respondió el protagonista involuntario de mi vídeo al otro lado. Su voz sonaba ronca y el hombre tuvo que aclararse la garganta al terminar de saludar, señal de que llevaba varias horas sin hablar.

—Buenas —saludé—. ¿Hablo con...? ¿Con quién hablo?

—¿Qué es lo que quiere? —respondió el hombre conteniendo un primer arrebato de mal humor. Por su tono seco y poco «comercial», muchas llamadas para comprar muñecos no debía de tener, pensé.

—La pregunta correcta sería: ¿qué es lo que quiere usted?

—Creo que se ha equivocado, joven —«¡¿Joven?!». ¿Quién menor de 60 años habla así? Aunque por su voz, calculaba que tendría cuarenta y pico.

—Eso parece..., «mayor» —respondí aguantando la risa—. Creí que hablaba con un artista, un creador, un... un... Leonardo da Vinci de los muñecos. Pero debo de haber marcado mal el número. Un saludo —dije a modo de órdago.

—¡Espere, espere! Está llamando al número correcto. ¿En qué puedo ayudarle? —como suponía, mi interlocutor reaccionó de inmediato suavizando el tono.

—¿No ha pensado que quien necesita ayuda es usted?

—¿A qué se refiere? —dijo con una amabilidad forzada.

—En general, a todo.

—¿... Todo? —respondió desubicado.

—Vamos por partes —respondí resuelto—. Atención telefónica. Cero. Trato con el cliente. Cero. Habilidad comercial. Cero. ¿Quiere que siga?

—Yo... Bueno, le pido disculpas si se ha sentido molesto...

—No es molesto, caballero. Es... ¿Cómo lo diría? Perplejo. En la vida me habían tratado así cuando iba a comprar algo. Como comprenderá, a nadie le gusta pagar para ser tratado mal.

—En nombre de M-M insisto en mis disculpas y le ofrezco un diez por ciento de descuento en su próxima compra.

—¿M-M? —pregunté desconcertado. Esto se ponía interesante— ¿«M» de... Mierda? Porque si es así, estamos hablando de doble mierda.

—No, señor... —respondió conteniéndose— M-M, de Magical Muppets, ¿no es donde está llamando? —Casi me doblo de la risa en el asiento al escuchar el nombre de su «empresa», por llamarla de alguna forma.

—Si le digo la verdad, no sabía dónde llamaba. Olvidó poner el nombre del negocio en su anuncio —dije cuando pude volver a articular palabra.

—¿Cómo? —Al otro lado de la línea escuché al señor revolviendo entre papeles—. Ya, esto... Debieron cortarlo mal en la imprenta.

En la imprenta, claro. Quería convencerme de que una fotocopia cutre que luego había cortado a mano en su casa era un trabajo de imprenta. Ese hombre era un filón.

—En segundo lugar, ¿qué le hace pensar que tengo intención de realizar una compra?

—¿Cómo dice?

—Me acaba de ofrecer un descuento. ¿Cree que llamo para realizar una compra? —insistí.

—Bueno, yo... —estuvo a punto de volver a perder la compostura, aunque aún mantenía el tipo—. ¿Por qué llama, entonces?

—Verá —empecé fingiendo un leve tono amenazante—, le llamo de la oficina de *Management* de CR7 en Londres. Hemos visto su anuncio y queríamos preguntarle por su número de licencia para reproducir su imagen.

—E-el... ¿número de licencia? —respondió desconcertado, aunque lo que me transmitía su voz en realidad era pánico.

—Supongo que dispone de licencia para usar la imagen de nuestro cliente. Aunque, ahora que lo compruebo... —tecleé a lo loco en mi teclado solo por hacer ruido— ... Magical..., ¿cómo era?

—Muppets —respondió con voz casi inaudible.

—Magical Muppets... —seguí tecleando— ... no aparece en nuestra base de datos. A no ser que se le concediera una licencia gratuita como organización benéfica. ¿Es ese el caso? ¿Es Magical... lo que sea, una ONG?

—Eh... No.

—Entonces, ¿quién le ha autorizado a fabricar muñecos con la imagen de CR7? ¿El propio señor Ronaldo?

—Bueno, verá... —empezó a explicarse el señor sin saber qué iba a decir—. Yo... a ver. Yo soy artesano, no pensé que tuviera que pedir una licencia para usar...

—¿Tiene abogado? —interrumpí.

—¿Abogado? —Me imaginé cómo el hombre se iba encogiendo poco a poco en su silla—. Mi cuñado estudió Derecho, pero trabaja de contable.

—Y le hace la declaración de la renta, no me diga más.

—Sí —respondió avergonzado.

—Pues a lo mejor debería ir pensando en llamarle porque mi equipo jurídico está redactando una demanda para presentar ante la corte británica. ¿Su cuñado habla inglés?

—Chapurrea, como todo el mundo.

—Pues vaya invirtiendo las ganancias de su negocio en un curso de inglés para usted y para su cuñado. Pero uno intensivo, no de «inglés en mil palabras» ni chorradas de esas.

—A ver... No... no nos pongamos nerviosos —replicó acorralado.

—Ah, ya entiendo, que ganancias, poquitas. Encima de aprovecharse de mi cliente, no ha sacado un euro de ello. Le van a condenar antes por inútil que por delincuente.

—Va-vamos por partes —Parecía un ratoncito en una jaula, buscando una salida para escapar—. En primer lugar, yo no pretendía...

—¿Qué es lo que no pretendía? ¿Hundir a mi cliente? —le interrumpí. No quería insistir en el tema legal, pronto se me vería el plumero.

—¿Hundir... a quién?

—¡A Cristiano! ¿Es consciente del daño psicológico que le ha hecho?

—Creo que no le entiendo.

—Le he visto llorar —dije sin más y fingiendo que los ojos se me llenaban de lágrimas a mí también.

—¿Llorar? —El hombre no entendía nada. Justo lo que perseguía.

—Sí, como un chiquillo. ¿O es que no ha visto la crisis goleadora de la que es víctima?

—Yo... tampoco sigo mucho la actualidad deportiva.

—Se nota. Pues no es la edad, ni su estado de forma, ni que Messi le vaya a quitar otra vez el Balón de Oro. ¡Es usted! —sentencié.

—¡¿Yo?!

—¡Sí, usted! ¿No es consciente del muñeco que ha hecho..., mejor dicho, que ha perpetrado con su imagen? Desde que mi cliente lo vio, no duerme, no come, ¡no marca!

—Bueno, este domingo marcó un *hat-trick*. No es que esté al día, como le digo, pero ha salido en todos los informativos.

Pillado. Después de la política, los programas de La 2 y los Juegos Olímpicos de Invierno, el fútbol es la cosa que menos me interesa del mundo. Si no reaccionaba rápido, se me iba a caer todo el chiringuito.

—Caballero —proseguí—, mi cliente es, ante todo, un artista, lo cual no puedo decir de usted. Y a veces es capaz de meter la pelotita en la portería sin querer, aunque tenga los ojos bañados en lágrimas. ¿Sabe lo que quiero decir?

—Entonces, tan mal no está —dijo el hombre. Había encontrado una grieta y estaba dispuesto a tirar de ella hasta convertirla en una sima para colarse dentro y defenderse.

—¿Puedo hacerle una pregunta? —cambiar de tema, un viejo truco—. ¿Le gustaría encontrarse con un muñeco creado, en teoría, a su imagen y semejanza, y comprobar que no se parece en nada a usted?

—Llevo mucho tiempo practicando conmigo mismo. El de su cliente no es el primero que hago.

Se me estaba subiendo a la chepa, el tío. No era tonto, desde luego. Iba a tener que echar el resto para reconducir la situación.

—¡Pues venda los muñecos con su imagen, cabeza de alcachofa!

—¿Cómo dice?

—Pero, ¿cómo se le ocurre hacer semejante despropósito? ¡Hasta yo he creado obras mejores sentado en el «trono»!

—Le pido un poco de respeto.

—¿Respeto? ¿Me está pidiendo respeto? ¡¿Usted?! Que ha manipulado... ¡¿Qué digo manipulado?! ¡Profanado, violado la imagen del jugador más grande de todos los tiempos! Bueno, después de Di Stéfano. Y de Pelé. Y de Maradona. Y de Cruyff. Y de Messi, claro. Le voy a decir una cosa y espero no tener que repetirla: le pido..., no, le exijo, que retire inmediatamente del mercado todos los muñecos que existen de mi cliente.

—Solo hay uno. Es un prototipo.

—Pues... Pues... —era duro de pelar el hombre—. Destrúyalo. O, mejor, mándemelo por correo. Creo que la única solución va a ser practicarle un exorcismo delante de Cristiano para que se quede tranquilo.

—¿Un exorcismo al muñeco?

—Sí. Para que mi cliente pueda destrozarlo, destriparlo. Que vuelva a sentir que es único, que no hay ninguno como él, que no existe en el mundo ni una sola réplica, y menos de la pésima calidad que ha perpetrado usted.

—¿Es esto una broma?

—Broma es lo que usted hace. Y de mal gusto.

—Si esto es una broma, le pido por favor que pare.

—¡Pare usted de fabricar esos muñecos! ¿No ve que es peligroso? ¡El día que haga uno de Trump, a lo mejor provoca la tercera guerra mundial!

—Pues ya es demasiado tarde —se defendió—. Tengo una serie de muñecos de líderes mundiales: Trump, Obama, Putin...

—¡Y de Rajoy, ¿no te digo?!

—No, de Aznar.

—Tócate los...

—También reproduzco escenas históricas, como el trío de las Azores.

Calificarle de friki se quedaba corto. Me estaba arrepintiendo de haber quemado ese filón en una llamada. Tenía que haberle pedido su catálogo, era incapaz de imaginar la cantidad de «maravillas» que debían de haber salido de su cabeza. Pero ya era tarde, estaba metido de lleno en el fregado y ya tenía que seguir.

—Ahora mismo llamo a la guardia civil para alertarles. No ya como manager de CR7, sino como ciudadano. ¡Tengo derecho a proteger a mis hijos de un monstruo como usted!

—¿Puedo saber su nombre? —contraatacó el hombre.

—¿Puedo saber el suyo? —repliqué a la defensiva.

—Donald Collins.

—Donald, como el pato —me mofé.

—Donald, como Trump —replicó amenazante.

—¿Es un chiste? ¿Qué es, cómico también?

—¡Deje ya esta broma! ¡No tiene gracia!

— Lo que no tiene gracia es que muñecos como los que usted hace circulen por ahí. ¡Que puedan verlos los niños!

—Como no cuelgue, llamo a la policía.

—Eso, hágalo, así me evito hacerlo yo.

—¡Cretino!

Mi «víctima» pasaba al insulto. Era hora de terminar antes de que la llamada se convirtiera en algo desagradable.

—Señor Collins —dije con otro tono, más conciliador—, tiene usted razón.

—¿Cómo dice? —respondió desconcertado.

—Esto es una broma. Soy Joel Graham y estoy realizando un vídeo para mi canal.

—¿De qué me está hablando? —no conseguía salir de su desconcierto.

—Que ni yo trabajo para CR7, ni CR7 ha visto sus muñecos, que yo sepa, ni nada.

—Esto es un vergüenza —respondió.

—No, solo es un vídeo —dije con la mejor intención. No quería más gresca, solo acabar de la mejor manera posible.

—Un vídeo humillante.

—Hombre, humillante... —repliqué a modo de excusa—. Dejémoslo en simpático.

—¿Usted cree que puede hacer estas cosas? ¿Llamar a cualquiera y hacerle pasar un mal rato solo para reírse de él?

—A ver, jefe, cualquiera, cualquiera, no es. No creo que a nadie se le ocurra vender muñecos tan... «peculiares».

—¿Y a usted qué más le da? Si no le gustan, pues no los compre y punto.

En eso tenía razón. No hacía daño a nadie fabricando y vendiendo sus muñecos. Solo a la vista, en cualquier caso.

—Esto no va a quedar así —amenazó.

—¿Qué va, a fabricar muñecos inspirados en mí? Me encantará verlos —dije con sorna—. Puede visitar mi canal para ver cómo soy y, de paso, darle al «me gusta». Aunque viendo el resultado, no creo que necesite fijarse mucho en el personaje original. Total, va a hacer el muñeco que le salga de las pelotas.

—¡Ya vale! —zanjó. Se estaba poniendo violento y eso me lo ponía muy difícil para poner fin al vídeo—. ¿No se ha reído lo suficiente de mí?

—A ver, señor Collins. —Esto era un duelo entre dos contendientes y ninguno de los dos estaba dispuesto a firmar la derrota—. No es reír, no lo malinterprete. Es... una labor social. Le estoy ayudando a que reoriente su carrera profesional y se dedique, no sé..., a jugar a la petanca, a mirar obras... Algo inofensivo para la humanidad.

—Estoy viendo ahora su canal y, por lo que veo, no soy la única víctima. ¡Ya está bien! ¿Se cree que puede hacer lo que le dé la gana? Se siente protegido, ¿verdad? Ahí, en su cueva, burlándose de cualquiera, con millones de seguidores que le ríen las gracias, como si fuera un dios. Pues no, niñato, aquí, al otro lado, hay gente a quien todo esto no le hace ninguna gracia.

Me venía bien que hablara. Cuanto más lo hiciera, más tiempo me daba a mí para pensar en qué le iba a contestar. Y no me iba a quedar corto, ni mucho menos.

—A ver, alcaparra...

—¡Cállese! —me cortó—. ¡No quiero escucharle ni una palabra más!

—¿Y cree que yo sí?

—Solo voy a decirle una cosa —dijo impostando un tono pausado, como queriendo hacerme entender que controlaba su ira—. Voy a ir a por usted.

—¿Qué va, a llamar al abogado de Cristiano Ronaldo? —repliqué—. Porque, si quiere, puedo pasarle el número.

—Escúcheme, porque solo voy a decirlo una vez: esto no va a quedar así.

—Desde luego, espero que quede mejor. Me refiero a sus muñecos —dije. Pero Donald ya había colgado.

Me quedé mudo. Una pausa dramática para que se calmaran las risas de mis seguidores al otro lado de la pantalla. El final había sido mejor de lo esperado.

—Este es de la camorra, por lo menos —dije mirando a cámara—. Escúchame, Donald Collins, si tienes estómago para hacer muñecos como los que pretendes vender, tienes que tenerlo también para aguantar las críticas. Que va en el precio, amigo, no todo el mundo va a saber apreciar tu arte. Arte satánico, eso sí. Oye, y quién sabe, a lo mejor dentro de cien años, o doscientos, llega alguien y reconoce tu talento. Venga, Donald, que en la casa de Mickey Mouse te van a querer igual. ¡Salud!

Y corté el vídeo.

2.

Si hay algo que me agota de ser *youtuber* es el *business*: propuestas de anunciantes, firmas de autógrafos, sesiones de fotos, «ponte aquí», «lleva esta gorra», «haz esta entrevista»... Todo eso es el *business*. Y Kevin, mi representante, parece obsesionado con él. Lógico, es su trabajo. Hay días que no me deja respirar. Aparece en casa a las nueve, me saca de la cama, me mete en su coche, me lleva a tal sitio, me trae a otro, me taladra con su verborrea, me programa los siguientes siete días y, cuando ya no sé ni quién soy, me devuelve a casa.

Esa mañana, en cambio, me había levantado a tiempo y cuando Kevin llamó al timbre de la calle, ya estaba listo.

—Subo café y donuts. Y vístete antes de que suba, no me obligues a verte en calzoncillos —me dijo sin saludar, como siempre.

—Ya he desayunado, papá —dije con retintín—. Bajo enseguida.

—¿Estás levantado ya? —preguntó con sorpresa.

—Sí, pero no te comas los donuts, que son para mí. —Colgué el interfono y salí de casa impaciente. Quería ver la cara de Kevin antes de que se le pasara el asombro.

Kevin era como un padre, solo que en plan joven. Tenía unos treinta años y había estudiado periodismo. Quería ser reportero de guerra: Siria, Irak, Gaza y Cisjordania; siempre nombraba estos cuatro lugares, como si solo hubiera guerra en ellos en el mundo. Era su vocación, creía, pero cuando consiguió su primer trabajo de redactor en un programa de televisión, se dio cuenta de que la única guerra que iba a conocer era la de lograr meter el micro entre el de sus compañeros para conseguir la declaración del famoso de turno.

Le conocí en el *Meet and Greet* de uno de mis shows. En teoría, los *Meet* están reservados solo a los fans, los periodistas no pueden entrar. Ellos tienen otros momentos para entrevistarme y hacerme fotos. Reconozco que no suelo darles mucha bola. Siempre hacen eso de «sacar de contexto». Si una declaración puede tener dos caras, ellos siempre escogen la que no es. Si dices: «Nunca había tenido un recibimiento como el de hoy», ellos publican: «Joel Graham, decepcionado por la fría acogida de sus fans». No falla. Haciendo eso, como mínimo, se aseguran una segunda noticia donde Joel Graham tiene que explicar que sus declaraciones se han sacado de contexto. El periodista se ofrece a entrevistarte y, así, se asegura una tercera noticia. Para ser reporteros de guerra, no sé, pero para estrategas, la facultad de periodismo les prepara a las mil maravillas. Cansado de que «me saquen de contexto», decidí que los periodistas, cuanto más lejos, mejor. Además, yo no soy noticia de nada. Soy un *youtuber*, punto. Ni mi vida, ni lo que hago fuera de mi canal, ni quiénes son mis amigos, le interesa a nadie.

En teoría, él no debía estar en el *Meet* donde lo conocí. Se coló. No aprovechó un descuido de la seguridad del show, ni se escondió en un armario, ni cosas por el estilo. Se hizo pasar por fan. Me siguió durante meses en mi canal, empezó a comentar mis vídeos, me escribía a mi correo. Firmaba como Sugar Kane, un nick como cualquier otro, pero con dos caras: era el nombre del personaje de Marilyn en *Con faldas y a lo loco* y el título de una canción de Sonic Youth, un grupo de la prehistoria que solo conocían padres enrollados de pasado *indie* y frikis como Connor. De hecho, fue Kevin quien me dio las dos referencias. Al principio, no reparé en él, de hecho, estaba convencido de que era una chica. Una «seguidora» más, pensaba. Pero sus comentarios destacaban sobre los demás y pronto llamó mi atención. Eran ingeniosos, diferentes, y sobre todo, divertidos. Llegó un punto en el que, cada vez que colgaba un vídeo, esperaba impaciente su comentario. Y siempre llegaba. Entre la tal Sugar Kane y yo se estableció un juego curioso. Yo metía guiños en mis vídeos y esperaba a ver si «ella» los pillaba. Y los pillaba.

Un día, cuando el juego estaba en pleno apogeo, Sugar Kane escribió un comentario en el muro de uno de mis vídeos en el que me reprochaba que era «repetitivo». Dijo algo así como: «... si segundas partes nunca fueron buenas, quintas, sextas, séptimas... Eso ya ni se comenta». Estoy acostumbrado a comentarios de todo tipo, no me voy a poner a llorar a estas alturas cuando me ponen verde (lo cual sucede con frecuencia); qué se le va a hacer, cosas de la fama. Pero en esa ocasión me dolió por venir de quien venía y, sobre todo, porque tenía razón. Había hecho un vídeo normalito, correcto, pero repitiendo ideas ya usadas. Mis seguidores lo habían acogido bien, pero Sugar me había cazado. No sabía quién era, si era una chica, un chico, joven, adulto. No sabía nada de esa persona, pero, tras meses de juego privado entre nosotros, su comentario me llegó al alma. Lejos de picarme, me propuse responderle a lo grande. Me encerré en casa durante varios días y estuve dándole vueltas a mi siguiente vídeo. Al final, se me ocurrió una idea. Fue entonces cuando hice mi primer vídeo de bromas telefónicas; hasta la fecha, el vídeo más visto de mi canal.

Sugar había logrado que me pusiera las pilas. Gracias a «ella» me había obligado a currármelo más y a sacar nuevas ideas. Sin sospecharlo, había logrado que mi canal pegara un salto hacia arriba. A cambio, Sugar desapareció. No volvió a comentar mis vídeos, ni a escribirme. Se esfumó. Parecía un ángel que había llegado a mi vida para cumplir una misión, y cuando la cumplió, se marchó.

La vida —y los vídeos— continuó. Al principio echaba de menos sus comentarios, pero al poco tiempo, mi cabeza se ocupó en otras cosas y Sugar quedó relegada a un curioso recuerdo. Hasta el *Meet* en el que se coló. Ese día, tras el show, me junté con unos cien fans. Me encantan esos momentos. Es cuando pongo cara a mis seguidores. Comentamos los vídeos, nos hacemos fotos, nos echamos unas risas. Tras la hora de rigor, cuando ya me despedía de ellos, escuché voces en la entrada de la sala. El guardia de seguridad trataba de impedir el paso de un chico.

—El encuentro ha terminado —insistía.

—Tengo entrada, soy fan, estoy en la lista —replicaba el chico nervioso—. ¡Solo una foto!

Me quedé mirando con curiosidad. Para ser fan, casi doblaba la edad del resto. Pero no fue eso lo que me llamó la atención. Fue la camiseta que llevaba: por delante, la foto de Marilyn y por detrás, el logo de Sonic Youth. No había duda. Era él.

—¿Sugar? —dije en voz alta— ¿Eres un tío?

Los casi cien fans que me rodeaban se giraron a la vez hacia la puerta y miraron a aquel chico al que el guardia trataba de llevarse de ahí agarrado de la cintura. La imagen merecía la pena: un tipo de dos por dos agarrando con los dos brazos a un tipo más bien gordito mientras este agitaba brazos y piernas en el aire, como si nadara en una piscina imaginaria.

—Joel, dile a este gorila que me suelte, que me está apretando la tripa y voy a acabar por echar la pota —dijo. Así es Kevin: espontáneo, deslenguado—. ¡Que me sueltes o te meto la punta de la bota por... —y, sobre todo, bastante macarra.

—¡Suéltalo! —dije conteniendo la risa. El guardia se quedó quieto sin estar seguro de qué hacer, mientras sujetaba a Kevin a la altura de su cadera a modo de paquete.

—¿No lo has oído, Hodor? —dijo Kevin.

Los presentes estallaron en una carcajada y «Hodor», el guardia, molesto, soltó a Kevin sin más. El que estaba a punto de convertirse en mi representante, cayó al suelo de golpe.

—No era literal —protestó desde el suelo.

Unos minutos más tarde, Kevin repasaba los moratones en codos y rodillas y yo le escuchaba asombrado. Nos habíamos quedado a solas en la sala y él no paraba de hablar. Me contó que era periodista y que se había fijado en mí para hacerme una entrevista para la web de noticias para la que trabajaba.

—Y todo por veinte euros de mierda.

—¿Veinte euros? —pregunté alucinado.

—Es lo que pagan por artículo. Veintitrés si lleva foto. Como ves, es un trabajo para forrarse.

Pero cuando supo mi relación con la prensa y lo difícil que era convencerme para conceder entrevistas, se le ocurrió una estrategia: infiltrarse como fan en mi canal, chica, para más señas, y llegar hasta mí de otra manera.

—Qué importante soy —dije con sorna—. Vas a conseguir sacarme los colores.

—De importante nada. Es que si logro colocar un reportaje en lugar de un artículo, me pagan cuarenta euros. Y me vales igual tú que las focas del Pacífico. El caso es que lo compre el jefe de redacción.

—Ya —respondí disimulando mi chasco—. Cuarenta y tres con foto, ¿no?

—No, cuarenta y seis. Los reportajes llevan varias fotos, pero a partir de la tercera ya no las pagan.

Empezó a comentar mis vídeos para llegar hasta mí y así lograr entrevistarme, pero, poco a poco acabó por engancharse al mismo juego al que me había enganchado yo con él: ese curioso diálogo virtual que mantuvimos durante algunos meses.

No se olvidaba de qué le había llevado hasta mí: el deseo de hacerme una entrevista y colocar el reportaje en la web por cuarenta y seis miserables euros, pero a medida que fue creciendo nuestra «relación», empezó a pensar que no era muy ético haberme llevado al huerto solo por un interés personal. Por eso decidió desaparecer. Aprovechó mi vídeo más flojo para darme un toque de atención y dejarme el recado de que me estaba acomodando. Fue su carta de despedida, me contó.

—Entonces, ¿por qué has venido hoy? —pregunté desconcertado.

—Porque me han echado de la web.

—Vaya, lo siento —dije con sinceridad.

—Publiqué el *repor* de las focas del Pacífico —dijo con un hilito de voz—. Un fracaso. No llegó a las cien visitas.

—Uf —exclamé. Acostumbrado a millones de visionados de mis vídeos, no llegar a ni a cien visitas me parecía inimaginable.

—Y de *likes* y *shares*, ni hablamos.

Por primera vez desde que había irrumpido en la sala, Kevin se quedó callado. Estaba afectado por lo que le había pasado. En esos instantes de silencio, me dediqué a mirarle con un poco más de atención. Su verborrea era tan arrolladora que no te daba tiempo a otra cosa que a escucharle. Pero ahora que se había callado y que miraba al suelo, pude observarle. Tenía algo más de treinta años y estaba, por decirlo de forma elegante, bien alimentado. Llevaba unas gafas más grandes de lo que el tamaño de su cabeza aconsejaba y eso le daba un aire contradictorio: inteligente y gracioso a la vez, como si quisiera decir al mundo que no se tomaba muy en serio a sí mismo.

—Es la hostia, no me digas que no —soltó como conclusión de todo lo que me había contado—. ¿No te parece?

—¿Cómo dices? —respondí despertando de mi letargo.

—¿Te lo tengo que grabar en vídeo para que te enteres? —dijo retomando su tono deslenguado—. Cómo sois los de tu generación, si no os dicen las cosas desde una pantalla, no os enteráis de nada.

—Como si fueras una anciano —respondí.

—Comparado con todos los que estaban aquí hace un rato, soy del Pleistoceno.

—¿Cómo te llamas? —pregunté. Kevin me miró con el ceño fruncido. No estaba acostumbrado a que le pillaran a contrapié—. Porque Sugar no creo que sea, ¿no?

—Kevin. Y desde hoy, soy tu representante.

Sonrió y me ofreció su mano para sellar el trato. La propuesta me cogió desprevenido, pero no era descabellada. Conocía mi trabajo, se había preocupado en mirarlo de otra manera, era vivaz y espabilado. Su atrevimiento me pareció tan sorprendente que se la estreché.

—Pero olvídate del diez por ciento de comisión. Cinco, y vas listo.

—Puto explotador —dijo.

Desde entonces, Kevin es mi representante. Hasta ese momento, yo era quien llevaba mis asuntos. Me echaba una mano un abogado, colega del hermano mayor de Jan, mi amigo. Pero todo el tema de contrataciones, reuniones con anunciantes y demás, lo hacía yo. Por eso me iba como me iba: si me apetecía, lo hacía, si no, no. En el momento en el que Kevin empezó a trabajar conmigo, me olvidé de todo eso: de negociar, de seleccionar, de pelearme con unos y con otros por la pasta que debía cobrar. Y, por primera vez desde que empecé a ser *youtuber* tuve una agenda organizada. Y una vida organizada, también.

—Buenos días, Mary Poppins —dije nada más verle apoyado en el coche frente al portal de mi casa. Le llamaba así porque siempre lo arreglaba todo. Kevin lo odiaba, pero había decidido dejar de protestar: sabía que eso me motivaba para insistir.

—Buenos días, Peter Pan —respondió dando un bocado a uno de los donuts.

—Eh, que eran para mí.

—Tú tienes que cuidar la línea, que la pantalla engorda.

—Te lo descontaré de tu sueldo —repliqué mientras me subía al coche.

—Para lo que me pagas... —protestó.

—No te quejes, que al final me has sacado el quince por ciento.

—Y para lo que hago, me parece poco.

—¿A que te vuelves a la web de noticias a veinte euros el artículo publicado? —amenacé de broma. Comentarios así eran el pan de cada día entre nosotros.

—Al menos ahí el café era gratis. ¿Quieres uno? —dijo con una sonrisa irónica mientras me ofrecía uno en vaso de cartón. Se lo cogí y arrancó.

De camino, Kevin me puso al día. Íbamos a reunirnos con los organizadores de un evento que iba a reunir a varios *youtubers* para una convención de cultura digital o algo así. Pero pronto la conversación tomó otro camino.

—Menudo bombazo el vídeo del tipo ese de los muñecos —dijo.

—Un crack, el tío. No quiero ni pensar cómo serán el resto de los muñecos que hace. Nunca había visto nada igual.

—Pues tus seguidores están como locos por comprarlos.

—No, si encima le voy a hacer rico.

—Pero ha desaparecido. No hay manera de contactar con él.

—¿Lo has intentado? —dije asombrado.

—Claro —dijo con una sonrisa afilada. De todas las sonrisas de su repertorio, esa era la que más miedo me daba—. ¿O es que crees que voy a dejar pasar una oportunidad de hacer negocio?

—Me das miedo —dije, arrugando el vaso del café que acababa de terminar.

—Pensé que podíamos asociarnos con él y vender los muñecos desde tu canal. En plan de coña, ¿sabes?

—Ni se te ocurra. No quiero que se me asocie a un producto como ese.

—Piensa con la cabeza, Joel —cuando adoptaba el tono de padre había que ponerse alerta—. Pensé que podíamos hacer un sorteo entre tus seguidores y el premio sería un muñeco del ganador hecho por ese pavo. La gente iba a pillar la gracia.

—Ni hablar —dije tajante—. No mezclemos las cosas. Además, el tío se mosqueó un huevo.

—No, si ya. Además, ha desaparecido del mapa, así que nada.

—Mejor —sentencié para zanjar el asunto.

—Pero es raro —reflexionó Kevin—. Nadie desaprovecha una oportunidad así para ganar pasta, aunque sea porque te has reído de él.

—Allá él —y no dije nada más. No quería darle más vueltas. El tío de los muñecos era pasado y ahí quería que estuviera: en el pasado.

La reunión fue aburrida y larga. Yo me dediqué a escuchar y a decir «sí» o «no», mientras Kevin negociaba los términos de mi participación con claridad y sin dejarse liar. Cuando la situación se ponía tensa y el cliente me miraba buscando complicidad, yo me limitaba a sonreír:

—Estoy totalmente de acuerdo con Kevin —decía. El cliente sabía entonces que tenía que entenderse con él sí o sí. Kevin era el mejor en eso: bastaba una mirada para que supiera lo que yo pensaba y lo que él tenía que transmitir. Éramos un equipo perfecto y, lo más importante, nos los pasábamos muy bien.

Al tercer bostezo que traté de disimular, Kevin entendió que ya era hora de terminar la reunión. Firmé un par de fotos para los hijos de los organizadores y nos largamos de ahí.

—¿Te dejo en casa? —me preguntó de camino al coche.

—No, hoy tengo entrenamiento.

—¡¿Ahora?! —respondió con desagrado.

—Sí, ahora —respondí sonriendo—. ¿Me acercas?

El único punto de fricción entre Kevin y yo era el fútbol. No el deporte en sí, sino el hecho de quedar con mis amigos para jugar. Como representante intentaba que me dispersara lo justo y veía en mis amigos una amenaza constante.

—Un día te vas a partir la pierna y verás.

—Sería perfecto: un diario para mi canal donde se viera la evolución de mi lesión —dije bromeando pero, al mismo tiempo, considerando la opción.

—Uy, sí, interesantísimo —dijo con sarcasmo.

—¿Y si me escayolo y lo hago? Aunque no me parta la pierna de verdad.

—Ni hablar —dijo en serio.

Sonreí y me metí en el coche. Hacerle enfadar me encantaba.

En el campo ya me esperaban Connor, Jan, Silvestre y el resto del equipo.

—¡Tío! —me gritó Silvestre—. Llegas tarde.

—Lo siento, chicos —me disculpé—. Tenía que currar. Sabéis lo que es eso, ¿no?

—Expediente disciplinario —me amenazó Connor—. Quédate con esa idea.

Jugar al fútbol era mi vía de escape. Llevaba en ese equipo desde los quince años y no pensaba dejarlo por nada del mundo. Fue un poco incómodo cuando empecé a ser conocido por mi trabajo de *youtuber*: venía más gente a los partidos, los rivales me entraban con más dureza, mis compañeros me la pasaban más. Tonterías. Cuando vieron que soy peor que un jugador de regional, se relajaron y, aunque a mi equipo se le conoce como «el equipo del *youtuber*», ya están acostumbrados a jugar contra mí y me tratan como a uno más.

Entrenamos algo más de una hora, como era habitual, con partidillo incluido. Íbamos antepenúltimos en la liguilla y si no nos poníamos las pilas, corríamos el riesgo de descender. O desaparecer, porque en la competición en la que estábamos ya no se podía descender más. Mis compañeros estaban preocupados por eso, pero yo me lo tomaba con filosofía.

—Ya puestos, es mejor quedar los últimos: último clasificado de la última liguilla de la última competición del país. Destacar, destaca —dije para relajar los ánimos camino del vestuario.

—Típico consuelo de perdedor —replicó Connor.

—¡Es que no damos ni una! —protestó Silvestre con su tono de agonía habitual—. Ni achicamos, ni alineamos la defensa, ni respetamos en rombo...

—¡Para el carro, Van Gaal! —dije—. Que somos aficionados, hacemos lo que podemos.

—Que es poquito, por lo visto —dijo Connor.

—Como sigamos así, yo pago mi cláusula de rescisión y me largo a un grande —dijo Jan de broma—. Que tengo ofertas, ¿eh?

—Sí, de recogepelotas —le respondió Connor.

—¡Venga esos ánimos! —insistió Jan—. Hoy invito yo al aperitivo.

—Invitas porque te toca, no vayas de enrollado. Que te he hecho tres caños —puntualizó Silvestre. Era el único que se lo tomaba en serio, estaba desesperado.

—Para Sil, una tila —dije mientras abría mi taquilla.

Pendiente como estaba de la charla, tardé una décima de segundo en darme cuenta de lo que acababa de suceder: al abrir la puerta de la taquilla se me vinieron encima un montón de bultos que se liberaron de la presión de estar embutidos dentro.

—¿Qué cojones...?

No me fue fácil procesar lo que veía. Los bultos no eran otra cosa que decenas de muñecos de peluche de un palmo de tamaño.

—Oh, nuestro mediocentro se trae los juguetes para jugar en el recreo —bromeó Connor.

Pero no tenía gracia. Mucho menos cuando me di cuenta de que los muñecos que se esparcían entre mis pertenencias dentro de la taquilla y mis pies eran obra de Donald Collins.

3.

La primera sensación que tuve fue de ira. Empecé a mirar a todos lados como si el responsable de haberme llenado la taquilla estuviera ahí, esperando a ver mi reacción y eso me permitiera ir hacia él para pedirle cuentas. Ser consciente de que eso era imposible me dejó desconcertado. Miré uno a uno a los presentes, como si ellos pudieran darme una explicación. Pero ni Connor, ni Jan, ni Silvestre, ni el resto de los chicos del equipo sabían de qué iba todo eso y me miraban interrogantes.

—Es el capullo de los muñecos —aclaré—. ¿Alguien ha visto algo?

Nadie contestó. Solo Connor se acercó hacia mí y se agachó para inspeccionar el «regalo».

—Al natural son mucho peores —dijo—. Una auténtica mierda.

—¿Cómo ha podido...? —No era capaz de entender lo que acababa de pasar.

—¿Está todo? —preguntó Silvestre.

—¿Cómo, todo?

—Tus cosas, tío. Si te ha abierto la taquilla, puede haberse llevado algo.

—¡Hostia!

Me giré hacia mi taquilla, tiré al suelo los muñecos que quedaban dentro y saqué mi bolsa. Dentro estaba mi ropa, mis deportivas, mi toalla... Y mis llaves y mi cartera. Respiré aliviado. Era una victoria ridícula en comparación con lo que me acababa de suceder, pero al menos podía entrar en casa.

—Tranqui, Joel, esto ha sido solo por joder —me tranquilizó Silvestre.

—Tómatelo como una coña —dijo Jan. Siempre tan generoso y conciliador. Era su virtud, pero hay ocasiones en las que no se puede ser tan bien pensado.

—Pues no ha tenido ni pizca de gracia —dije—. Esto ha sido demasiado. ¡Me ha abierto la taquilla! Es mi intimidad.

—Tienes razón. Si yo usara calzoncillos de Pitufos como tú, tampoco me gustaría que nadie lo supiera —dijo Connor bromeando. Pero yo no estaba para risas.

—¿Y si no ha sido él? —preguntó Jan—. A lo mejor es algún seguidor tuyo.

—¿Y de dónde ha sacado todos estos muñecos? —La idea de Jan me parecía una tontería—. Nadie va a molestarse en fabricar... —intenté contar los muñecos que se esparcían bajo mis pies. Habría más de veinte— ... todo esto para hacer una gracieta.

—No es la primera vez que alguien te «acosa» —insistió Jan.

—Ya, pero nunca han llegado tan lejos. Esto es cosa del tío de los muñecos.

—Pues denúnciale —sugirió Silvestre.

¿Para qué?, pensé. Sí, podía hacerlo, protestar en la recepción del polideportivo. ¿Y qué? Nadie haría nada, nadie sabría nada.

—¿Y qué pruebas tengo?

—¿Necesitas más? —preguntó Connor levantando uno de los muñecos.

—Esta mierda no prueba nada. Vosotros mismos lo estáis diciendo: podría ser uno de mis seguidores. Aunque yo sepa que no, cualquiera puede pensarlo.

—Pues entonces, mira el lado positivo: ya tienes regalos para todo el mundo las próximas navidades —dijo Connor sonriendo. Todos sonrieron. Yo también.

Agradecía el esfuerzo de Connor por quitarle hierro al asunto, pero lo que acababa de suceder era demasiado como para mirar hacia otro lado. Por primera vez desde que me dedicaba a hacer vídeos para mi canal, alguien traspasaba la línea que separa mi trabajo de mi vida. Siempre pensé que, a pesar de que mi canal soy yo y el que sale ahí soy yo y no un personaje, todo el mundo distinguía entre lo que sucede detrás de la pantalla y lo que sucede en mi vida real.

Es cierto que desde que mi canal tiene éxito, mi vida es diferente: me reconocen por la calle, me piden fotos, a veces la gente se pone un poco pesada —los padres de mis fans, los que más. Pero todo eso forma parte de mi vida. Trabajar con tu cara es lo que tiene. La fama me ha obligado a cambiar ciertos hábitos: salir menos de casa, no ir a lugares muy concurridos, cuidar mucho lo que digo y hago en público. Y lo acepto. A cambio tengo un montón de cosas y, sobretodo, puedo vivir de lo que me gusta. Pero eso no significa que vaya a pagar cualquier precio. Abrir mi taquilla y llenarla de muñecos era una intromisión que iba más allá de las reglas que yo y mis seguidores habíamos establecido de manera tácita: yo, aquí y ellos, allí. Cada uno tiene derecho a tener su espacio. Si ellos respetan el mío, yo respeto el de ellos. Lo que Donald había hecho no podía ser otra cosa que una declaración de guerra.

—Bah —dijo Jan—. Déjalo estar. Tampoco es para tanto.

—No, Jan —respondí con firmeza—. Esto no puede quedar así.

—Eso es justo lo que dijo el pavo de los muñecos al final de tu vídeo —me recordó Connor.

—Pues mira, en algo estamos de acuerdo —respondí.

Al abrir la puerta de mi casa me encontré un sobre en el suelo. El día iba de sorpresas, por lo visto. «Donald», pensé al tiempo que deseaba que fuera un aviso de lectura del contador del gas. Abrí el sobre apresurado, más que abrirlo, lo rompí. Dentro encontré un *flyer* parecido al anuncio que cogí del videoclub de Silvestre.

—Donald —afirmé en voz alta. Como temía, todo era peor de lo que imaginaba.

El *flyer* tenía la foto de un muñeco de Trump. Era igual de pésimo que el de Cristiano Ronaldo, pero el significado era muy distinto. Le gustaban los juegos al hombre, pensé.

Al lado, un texto, cómo no, escrito en Comic Sans. ¿Qué clase de hortera sigue utilizando esa letra?

¿Te ha gustado mi regalo? Pensé en llevártelo a casa, pero me pareció que compartirlo con los tuyos era mejor idea. Porque esto va de eso: de los «tuyos». No los del fútbol que, por cierto, son malos de narices, sino los que te siguen en tu canal. Esos millones de mocosos que te ríen todas las gracias. A ellos deberás dirigirles tu próximo vídeo: una disculpa pública por la llamada que me hiciste. Ya sabes cómo se las gasta nuestro amigo Trump. Y por si no lo sabes, él y yo somos bastante parecidos.

Leí el mensaje varias veces. En esas líneas había tantas cosas preocupantes que tardé varios minutos en moverme de la entrada de mi casa. No solo sabía dónde jugaba al fútbol, sino que sabía dónde estaba mi casa, quiénes eran mis amigos y, lo peor, quería que hiciera un vídeo a medida para él. ¿Qué clase de demente era ese tío?

—¡Ni hablar! —dije en voz alta.

Decidido, me dirigí al estudio. Iba a hacer un vídeo, sí, pero no exactamente el que me pedía Donald. Tal cual estaba, sin cambiarme, sin duchar, me senté frente a la cámara y empecé a grabar. Me salté mi clásico saludo y fui al grano.

—Esto no es un vídeo —empecé serio—. Es una carta. Una carta, un mensaje, una notificación... Sí, como las que te mandan de Hacienda. O las que te aparecen en las aplicaciones del móvil. Da igual. Un aviso. Es todo eso. Y, como me ha pedido mi..., ¿cómo llamarlo?..., «amigo» Donald, la hago pública, aunque en realidad solo va dirigida a él.

Hasta yo me estaba asustando de mi tono. Sentía tal rabia dentro de mí que tenía que hacer verdaderos esfuerzos por no perder los papeles. Respiré hondo antes de continuar.

—Os acordáis de Donald, ¿no? El gran artista de los muñecos —hice una pausa. Aquí iba a editar un fragmento del vídeo de la llamada—. Pues parece que no ha tenido suficiente. El hombre está dolido. Sí. Muy dolido. No entiende de qué va esto: una llamada, una broma, unas risas y todos amigos. No. Él no está dispuesto a pasar página. Hoy el tal Donald ha dado un paso importante. Para él, sin duda, pero para mí también. Ha traspasado todos los límites y me ha pedido, en realidad, me ha exigido, que grabe un vídeo de disculpa —silencio. Era el momento en el que esperaba que mis seguidores digirieran lo que acababa de decir—. Sí, quiere que me disculpe por la llamada que le hice el otro día.

Hice una nueva pausa. Pensaba editar aquí alguna de las amenazas que me dirigió durante la llamada.

—¿Disculparme? A ver, Donald, uno se disculpa cuando ha hecho algo mal y una broma, puede que no te guste, pero no es algo que esté «mal». No es un delito, no es un ultraje, no es más que una broma. En cambio, amenazarme, amedrentarme, violar mi intimidad —no quería dar detalles de lo que había hecho, abrirme la taquilla o dejar un anónimo en mi casa, no fuera que eso le diera ideas a algún pirado más—, eso sí que es algo por lo que pedir disculpas. Lo entiendes, ¿alcaparra? Seguro que no —mi tono iba subiendo de intensidad—. Por eso, voy a hacer lo que me pides. Sí, te voy a pedir disculpas pero no aquí, no ahora. Te las voy a pedir cara a cara. Tú me ves, ¿no? Sabes quién soy —y dónde vivo, pensé—, pues yo quiero lo mismo. Quiero verte. En persona. Donde quieras y cuando quieras. Y ahí, en tu cara, te pido disculpas. Si quieres, lo grabamos y lo cuelgo. Pero que todo el mundo te vea, que te escuche, que entienda por qué yo me tengo que disculpar y tú no. Porque yo no lo entiendo. A lo mejor, si nos lo explicas bien a mí y a los «mocosos» que me siguen, todos aprenderemos algo de ti. No a hacer muñecos, está claro, eso mejor no se lo enseñes a nadie. Pero sí a ser mejores personas, como tú. Así que, cuando quieras, quedamos para que nos des esa clase. Te espero, Donald.

Y corté la grabación.

Lo odiaba. Odiaba despertarme con el timbre de mi casa. Mi cerebro estaba entrenado para no activarse cuando sonaba, pero todo tenía un límite y cuando llevaba varios minutos escuchándolo dentro de mis sueños acababa por desvelarme y ponerme de mala leche. Solo podía ser Kevin. Y esperaba que fuera él, porque como fuera otra persona, estaba dispuesto a acabar con su vida. Me levanté tambaleándome y me dirigí a la puerta chocándome con todo mueble que había en mi camino. Al llegar a la puerta, la abrí sin más.

—¿Tú te crees que puedes llamar de esta manera? —Efectivamente, era Kevin. Entró sin decir nada—. Buenos días, ¿eh? —Respondí molesto.

—Si me dieras un juego de llaves, esto no pasaría —respondió sin mirarme y yendo directo a mi estudio.

—¿Adónde vas? —pregunté alarmado.

—A borrar tu último vídeo —dijo entrando en el estudio—. Y vístete, anda, que no me pagas para verte en gayumbos.

Apreté varias veces los ojos para despejarlos de legañas. No estaba seguro de ver lo que estaba viendo. O, mejor dicho, de escuchar lo que Kevin me decía.

—¡¿A borrar, qué?!

Fui directo al estudio tropezándome de nuevo con los mismos muebles que antes y tirando, de paso, una estantería de DVD. Al entrar, me encontré a Kevin manejando el ratón frente a mi ordenador. En condiciones normales me hubiera abalanzado sobre cualquiera que se atreviera a hacer algo así. Pero que fuera Kevin, con quien tenía total confianza, solo me hacía pensar que estaba presa de un ataque de enajenación, lo cual me aconsejaba actuar con prudencia.

—Kevin, tío, vale que seas mi *repre*, pero... Mi ordenador es sagrado.

—Si te levantaras a la misma hora que el resto de los mortales, ya sabrías de qué va todo esto. Tu vídeo es *trend topic*, ha batido récord de visitas, no se habla de otra cosa en las redes sociales —dijo mientras movía el ratón frenético entre las carpetas de mi escritorio—. ¿Dónde coño...?

Me acerqué a él y le arrebaté el ratón de las manos.

—Si me dices que buscas, igual puedo ayudarte. Total, es mi disco duro —dije con ironía. Kevin me miró con los ojos fuera de sus órbitas. No tenía duda: mi representante estaba poseído por el maligno.

—¿No eres consciente de la que has montado? —gritó.

—Eh, eh... —respondí—. No me hables así, que no eres mi madre ni nada que se le parezca.

—¿Cómo se te ocurre hacer un vídeo así? —continuó furioso, ajeno a mi comentario.

—Un vídeo... ¿Cómo?

—Me dijiste que ibas a dejar estar el tema del tío de los muñecos.

—No sabes lo que pasó ayer —respondí a la defensiva—. Ese tío me llenó la taquilla del vestuario de muñecos. No podía dejarlo pasar. Si no corto este tipo de cosas de raíz, me comen.

—¿Y la mejor manera de hacerlo es humillándote? —No entendía a qué se refería, no entendía nada.

—¿Humillándome? Al contrario. Le he dejado las cosas claras. Es lo que se merecía.

—Pues no pillo la gracia, Joel. Nadie la pilla.

—Gracia, ninguna. —Ya me estaba hartando de no saber qué pasaba—. No sé qué mosca te ha picado, pero esto está empezando a tocarme las narices.

—¿A ti esto te parece normal?

Me arrebató de nuevo el ratón de las manos y abrió la página de mi canal. Mi primera mirada se dirigió al contador de visitas, un tic que ya no podía quitarme. Como me acababa de decir Kevin, tenía más visitas que ningún otro de mis vídeos. No voy a negar que en ese momento me sorprendió. Pero la sorpresa fue mayor cuando el audio del vídeo empezó a penetrar en mis oídos.

—*... perdóname, Donald, te lo suplico...*

—¿Qué cojones...? —murmuré.

Levanté la mirada del contador a la imagen y lo que vi casi me fulmina. Un muñequito que, en teoría me representaba a mí, aparecía de rodillas frente a otro que representaba a Donald Trump. Era una animación cutre, solo superada por la pésima calidad de los muñecos. Era tan alucinante que en décimas de segundos recorrí la pantalla para asegurarme de que estaba viendo mi canal.

—*... No, pequeño Joel. ¡No hay perdón para los malvados!* —Se escuchaba en el vídeo.

—¿De dónde ha salido esta mierda?

—Llevo haciéndote esta pregunta desde que he entrado en tu casa.

Paré el vídeo y miré a Kevin. Era incapaz de seguir mirando. Era incapaz de decir nada.

—Supongo que tienes una explicación. Esto no es que baje el nivel de tu canal. Lo deja bajo tierra.

—Yo... —Me costaba hasta encontrar las palabras—. Yo no he hecho esto.

En cuanto pronuncié estas palabras, como me pasó frente a la taquilla del vestuario la tarde anterior, reaccioné y, sin dudarlo, me pegué a la pantalla del ordenador. Quería entrar en mi cuenta y eliminar el vídeo de inmediato.

—¿Qué haces? —preguntó Kevin. A pesar del momento de nervios, parecía más tranquilo. No le había costado mucho creer que no había sido yo quien había hecho esa basura.

—No sé cómo, pero el capullo de Donald lo ha colgado en mi nombre. Voy a borrarlo.

Aún no había procesado lo que estaba sucediendo. Otro ataque de Donald, otra intromisión en mi intimidad, *hackear* mi cuenta. De eso me ocuparía después. En esos momentos la prioridad era eliminar semejante despropósito de mi canal. Pero cuando traté de acceder a mi cuenta, fui consciente de la envergadura de lo que tenía sobre mis hombros.

—No me deja —dije desconcertado.

—No te deja, ¿qué?

—Acceder.

—¿Estás metiendo bien la contraseña? Mira que aún no te has lavado la cara.

—Tranquilo, se me han caído las legañas del susto. —Volví a teclear mi contraseña, tecla a tecla, por si se me estaban yendo los dedos de sitio. Nada, imposible—. No. No puedo entrar.

En la pantalla apareció un aviso de la plataforma. Se denegaba el acceso a la cuenta desde mi IP por introducir la contraseña incorrecta tres veces.

—Cojonudo —dijo Kevin—. ¿Dónde tienes el whisky?

—No bebo, ya lo sabes.

—Pues saca el cianuro, va a ser más eficaz.

Miré a la pantalla y actualicé el navegador. En esos pocos minutos, el número de visitas había crecido en varios miles.

Seguía en *shock*. Sentado en el sofá, miraba a una pelusa que bailaba al ritmo de los pasos de Kevin mientras hablaba por su móvil caminando de un lado a otro del salón.

—... Ha habido un acceso fraudulento a la cuenta de mi cliente, ¿no lo entiende? —bramaba al auricular—. ¡Es uno de los canales más visitados, no pueden quedarse de brazos cruzados!

No sabía qué hacer. En mi vida me había sentido tan acorralado. De repente, todas las normas con las que había vivido se habían desmoronado. Cuando eres niño te dicen: «no te quedes mirando a la gente, no señales con el dedo, no hagas esto o aquello que pueda hacer sentir mal a los demás». Luego te dicen: «respeta a los que te rodean, no te metas con nadie...». Mensajes para no invadir el espacio del otro. Es lo mínimo para que podamos vivir juntos en el mismo mundo. Así te sientes a salvo, protegido. Es tu intimidad, tu propio reino. No imaginas que nadie se atreva a violarlo.

—Si no actúan de inmediato, mi cliente está dispuesto a cerrar el canal e irse a Vimeo —amenazaba Kevin.

Su voz me llegaba como si yo estuviera bajo el agua y él en la superficie. Todo me parecía lejano. Que Donald hubiera entrado en mi taquilla el día anterior me hizo sentir furioso. Que entrara en mi canal, era peor. Era equivalente a haber entrado en mi habitación para fisgonear en mi cajón de la ropa interior. Mi canal era mi espacio, mi casa. Era un lugar en el que solo yo tenía derecho a entrar.

—De acuerdo, gracias —dijo Kevin. Y colgó. No había escuchado las últimas frases, perdido como estaba en mis pensamientos, pero por la cara de satisfacción de Kevin, entendí que había resuelto el problema—. Lo eliminan ahora.

—Gracias —respondí lacónico. Kevin vino a sentarse junto a mí. El impulso de sus pasos hizo que la pelusa describiera un arabesco en el aire y terminara perdiéndose debajo del mueble de la tele.

—¿Estás bien? —preguntó preocupado.

—No.

—Vístete, anda, tenemos que ir a comisaría.

Seguía en calzoncillos y camiseta. Ni siquiera había desayunado.

—Paramos a comer antes, ¿no? —dije.

—Claro —dijo paternal. Por lo general, la pose de padre de Kevin era para echarme la bronca. Solo a veces, como esta, era para darme ánimos—. Vamos a pasar página. Esta tarde actúas.

—¿Cómo?

—Tienes show, ¿no te acuerdas?

Lo que había sucedido me había sacado del mundo real. Un show delante de cientos de personas es lo último que quería hacer esa tarde.

—Suspéndelo —respondí.

—No es la mejor idea. Después de esto, hay que aparentar normalidad.

—No puedo aparentar algo que no es.

—Voy a emitir un comunicado en las redes sociales explicando lo sucedido. Es tan obvio lo que te ha pasado que todo el mundo lo va a entender —explicó Kevin.

—El problema no son mis seguidores. El problema soy yo. ¿Crees que estoy para actuar hoy?

—Pues lo estarás —dijo Kevin regresando al modo «padre-bronca»—. Aún quedan unas horas. Te duchas, comemos, nos calmamos... y cuando sea la hora del show, ni te vas a acordar de lo que ha pasado.

—Ni de coña —afirmé.

4.

A las ocho de la tarde estaba en el *backstage* de la sala donde se iba a celebrar el show. Como era de esperar, Kevin se había salido con la suya. No voy a negar que tuviera razón: seguir con mi actividad normal era la mejor respuesta que podía dar después de la jugada de la que había sido víctima por parte de Donald. Antes de ir al show, habíamos parado en una comisaría donde habíamos denunciado lo sucedido. No confiaba mucho en la utilidad de hacerlo, pero Kevin había insistido. No podíamos quedarnos de brazos cruzados, decía. La persona que había hecho eso no podía quedar impune. Tampoco pude negar que tuviera razón en eso.

Kevin había colgado una nota en las redes sociales explicando lo sucedido. Decía que mi cuenta había sido *hackeada* y el vídeo que todo el mundo había visto no era obra de Joel Graham. No daba más detalles, ni citaba a Donald, ni hacía referencia al vídeo de la llamada que había generado todo lo sucedido. No quería darle protagonismo a mi acosador, me explicó. Tan solo defendía mi derecho a que se respetara mi privacidad y se mantuviera la línea que separaba mi trabajo de mi vida.

A pesar de los esfuerzos de Kevin, lo sucedido era la noticia del día en la comunidad *youtuber*. Una sociedad ávida de sucesos a cada segundo solo necesita que se prenda la mecha para tener algo de lo que ocuparse el resto del día. O algo sobre lo que escribir en los muros de sus perfiles. De la noche a la mañana me había convertido en el blanco de todos los comentarios. Unos, los menos, me defendían. Otros, los más, aprovechaban para hacer chistes, memes o, los peores, para cebarse conmigo. El éxito de mi canal era mi mejor escudo ante mis detractores. Hasta ese momento, que mis vídeos gustaran y funcionaran restaba argumentos a todos aquellos que me tenían ganas. El poder del «me gusta» era imbatible y cualquier disidente que me pusiera verde sin motivo entraba de inmediato en la categoría de *troll* y era silenciado por todos los demás. Mis propios seguidores actuaban como centinelas de mi canal, lo cuidaban y lo protegían. Una «policía» cibernética espontánea. Es una de las cosas que más me gustan de internet: la autogestión que surge en un medio donde apenas hay normas y donde, desde el anonimato, se pueden decir barbaridades. Si eres legal con los demás, los demás lo son contigo. Es un acuerdo no escrito entre las partes que permite que, en la jungla de la red, la convivencia sea posible.

A cambio, cuando alguien salta la barrera y le sale bien, los efectos son incontrolables. Era lo que me acababa de suceder con Donald. Su disparo había dado en el centro de la diana. El vídeo que había colgado en mi canal había desbordado cualquier intento de mis seguidores más fieles por contenerlo. Primero, porque nadie imaginaba que no fuera mío.

Luego, porque, una vez hecho el daño, cualquier explicación llegaba tarde y sonaba —como había advertido Kevin—, a excusa barata. Cuando el vídeo hubo desaparecido del canal, ya podía verse en decenas de cuentas de Twitter, en muros de Facebook y en otras plataformas de vídeo *online*. Otra de las cosas de internet que, a veces, se vuelven en tu contra: lo difícil que es tener control sobre lo que cuelgas. Cuando va a tu favor, todo es maravilloso. Pero cuando se trata de algo que quieres que nadie vea, es una pesadilla.

—Sales en cinco —me dijo uno de los organizadores.

—¿Ya? —respondí sorprendido—. Si aún no hay gente.

—Está a tope.

Era raro. Siempre escuchaba el rumor de la gente que esperaba mi aparición en la sala antes de salir. Y según se acercaba la hora, el rumor iba creciendo. Pero esta vez, no llegaba nada a mi camerino.

—¿Y hoy que han venido, mudos? —pregunté con mala idea.

—Están tranquilitos —me soltó el organizador con prudencia—. Pero se mueren de ganas de verte actuar. Ahora vengo a buscarte para llevarte al escenario. —Y salió.

Tranquilitos. Ya. Algo pasaba y no acertaba a saber el qué. Kevin entró sin mirarme y fue directo a la mesa de las bebidas sin decir nada.

—¿Qué pasa? —pregunté extrañado. Si de normal Kevin era un torbellino, antes de un show, era un terremoto.

—Nada —dijo con una sonrisa tímida—. Está a reventar. ¿Quieres calentar la voz?

—¿Qué coño pasa, Kevin? —insistí molesto.

—¡Nada, joder! —respondió nervioso. No me gustaba el tono—. ¿Calentamos?

—Kevin, tío... —di dos pasos y me puse frente a él—. Pasa algo y no quieres decírmelo.

—Me han llamado de comisaría —dijo tragando saliva—. No existe nadie con el nombre de Donald Collins.

—¿Cómo? —No entendía.

—Que no existe. Es un nombre inventado.

—¿Y el teléfono?

—No da señal. Está dado de baja.

—Pero podrá saberse a quién pertenecía, ¿no? —Me parecía tan fácil averiguarlo, que no entendía cómo Donald, o como se llamara ese tío, no estuviera detenido ya a esas horas.

—Supongo —respondió sin más. Apremiado por mi mirada interrogante, se vio obligado a continuar—. Pero tu caso no es una prioridad, entiéndelo.

—¿Ah, no? —respondí furioso—. ¿Que destrocen mi reputación no es una prioridad?

—No —afirmó Kevin—. En un mundo donde hay robos, asesinatos, estafas y esas cosas, *hackear* un canal de YouTube no lo es. Las cosas son así.

Genial. Una agresión de esa magnitud iba a quedar impune. Lo que me faltaba. Ya no solo me sentía acorralado, humillado, despreciado. Ahora también me sentía desprotegido por la ley.

El organizador se asomó por la puerta.

—¿Vamos, jefe? —Le miré desubicado. ¿Era de verdad el mejor momento para salir a un escenario?

—Luego nos ocupamos de esto, Joel —dijo Kevin—. Ahora hay que salir ahí a darlo todo.

Resoplé y traté de recorrer en mi cabeza el camino que había entre mis problemas y lo que iba a suceder en unos segundos. Era como si tuviera que hacer un viaje transoceánico en medio minuto. Salí del camerino. Kevin me miró con una media sonrisa mientras sujetaba un vaso de zumo de naranja en sus manos. Por primera vez en mi vida le vi frágil. Era una roca y me metía mucha caña, pero en ese instante me di cuenta de que todo lo que había pasado también le afectaba. Por un instante se me encogió el corazón. Pero si no podía permitirme dejar sitio a la rabia que sentía en ese instante por las malas noticias sobre Donald, tampoco podía hacerlo para ocuparme de la impotencia de Kevin. Así que vacié mi cabeza de cualquier pensamiento y fijé mi mirada en la espalda del organizador que me precedía por el pasillo que conducía al escenario. Al llegar, el organizador me hizo una señal para que me detuviera. La megafonía anunció mi nombre y el chico me abrió el paso moviendo la palma de su mano hacia delante. Como un autómata, salí al escenario sin ser consciente de verdad de lo que estaba haciendo. Y os juro que en ese momento, mi cabeza estaba en cualquier sitio menos en ese.

—¡Buenas noches! —grité al micro.

Silencio. Murmullos. Miradas y risitas. Antes lo había dicho de coña, pero, ¿eran mudos? Los focos me impedían ver con claridad, pero, como me habían advertido, la sala estaba hasta la bandera. Sin embargo, por un instante no se oía ni una mosca.

—¿Buenas noches? —pregunté intimidado. Algo no estaba cuadrando: tal vez el micro no funcionaba; tal vez, no estaba bien iluminado...— ¿Hay alguien ahí? —insistí tratando de hacer un chiste.

—«Perdóname, Donald, te lo suplico» —dijo alguien entre el público imitando burlón la voz del vídeo. Al instante, la sala entera estalló en una carcajada.

—¿Cómo? —dije sin pensar. Lo había escuchado a la perfección, pero no podía creerlo. La sala estaba revolucionada, nadie parecía prestarme atención—. ¡¿Qué cojones os pasa?!

Se hizo el silencio. Solo escuché los pasos de Kevin acercándose corriendo entre bambalinas.

—¿Alguien quiere decirme algo? Porque si es así, le invito a que suba aquí y estaré encantado de hablar con él. O ella.

Miré al público desafiante. Nadie me miraba a los ojos. Medio cegado por los focos solo podía advertir alguna cara de cachondeo. Me sentí como el típico profesor al que se le revoluciona la clase y no sabe cómo reconducirla. Echar la bronca nunca funcionaba en esos casos, pero ahora entendía que era el único recurso. Cómo me compadecí de todos los profesores que había tenido en mi vida.

—«¡No hay perdón para los malvados!» —dijo otro. Nueva carcajada.

—¡Dad las luces de la sala! —grité—. ¡Quiero veros!

Esta vez, los asistentes respondieron con abucheos. El nivel de provocación crecía por momentos.

—¡Que deis las putas luces! —insistí fuera de mí. Solo el micro me daba una ligera ventaja. Pero ellos eran más y tenían ganas de pasarlo bien a mi costa. Como las luces no se encendían, me dirigí al borde del escenario dispuesto a bajar y enfrentarme con todos ellos. No veía caras, solo móviles enfocando hacia mí.

—Uhhhhhh —respondieron con sorna.

—Os vais a enterar, desagradecidos —ya iba a saltar al patio de butacas cuando sentí unas manos en mis axilas que me levantaron en el aire y me sacaron de ahí. Después de eso, apenas recuerdo nada.

Según me contó Kevin después, fueron dos *relaciones* de la sala los que me sacaron del escenario. El trayecto hasta sacarme de ahí fue patético —eso no me lo dijo Kevin, pero está grabado desde infinidad de puntos de vista. Soy yo suspendido en el aire y pataleando mientras gritaba furioso al público. En el camerino, hicieron falta varias personas para reducirme y hasta que llegaron del Samur y me inyectaron un tranquilizante, no lo consiguieron del todo. Por suerte, nadie grabó esa escena. Después de eso, me llevaron a casa. O eso me ha contado mi *repre*, porque yo solo recuerdo abrir los ojos a las doce del mediodía y no saber dónde estaba. Había dormido desde la noche anterior y al levantarme de la cama, casi me desmayo de debilidad.

—Come, hijo, estás en los huesos. —Era mi madre quien me insistía. Debe de ser una frase que injertan en el cerebro de todas las madres del mundo. En esta ocasión le hice caso, estaba canino—. Ya te dije que esto de internet no era de fiar. Que si te lo pasas bien, vale para un ratito, pero que tenías que buscarte otra cosa por si acaso. —Otra típica reflexión de madre.

—Es mi trabajo, mamá.

—Trabajo... —respondió escéptica mientras ahuecaba los cojines de mi sofá. Kevin la había llamado y le había faltado tiempo para venir a mi casa para cocinar para mí y ya, de paso, recoger la casa. Típico de madre. No tenía duda: las madres tienen un chip implantado que solo tienen ellas.

—Y bien que me gano la vida —me defendí.

—Pues no es lo parece, hijo. Mírate —Me observó con pena—. Come, anda.

Mi hermanita Grette asomó desde el pasillo.

—Joel... ¿Me dejas la *tablet* para jugar a *Frozen*?

—Claro —sonreí—. Ya sabes dónde está.

Grette tenía nueve años y era adorable. En su vida había dos pasiones: sus amigas del colegio y yo. Nos veíamos poco, mi día a día no era muy familiar, sobre todo desde que me fui a vivir solo hacía ya unos años. Mi trabajo, o «eso que hacía en internet», según mi madre, me tenía bastante ocupado. Pero siempre que podía, buscaba el momento para estar con ella.

Grette salió por la puerta feliz, momento que aprovechó mi madre para sentarse frente a mí en la mesa. Yo seguía devorando los macarrones de mi plato, aunque sabía que se avecinaba charlita de madre.

—Kevin me lo ha contado todo. —¡Maldito Kevin!—. Me ha dicho que tuviste un ataque de ansiedad.

—Bah, no fue nada. Estrés —disimulé.

—¿Seguro? —Metió su mano en un bolsillo de la chaqueta y sacó una caja de comprimidos—. Me dijo que te diera esto, es lo que ha recomendado el médico que tomes.

Miré la caja sorprendido. Eran tranquilizantes.

—A ver... —dije tratando de controlar mi enfado—. Que un ataque de nervios lo tiene cualquiera.

—De ansiedad —puntualizó mi madre.

—¡¿Qué más da?! —exploté. De inmediato me di cuenta de que mi reacción había estado fuera de lugar.

—¿Lo ves? —dijo mi madre otra vez con ese tono de madre que te indica que tiene razón—. ¿Por qué no vienes a casa unos días y descansas?

Te pase lo que te pase en la vida, solo hay una cosa segura: tu madre siempre te va a dar cobijo. No lo valoramos lo suficiente, pero es la única persona que va a salvarte cuando ya no quede esperanza.

—Gracias, mamá —respondí avergonzado por mi reacción anterior—. Pero...

—¡Pero nada! —afirmó autoritaria—. Te vienes y punto.

—Te lo agradezco, mamá, pero estoy bien, de verdad. He tenido algún problemilla con mi canal, pero todo va a solucionarse.

Mi madre me miró compasiva. Sabía que no iba a ir se pusiera como se pusiera. Si ellas tienen un chip, los hijos tenemos otro, y es el de no hacerles ni caso. Y menos a cierta edad como la que yo tenía.

—¿Estarás bien? —me preguntó preocupada.

—Sí, tranquila —sonreí.

Un rato más tarde, mi madre y Grette se despedían de mí no sin antes prometerle que comería y dormiría lo necesario. Sahara, mi nevera, estaba repleta y la casa olía de maravilla. El orden que había dejado mi madre a su paso contrastaba con el caos que había en ese momento en mi canal. Por eso, cuando se cerró la puerta y me quedé solo, miré hacia el fondo del pasillo con pavor. La puerta de mi estudio estaba entreabierta y de él salía el leve zumbido de los ventiladores de mis discos duros. Había una fuerza extraña que salía de ahí, algo que me llamaba pero que, al mismo tiempo, me impedía acercarme. Después de todo lo sucedido, me di cuenta de que tenía miedo a mi propio canal, a mi trabajo, a mis vídeos. A mis seguidores. El corazón empezó a latirme con fuerza. Recordé las pastillas que me había recomendado el médico. ¿Estarían en la salita? Alguien llamó a la puerta con los nudillos. Me sonó a gloria, a una buena razón para no tener que enfrentarme a lo que estaba al final del pasillo. Abrí sin pensar.

—¿Qué os habéis dej...? —dije dando por hecho que eran mi madre y Grette. Pero no, eran Connor, Jan, Sil y Flavia.

—Tío... —protestó Silvestre—. Seis a uno.

—Y menos mal que he marcado el del honor en el último minuto —apuntó Jan.

—Porque te necesitamos en el equipo, que si no, te dábamos la carta de libertad —amenazó Connor.

Los cuatro hicieron ademán de entrar en casa, como hacían siempre, pero esta vez no me moví para abrirles paso. No lo hice de manera consciente, fue un acto reflejo. Eso provocó que Flavia se diera de bruces con la espalda de Silvestre.

—¡Flavia, tía, mira por dónde vas! —protestó Sil.

—Si no entras... —se quejó Flavia.

La situación era incómoda: yo, frente a ellos, con el brazo extendido sujetando la puerta, haciendo una barrera para que ninguno de los cuatro entrara.

—Tío, ni que fuéramos comerciales de Tecnocasa que venimos a tasar tu piso —dijo Connor consciente de que se habían quedado a medio camino de entrar en mi casa.

—Estoy liado ahora —dije como excusa, poco creíble, por cierto.

—¿Estás bien? —preguntó Jan preocupado.

—Sí, sí... Lo único que necesito es estar solo.

—¿Después de lo que te ha pasado? Anda, quita —dijo Silvestre tratando de avanzar hacia el interior de la casa y haciendo honor a la frase de que «la confianza da asco».

Me mantuve firme. No quería compañía en esos momentos. Saber que mis mejores amigos estaban al corriente de lo que había pasado me avergonzaba bastante.

—Venga, Joel, hemos traído un huevo de frikadas para hacer un maratón —dijo Connor levantando una bolsa a rebosar de películas.

—De Serie Z para abajo —puntualizó Jan—. Hay hasta gore indonesio, ya conoces a Connor.

—¿No las habrás cogido de mi videoclub? —preguntó Silvestre alarmado. Connor le respondió con una sonrisa pícara—. Joder, cómo se entere mi jefe, me mata.

—Que no, tíos. Otro día —afirmé rotundo. Los cuatro me miraron decepcionados.

—¿Puedo ir al baño, al menos? —preguntó Flavia, como siempre, a lo suyo.

—No, Flavia —dijo Jan consciente de que era el momento de irse.

—Nos vemos otro día, ¿vale? —dije.

—En el entrenamiento, ¿no? Solo quedan tres partidos para acabar la temporada y aún podemos evitar el descenso —preguntó Silvestre, siempre preocupado por cualquier cosa.

—¿Descenso a dónde? Ya no se puede bajar más de nuestra categoría —precisó Connor.

—Ya veremos —respondí. Y avancé un paso hacia delante mientras cerraba la puerta de casa. Los cuatro retrocedieron al rellano a la vez—. Chao.

Cerré la puerta y me arrepentí en seguida. No estaba seguro de querer estar solo, pero aunque no sabía por qué, era la decisión que había tomado. Pasar la tarde con mis amigos viendo gore indonesio era un plan que, en otras circunstancias, nunca habría rechazado. Pero esa tarde, no era lo que necesitaba. Tenía que ordenar mis ideas, tomar tierra después de un vuelo con demasiadas turbulencias. Decidido, avancé por el pasillo camino de mi estudio, pero al llegar a la altura del salón me detuve. El estudio, mejor para más tarde, pensé. Una fuerza extraña me impedía entrar ahí por el momento. Lo que tenía que hacer entonces, bien podía hacerlo en el sofá.

Tumbado, mirando al techo, traté de dibujar un mapa mental del lugar en el que estaba. Todo era normal hasta que un maldito *flyer* cayó en mis manos. Por alguna razón intuí que ese papelito ridículo era especial. No imaginaba que lo fuera de la manera en la que lo estaba siendo; más bien creí que tenía en mis manos una gran idea para mi canal. El vídeo había sido un éxito, pero terminó lleno de amenazas y reproches. No era inusual, tampoco nos engañemos: muchas llamadas terminaban así. Pero sí era cierto que el tono de Donald —aunque ya sabía que no era su nombre real, era la única manera que tenía de referirme a él— era algo diferente. Había un punto de dolor en sus amenazas, como si la broma no solo le hubiera enfurecido, sino que también le hubiera tocado algo por dentro. Algo doloroso. Era imposible para mí imaginar el qué. Era imposible imaginar que una tontería sin importancia como una broma telefónica provocara ese daño. Pero así había sido. Y, como consecuencia, Donald había atacado como un animal herido: con los dientes y las garras afiladas. Y provocando, de paso, un daño enorme.

Un punto negro en el techo parecía moverse. ¿Un insecto? Estaba demasiado concentrado en mis pensamientos para ocuparme de ello. Además, cuando miras mucho rato un punto lejano parece que se mueve aunque no lo haga. Sonreí para mí. Era como me sentía yo: inmóvil, incapaz de moverme por mucho que alguien me mirara mucho rato. Donald no había actuado de manera azarosa y desordenada. Tenía un plan y lo había llevado a cabo sin fisuras. Primero, abrió mi taquilla y la llenó de muñecos. Ahora entendía que lo único que perseguía con eso era provocarme, cosa que consiguió, ya que corrí a casa a grabar un vídeo de amenaza. Ese vídeo fue su excusa para entrar en mi cuenta y colgar uno que se había tomado la molestia en grabar, molestia mínima porque el vídeo era un despropósito. Gracias a eso, perdí los papeles en el show e hice el mayor ridículo público que se pudiera imaginar. Visto así, una cosa siempre había llevado a la otra. Donald actuaba con un plan, eligiendo sus movimientos con esmero y logrando mi respuesta, siempre para hacerme el mayor daño posible. ¿Cómo no me había dado cuenta? Lo que estaba haciendo mi acosador era dialogar conmigo. Solo que, hasta ese momento, el que llevaba las riendas de la conversación era él y yo no podía más que responder a la desesperada.

Suspiré profundamente. Intenté localizar el punto negro en el techo, pero fui incapaz. O era un insecto y había volado, o nunca hubo tal punto negro. Llegar a esa idea, la del diálogo que Donald había establecido conmigo, me dio cierta tranquilidad. Al menos podía entender algo de lo que estaba sucediendo. Sin embargo, una nueva sombra apareció en mi cabeza. Si esto era así, la siguiente línea la iba a escribir él. Después del incidente del show, era su turno. Y conociéndole, ya estaba tardando. Aunque, al mismo tiempo, acariciaba la idea de que la conversación siniestra que manteníamos hubiera llegado a su fin. Más bajo no podía hacerme caer, pensaba. O sí. Su exigencia había sido clara: quería un perdón público por mi parte. Y eso no lo tenía. Mi corazón empezó a latir con fuerza de nuevo. Cuando me incorporé del sofá no me cabía ninguna duda: Donald iba a volver a atacar y era imposible saber dónde y cómo iba a hacerlo. En ese momento, sonó el teléfono. Agradecí la interrupción; no quería seguir con la losa que representaba la supuesta amenaza Donald sobre mi cabeza. Era el fijo, cosa rara, nadie llama ya a los fijos. Corrí a descolgar cuando recordé dónde estaba el aparato.

—¿Quién es? —contesté al tiempo que la idea de que se tratara de Donald cruzaba por mi cabeza.

—Inspector Harris, de la comisaría de centro. ¿Podría acercarse a responder a unas preguntas? —dijo de forma contundente, como si estuviera enfadado.

—¿Sobre qué? —quise saber, asustado.

—Sobre el caso de Donald Collins. Creo que usted y yo tenemos mucho de qué hablar.

Fui incapaz de responder. En lo más profundo de mí temía que estuviera ante el siguiente movimiento de Donald.

5.

No puedo decir que me gusten las comisarías. Tampoco que no me gusten. En realidad, hasta que acudí aquella tarde a la llamada del inspector Harris, nunca había pisado una. No soy de meterme en líos, mucho menos en líos que acaben delante de la policía. Lo que más me sorprendió cuando entré fue descubrir lo poco que se parece una comisaría de verdad a las que salen en las películas. Pero, sobre todo, lo poco que se parecen los polis a los que salen en ellas.

Al entrar, me acerqué dubitativo al mostrador donde una mujer de uniforme tenía la cabeza entre un montón de papeles. «No tengo nada que temer», me dije. «Estoy en un lugar seguro». Pero después de todo lo que me había pasado en los últimos días, no tenía la certeza de que eso fuera verdad. ¿Qué era lo seguro y qué no? Un manotazo y todo lo que creemos sólido se desmorona como un castillo de arena en la orilla de la playa.

—¿Denuncia? —preguntó la mujer sin levantar la vista de sus papeles.

—¿Perdón? —dije como un chaval asustado. La mujer me miró con los ojos cansados.

—Que si viene por una denuncia. —Como tardaba en responder, resopló—: Aquí no comemos a nadie, joven. A no ser que venga a entregarse —añadió tratando de hacer un chiste.

—No, yo... Me ha llamado el inspector Harris.

—Ah, usted es... —no recordaba mi nombre, pero en seguida supo quién era— el de internet. —Y su cara anunció una sonrisa, tan imperceptible, que solo se manifestó en las patas de gallo de sus ojos. Hasta esa mujer sabía lo que me había pasado. Se volvió a un lado y gritó—: ¡Harris!

Harris se asomó al instante, la camisa arrugada, la cara arrugada, el humor arrugado. No era lo que se podía esperar de alguien que inspira confianza.

—¿Graham? —dijo con el mismo tono que había empleado por teléfono—. Acompáñeme. —Y desapareció por la misma puerta por la que se había asomado. Me quedé inmóvil, sin saber si seguirle o salir corriendo de allí.

—Vaya, joven. Harris tiene muy malas pulgas —me advirtió la mujer. Me vio tan cohibido que se vio forzada a adoptar un tono algo más maternal—. No comemos a nadie, recuerde.

Harris me invitó a sentarme frente a él. Lo hizo señalándome una silla al otro lado del escritorio mientras rebuscaba en sus carpetas.

—¿Pasa algo, inspector? —pregunté temeroso. La sospecha de que me hubiera llamado por algo que desconocía crecía por momentos. Era incapaz de imaginar qué podía haber tramado Donald para llevarme hasta ahí.

—Eso me lo tendrá que decir usted —respondió sin mirarme. No iba a ponérmelo fácil, estaba claro—. Aquí está —dijo malhumorado. Abrió la carpeta; dentro solo había un folio—. Bien. Delito informático, ¿no?

—No sé, inspector —respondí siguiendo su juego de ambigüedades—. Eso me lo tendrá que decir usted, no conozco la jerga.

Harris me miró por primera vez y sonrió. No debía de estar acostumbrado a que la gente le replicara con ironía. Era un riesgo, sin duda. Siempre es un riesgo retar a la autoridad: ellos llevan esposas y pistolas y tú, no.

—Delito informático —concluyó—. El denunciado está ilocalizable y su número de teléfono no está operativo.

Respiré un poco más tranquilo. Parecía que Donald no estaba detrás de mi presencia allí esa tarde.

—¿Han hablado con la compañía telefónica para averiguar a nombre de quién estaba la línea?

—No hemos tenido tiempo. En este momento hemos movilizado a todas nuestras unidades terrestres y aéreas para rastrear al sospechoso. Los servicios secretos también están sobre el caso —dijo con total seriedad.

—¿Y el ejército? —dije. No me hacía gracia que me tomaran el pelo, aunque la interpretación del inspector hubiera sido impecable.

—Eh, compañeros —dijo Harris levantando la cabeza al resto de la oficina—. Tenemos a una estrella del humor aquí. —Por suerte, nadie le hizo el menor caso—. Señor Graham, estamos hablando de una gamberrada de internet. Le he llamado porque aquí atendemos todas las denuncias, pero, como comprenderá, su caso es el último del que me apetece ocuparme.

Su actitud me pareció tan desagradable que por un momento estuve tentado de levantarme e irme. Harris sería una buena víctima de una de mis bromas telefónicas, pensé. «Pero ellos llevan esposas y pistolas y tú no», me repetí para ahuyentar cualquier impulso de hacerlo.

—Bien —respondí tranquilo—. Entonces solo estoy aquí para que los dos perdamos el tiempo un rato.

—Exacto, veo que nos vamos entendiendo. —Volvió a mirar el solitario papel que mi caso merecía—. Y ya que estamos, sigamos el procedimiento. ¿Sabe en qué ciudad vive el denunciado?

—Ni idea.

—¿Qué relación tenía con el denunciado?

—Ninguna. Solo le llamé por su anuncio.

Harris miró en el papel.

—El hombre vende muñecos, ¿no?

—O eso intenta.

—¿Le compró alguno?

—No, no llegué a hacerlo —respondí sorprendido. No podía creer que fuera la única persona en el mundo que no estuviera al tanto de la burla de la que el hombre había sido víctima.

—¿Algún número de cuenta para ingresar el dinero de los pedidos?

—¿Para qué me lo iba a dar?

—¿Tiene usted algo que nos sirva para localizarle? —dijo irritado.

La pregunta era más seria de lo que parecía. Me hizo ver que no tenía nada. En cambio, Donald lo tenía todo: sabía quién era, dónde vivía, quiénes eran mis amigos, dónde entrenaba. Todo. Era la diferencia entre estar a un lado o estar al otro de la pantalla. Aunque mantuviera mi vida privada al margen de mi trabajo, mi nivel de exposición era inmenso. En cambio, el de mis seguidores o el de cualquiera que me viera, era mínimo. ¿Qué tenía de Donald? Solo una voz y un *flyer*. Harris acababa de ponerme un espejo delante y había visto quién era yo en realidad y quién mi adversario.

—Nada —respondí lacónico—. Abrió mi taquilla en el vestuario del campo de fútbol donde entreno, igual hay huellas... —Al ver la cara de incredulidad de Harris, no continué—. Pero vamos, que la chica de la limpieza seguro que las ha borrado.

—Seguro. Haremos todo lo que podamos, señor Graham. —Y me tendió la mano para despedirme. Me la estrechó con firmeza y mirándome a los ojos. Era un capullo, pero ese gesto me reconfortó.

—Gracias, inspector.

La visita a la comisaría no había servido para nada. No para dar con Donald, al menos. Solo una sucesión de casualidades podría hacer avanzar el caso. Era una vía muerta, pensé. En esos momentos, más que nunca, supe que estaba solo en eso. Solos Donald y yo.

Caminé por la calle hasta mi casa. No era demasiado tarde, pero apenas había gente. Tuve la sensación de que me observaban. Miré hacia atrás, a los lados. Donald podía estar en cualquier sitio y yo no iba a enterarme. La lucha era desigual y yo no tenía ninguna ventaja. Podría ser ese señor que paseaba a su perro, ese que cruzaba hablando por el móvil. Cualquiera podía ser mi acosador. Descubrir que no sabía nada de él me puso en mi sitio. Y me hizo sentir peor. Por un instante asomó cierta culpa: ¿había utilizado a Donald para mi beneficio sin pensar en nada más? Sin preocuparme por saber quién era, qué hacía, dónde vivía. No hubiera tenido sentido hacerlo, en realidad. La inmediatez de internet era así. Todo va muy deprisa en la red y una cosa sucede a otra antes de que nadie pueda digerirla. Eso tenía una ventaja: antes de lo que imaginaba, lo que había pasado conmigo pasaría al olvido. A no ser que Donald se encargara de mantener la llama encendida. Y ahí fue cuando cualquier tentación de sentirme culpable desapareció: fuera lo que fuera lo que yo había hecho, nunca podría causar una respuesta tan desproporcionada por parte de nadie. En caso de que Donald hubiese tenido razón, después de todo lo que había hecho, la había perdido.

—Tallarines fritos con curry rojo, teppanyaki de pollo y... un Shao Mai —al llegar a casa lo primero que hice fue encargar comida asiática. Aunque mi madre me había dejado la nevera llena, esa noche me apetecía darme un homenaje.

—¿Quiere algo más? —preguntaron al otro lado de la línea.

—¿Le parece poco? —Reí—. No, nada más.

Era mi restaurante a domicilio favorito. Casi todas las semanas hacía al menos un pedido. Después de varios días intensos, me apetecía comerme un buen menú asiático, lo veía como si fuera a hacerme un *reset*. Seguro que después de eso, vería las cosas de otra manera.

—Dieciséis con veinte —me anunció el repartidor cuando llegó a casa. Llevaba el casco puesto y su voz sonaba apagada. Le di diecisiete.

—Quédate con el cambio.

—*Sus órdenes*, míster —dijo con un tono entre servicial y burlón.

Sentado en el sofá, me dispuse a desplegar toda la comida. Saqué las tarrinas, los envases con las salsas, la servilleta, los palillos. Al fondo de la bolsa de papel descubrí un papel. No era el tique, era una hoja arrancada de una libreta de cuadrícula. Desconcertado, la saqué y la desdoblé. En ella, confeccionada con letras recortadas, una dirección web.

—Donald. —Suspiré. Ahí estaba su siguiente movimiento.

El corazón volvió a latir con fuerza, pero esta vez, además, la intensidad de los latidos era muy superior: profunda y poderosa, como si alguien estuviera tocando un tambor dentro de mi pecho. Miré alrededor en busca de la caja de tranquilizantes. ¿Dónde narices la había puesto? No. No quería recurrir a ellos. Podía con eso. Con eso y con todo, me dije. Me olvidé de la cena, cogí el papel, me levanté y salí hacia mi estudio. Esta vez no me detuve en la puerta. La abrí de golpe y entré.

La primera sensación al entrar fue extraña. Si antes me había quedado clavado en el pasillo incapaz de entrar, ahora me detuve nada más cruzar la puerta. Una fuerza invisible me impedía avanzar más allá y acercarme al escritorio donde estaba mi ordenador. Con el papelito en la mano, miré hacia mis cosas, tan familiares que hacía tiempo que no les prestaba atención: la mesa, la silla acolchada, la pantalla ahora en reposo, mis botes de bolígrafos, mis muñequitos, mis fotos colgadas en la pared. Ese era mi espacio: el lugar donde pasaba la mayor parte del tiempo y que ahora me costaba sentir como propio. Me lo habían arrebatado, ya no era mío.

Despacio, me acerqué a la silla. Me acompañaba el zumbido de los ventiladores del disco duro que, según me aproximaba, iba en aumento. Parecía el rugido de la afición de un equipo de fútbol que, según te acercas al estadio, se escucha más cerca. Pero no era un estadio el lugar al que iba. No iba a ponerme delante de mi afición que me esperaba impaciente. Tenía la sensación de que, más bien, me dirigía al circo romano, a luchar con animales salvajes con la única ayuda de un machete y bajo la mirada de un público ávido de sangre y vísceras. Me senté en la silla y miré la pantalla en negro. Respiré hondo y pulsé una tecla cualquiera para sacar a mi ordenador del reposo. El zumbido de los ventiladores aumentó. Era el público enloquecido ante la inminencia del comienzo de la función. El espectáculo estaba a punto de comenzar.

La dirección que figuraba en el papelito era la de un portal de videoconferencias en directo. No lo conocía, pero imaginé que era uno de tantos de los que había para hablar por la red. Tecleé la dirección, pero antes de dar al *enter*, me tomé un instante para respirar. Estaba a punto de empezar un nuevo *round* y no quería caer sobre la lona al primer asalto.

Enter.

Tras un segundo, la página se cargó y, ante mí apareció la imagen del muñeco de Trump sentado en un butacón. Ridículo. Acepté activar mi cámara y mi micro. Quería demostrar que yo sí daba la cara aunque a quien tuviera delante fuera a una patética representación del loco más grande que había en el mundo en ese momento.

—¿Me vas a hacer hablar con un muñeco, Donald? ¿O cómo debería llamarte? —dije para tomar la iniciativa de la conversación. Esta vez no quería ir a remolque de Donald.

De fondo solo se escuchaba una melodía apagada de violín. Frases de una partitura que se repetían una y otra vez. Alguien estaba practicando en algún lugar cercano al ordenador desde el que trasmitía Donald. Al cabo de unos segundos, unos pasos se acercaron al ordenador.

—Amigo Joel —respondió Donald con una voz sorprendentemente jovial, nada que ver con el tono que escuché en la primera llamada, sombrío y cansado—. Pensé que antes de hablar conmigo cenarías.

—Al grano. —No quería empezar ninguna conversación intrascendente con él—. ¿Qué quieres?

—Saludarte, nada más.

—Pues ya me has saludado. Hasta luego. —E hice ademán de cortar la llamada. Esperaba que Donald lo evitara.

—Adiós, amigo —respondió tan tranquilo. Me equivoqué en mi suposición: Donald estaba dispuesto a terminar ahí. Me quedé con la mano suspendida en el aire camino del ratón.

—Adiós. —No iba a ceder, no esta vez.

—¿Todo bien, entonces? —dijo cuando el puntero de mi ordenador ya se estaba posando sobre el icono de cerrar ventana.

—¿Te interesa, acaso?

—No sabes lo que me está divirtiendo todo esto, amigo.

—¡No me llames amigo, desgraciado! —En seguida me arrepentí de haber levantado la voz, pero no pude contenerme.

—Tranquilo, Joel. —Su tono era condescendiente. Mi reacción había sido una metedura de pata; perdiendo los nervios solo conseguía darle a Donald toda la ventaja—. ¿Por qué no te relajas y disfrutas del juego, como hago yo?

—No he dicho que quiera jugar. Y esto será un juego para ti, pero te puedo asegurar que para mí no lo es.

—¿Ah, no? ¿Y qué era tu llamada sino eso?

—No compares. No es lo mismo una llamada inocente que destrozar la reputación de una persona.

—¿No hiciste tú lo mismo riéndote de mí y de mi trabajo delante de millones de personas?

—Tu trabajo es ridículo por sí mismo.

—Eso es opinable —respondió. La melodía de violín seguía sonando de fondo.

—Claro. Siempre habrá algún tarado al que tus muñecos le parezcan buenos.

—A mí.

—Un tarado —sentencié.

—Un tarado al que tus vídeos le parecen una mierda.

—Eso es opinable —dije utilizando sus mismas palabras. Mostrar mi cara me permitía dar matices con gestos y miradas a lo que decía. Esto último lo subraye bien con una amplia sonrisa irónica.

—Y lo único que he hecho —prosiguió—, es lo mismo que tú: mostrarle al mundo que tu trabajo me repugna, igual que tú mostraste al mundo lo que te parecía el mío.

—Hay una diferencia —me defendí—: yo lo hice en mi canal y a cara descubierta. No cometí ningún delito.

—La justicia... —dijo Donald dejando en el aire la última sílaba, prólogo de una reflexión—. Solo nos acordamos de ella cuando nos sentimos agredidos, ¿verdad? Pero, ¿qué pasa cuando se insulta, se humilla, se mofa de los demás? De eso no se ocupa la justicia. De eso solo se ocupan las personas.

—A no ser —repliqué—, que por el camino uno se salte la ley. Y eso es lo que tú has hecho abriendo mi taquilla o *hackeando* mi cuenta. Estaba respondiendo a sus argumentos y no me gustaba. Otra vez caía en sus redes.

—Es una cuestión de matiz —resumió.

—A los jueces les importan un pimiento los matices. Pero el día del juicio eres libre de contarles toda esta filosofada que me estás vendiendo.

—Lo haré, no te preocupes. Pero antes espero llevarme por delante todo esto. —Su tono se volvió agrio y duro al decir esto.

—¿Todo esto? —quise saber, aunque me lo imaginaba.

—Sí: a ti y a todos los niñatos como tú que os creéis los amos del mundo, que pensáis que una pantalla os da todo el poder para decir lo que os venga en gana. El mundo era mejor cuando había normas, cuando se respetaban los límites entre lo que está bien y lo que no...

—Y tú te los has saltado para dar ejemplo, ¿no? —dije sarcástico.

—Me los he saltado porque jugando con mis reglas no tengo nada que hacer. Así de triste es este mundo.

—Yo no pongo las reglas, no puedo ayudarte.

—Lo sé, pero bien que te beneficias de ellas.

—Simplemente sigo la corriente, tío, ¿qué quieres que haga? Es lo que hay, acéptalo.

—¡Me niego! —gritó. Bien: empezaba a perder los papeles, la ventaja volvía a mí—. Me niego a ser un borrego que sigue a la manada. Tu llamada me ha abierto los ojos. Alguien tiene que acabar con todo esto y ese voy a ser yo.

Qué pena no estar grabando la conversación. A pesar de lo que me acusaba Donald, yo tenía una ética, y una conversación privada, era privada. Aunque, lo reconozco, me arrepentía de no poder usar lo que estaba pasando para mi canal.

—Ahí le tenemos: el justiciero de YouTube —dije riéndome—. El Donald Trump de internet.

—Me gusta eso —respondió más calmado—. No sé si justiciero o combatiente. Pero sí: ya va siendo hora de que alguien os pare los pies a ti y a todos los críos maleducados que circuláis por aquí.

—No entiendes nada, «amigo» —dije—. Nada de nada.

Y era verdad. Gustara o no, el mundo ya no funcionaba como antes. No es que cualquiera pudiera llegar y hacer lo que le diera la gana, pero la libertad de decir lo que uno quisiera era mayor que antes. O, más bien, la libertad era la misma, solo que ahora había muchísima más gente escuchando al otro lado. Y eso significaba dos cosas: una, que cualquier tontería —a veces tonterías insufribles— tenían mayor repercusión; y otra, que se producía un curioso mecanismo de selección natural: lo que interesaba y era bueno, tenía éxito. Lo que no, era olvidado al instante. Eso era lo que no entendía Donald. Ante esa democracia espontánea en la que todo el mundo podía hablar, él quería sacar la espada y empezar a cercenar cualquier contenido que considerara «fuera de orden». Si no le gustaba algo, que mirara para otro lado, es lo que hacemos todos en internet.

—Creo que el que no entiende nada eres tú. Y por eso estás como estás. ¿Has visto el éxito de tus últimos vídeos? #joelgraham es eso que llamáis... *Trend Topic*, ¿no? Es tronchante.

—¿Qué quieres, Donald, dinero?

—Dinero... —río—. Primero los jueces, ahora dinero... Dices que no aceptas las normas, pero en cuanto puedes, recurres a ellas. Eres tan inocente.

—Entonces, ¿qué? ¿Qué quieres para acabar con esto?

—¿Quién quiere que se acabe la fiesta cuando te lo estás pasando bien? —Así que, para Donald, eso era todo lo que estaba pasando: una fiesta.

—¿No has tenido suficiente? Ya me has destrozado, ¡¿qué más quieres?!

—Acabar contigo.

—¡Cabrón!

Pero ya no lo escuchó. Había cortado la comunicación.

6.

Salí decidido de mi estudio. En cierto modo, la llamada de Donald me había liberado. Ahora sabía que no iba a parar y, aunque no tenía ni idea de qué era lo siguiente que iba a hacer, al menos tenía una idea clara: esto era una fiesta y yo estaba invitado a ella. Y cuando te invitan, hay que ser agradecido y estar a la altura.

Sentado en el sofá, aparté la comida que había pedido y que ya debía de haberse quedado fría y saqué una libreta. ¿Qué tenía? Poca cosa. El número de teléfono al que llamé la primera vez ya no pertenecía a Donald. Anoté «teléfono» en la libreta y lo taché. ¿Qué más? La nota en la bolsa del pedido. Alguien debió de dejarla ahí, incluso el propio Donald. No recordaba al repartidor. Era imposible, me entregó el pedido con el casco puesto. Era un chaval con acento latino, creí percibir. ¿Estaría compinchado con Donald? Podía ser, de él podía esperar cualquier cosa. Anoté en mi libreta: «nota», «repartidor», «ruta de reparto», «restaurante», «salida de pedidos a domicilio». La nota era una gran pista, me di cuenta. ¿Qué más? Pensé. Solo se me ocurrían las típicas cosas que salen en las películas: huellas dactilares, nada; cámaras de seguridad del polideportivo, nada; confidentes... Me reí. Aunque mi vida se había convertido en una película de terror, pensar en que iba a encontrar la solución en el cine me parecía una tontería.

Seguí dándole vueltas a ver si había algo más que pudiera ayudarme. Se me había pegado la melodía de violín que se escuchaba de fondo durante mi conversación con Donald y no dejaba de tararearla una y otra vez. Una y otra vez..., una y otra... ¡La melodía! Me resultaba familiar desde que empecé a oírla y no sabía por qué. Cogí mi *tablet*, entré en mi canal y busqué el vídeo de la llamada a Donald. Avancé unos segundos, cuando la conversación estaba en marcha y... Ahí la tenía. Durante toda la broma telefónica, como hacía unos instantes, se escuchaba esa melodía de fondo. Alguien que estaba estudiando una partitura. Anoté: «melodía», «estudiante violín», «¿academia de música?». Esto último lo dudaba, pero no estaba en disposición de descartar nada. «Profesor particular». Eso me sonaba mejor. Si había un estudiante de violín, podía haber un profesor a su lado. Mi hermana Grette era una de ellas. Para que no estuviera todo el día en el mundo de *Frozen*, mi madre la había apuntado a música. Por desgracia, escogió el violín como instrumento. Solo los que conviven con alguien que está aprendiendo a tocar un instrumento lo entienden. «Estudiante de violín en casa de Donald». ¿Tenía hijos pequeños? Es raro que un adulto empiece a estudiar música. Pero Donald parecía mayor, no le pegaba tener hijos menores de diez años. «Un vecino», apunté.

Me eché para atrás en el sofá y resoplé. Miré la libreta. La pista de la melodía era muy jugosa pero era inabarcable. ¿Cómo dar con un estudiante de violín en una ciudad con miles de habitantes? Aparté la idea de investigar por ahí de momento y me centré en lo otro: la nota que había aparecido en la bolsa del pedido de comida.

—Buenas noches —saludé al teléfono al encargado de coger los pedidos del restaurante unos minutos más tarde—. He hecho un pedido hace cosa de una hora...

—¿No le ha llegado? —preguntaron al otro lado de la línea.

—Sí, sí, todo bien. Solo que...

—¿Ha llegado tarde o algo? —El tono del encargado era nervioso y apresurado. Me estaba estresando.

—No, a ver, si me deja terminar, solo quiero saber quién me ha traído el pedido a casa.

—¿Por?

—Porque sí. ¿Puede ser? —respondí irritado.

—Sí, claro... —reculó el encargado. El cliente siempre tiene la razón, pensé. O casi siempre—. Lo que pasa es que servimos más de cien pedidos cada noche y tenemos diez repartidores, ahora mismo estamos hasta arriba. ¿Podría llamar más tarde?

—Es urgente.

—¿Ha pasado algo con el chico del reparto?

—No lo sé, por eso quiero saber quién es.

—Un segundo, ahora le atiendo. —Escuché cómo posaba el auricular sobre el mostrador y levantaba otro teléfono—. Buenas noches, ¿quiere realizar un pedido? —Oí.

Colgué el teléfono. No iba a conseguir nada de esa manera, así que me levanté de un salto y medio minuto después ya estaba en la calle rumbo al restaurante.

Al llegar comprendí por qué no era tan sencillo que me prestaran atención. Nunca había estado ahí, solo había hecho pedidos por teléfono y aquello parecía una factoría de cocinar y servir solo comparable a una cadena de montaje. Desde fuera se veía la cocina en la que se trabajaba a gran ritmo; en el mostrador, tres chicos atendían a los clientes que iban ahí a pedir su comida y cogían pedidos por teléfono; varios camareros servían comida en las mesas del local. La puerta era un enjambre de repartidores que salían con las típicas bolsas de papel con los pedidos. Observé el detalle de que iban cerradas en sus manos antes de meterlas en las cajas de reparto de las motos. Si esto era así, ¿en qué momento habían metido la nota en la mía?

Entré en el local y me invadió el mismo olor que desprendía la comida que recibía en mi casa. Eso me dio tranquilidad: era como estar en el sofá viendo la tele. Nadie parecía estar desocupado y, lo peor, nadie paraba quieto ni un segundo.

—Disculpa... —me aventuré a decir a un camarero. Me ignoró. Miré alrededor. Fui al mostrador—. Perdón...

—Póngase a la cola —me reprendió un cliente.

—Solo es una pregunta —dije disculpándome.

—Cuando sea su turno —me confirmó el dependiente.

No había manera. Al menos si no quería salir de ahí a golpes. Desesperado, busqué una solución. Había ido hasta ahí y no pensaba marcharme con las manos vacías. Seguí con la mirada a un repartidor y vi cómo iba directo a una ventanita que comunicaba con la cocina. Ahí recogía la bolsa con el pedido y, tras enfundarse el casco, salía pitando camino de su moto. Era mi última opción.

—Hola —dije a la ventana vacía. La persona al otro lado estaba a unos metros, de espaldas, metiendo tarrinas de un pedido en una bolsa al tiempo que consultaba una nota. No parecía más desocupado que los demás, pero al menos no estaba atendiendo a nadie y no tenía pinta de ir a moverse de ahí—. ¿Tienes un momento?

El chico que preparaba el pedido se giró, no porque quisiera hablar conmigo, sino porque esperaba encontrar a un repartidor en mi lugar.

—¿Trabajas aquí? —me preguntó desconcertado.

—No, solo quiero...

—¡¿No hay repartidores o qué?! —gritó hacia la puerta tras asomar su cabeza por la ventanilla. Ese gesto me obligó a echarme un paso hacia atrás. Un chico que no debía de tener más de dieciocho años acudió corriendo.

—Perdona, tío, llevo toda la noche sin parar, estaba echando un pito —se excusó.

—¿Te pagan por fumar? —respondió el chico autoritario. Tenía más o menos mi edad y parecía tener algo más de responsabilidad que el resto. El repartidor cogió la bolsa sin decir nada y se largó hacia su moto.

—Gilipollas... —murmuró entre dientes mientras salía. Miré al chico de la ventanilla sorprendido.

—Le he oído, no te preocupes. Es lo más suave que me han dicho hoy —dijo tan tranquilo—. ¡¿Las tarrinas de buey caramelizado cómo van?! —gritó a la cocina.

—¿Puedo preguntarte algo? —insistí.

—No —dijo el chico que metía más comida en una nueva bolsa—. Pero lo vas a hacer igual.

—Estoy buscando al chico que me ha traído el pedido esta noche a mi casa.

—Y yo estoy buscando una ración de Dim Sum. ¡Llevo esperando un Dim Sum desde hace cuatro horas! —gritó a los cocineros.

—¿Podría saber quién ha sido?

—Claro —respondió. Pero no dijo nada más.

—¿Y? —Le miré interrogante.

—Puedes saberlo, pero no ahora. ¿No ves cómo estamos? —hablaba abriendo bolsas, metiendo dentro tarrinas de comida, cerrándolas con grapas—. En una horita, baja la cosa. Si puedes volver entonces, te lo miro.

—De acuerdo. —Y me alejé satisfecho. Era el mejor trato que podía conseguir ahí esa noche.

Una hora y pico más tarde, vi, como me había asegurado el chico de la ventanilla, que la actividad bajaba bastante. Durante ese tiempo había estado en la calle, junto a la puerta del local, observando las idas y venidas de los repartidores. Nada hacía sospechar que hubiera sido alguno de ellos quien metió la nota en mi bolsa. Al menos ahí. Si fue un repartidor, tuvo que parar la moto, abrir la bolsa y meter dentro la nota. De locos.

—Eh, detective —me llamó el chico de la ventanilla. Había salido a la puerta del local con un refresco. Me acerqué a él.

—¿Servís comida todavía? —dije. A esas horas, tras estar un buen rato viendo circular pedidos delante de mis ojos, estaba muerto de hambre.

—Cocina cerrada —respondió con una sonrisa—. Anda, entra, que siempre sobran un huevo de cosas. Soy Will.

—Joel. Gracias.

Un rato más tarde, devoraba unos tallarines mientras el chico miraba uno a uno los tiques de pedidos de esa noche. Había un buen taco. Está claro que a la gente no le gusta cocinar en casa.

—Un pedido con Shao Mai, ¿no? —me dijo Will—. Va a ser fácil, nadie pide ese plato.

—Pues está cojonudo.

—Totalmente de acuerdo. —Me miró—. La gente no tiene ni idea. —Volvió a los tiques—. Este es —dijo apartando un tique del resto.

—Genial. —Y alargué mi mano para cogerlo.

—Eh, eh... —dijo apartando el tique—. Antes podrías decirme por qué tanto interés en saber quién es, ¿no?

—Me gustaba su casco —mentí—. Es una historia muy larga. Dime quién es y ya.

—Soy el encargado de los pedidos del turno. —Se puso serio de golpe—. Tengo que saberlo.

—Ya. —Resoplé. No tenía muchas ganas de contar la historia, pero si quería la información, no tenía más remedio que hacerlo—. En resumen: me he encontrado un mensaje dentro de la bolsa.

—¿Un mensaje? —preguntó extrañado.

—Sí, un mensaje dirigido a mí. No puede haber caído ahí por casualidad. Alguien tuvo que meterlo.

—¿Estás seguro?

—Completamente.

—¿Y qué decía el mensaje?

—Eso no tiene importancia —me excusé.

—Depende. Si era una amenaza o algo así, el restaurante tiene mucha responsabilidad. Bueno, y si no, también. Alguien ha manipulado el pedido y eso no es ninguna tontería. ¿De qué va todo esto?

Miré a Will un instante. Parecía un buen tipo. Y me estaba ayudando. Dudé si contarle la verdad o inventarme una película. Cualquiera de las dos cosas iba a resultar igual de inverosímil.

—¿Me dirás quién es el repartidor? —Quise saber.

—Claro. Y si ha sido él, hoy ha sido su último turno.

Le conté la historia completa, desde que vi el *flyer* en el videoclub de Silvestre hasta la videoconferencia de hacía unas horas, melodía de violín incluida. Will no cerró la boca ni un segundo del estupor.

—Menudo cabrón —dijo cuando terminé.

—¿De verdad no sabes quién soy? —pregunté con asombro—. Desde hace dos días nadie habla de otra cosa en la red.

—Yo paso de esos rollos. Ni estoy en redes sociales, ni veo vídeos online, ni nada. Costaba creerlo pero, ¿por qué no? No todo el mundo tiene por qué hacer lo mismo.

—¿Me vas a decir ahora quién es el repartidor?

—Rick. Un chaval majo. Lleva poco tiempo. Me extraña.

—Rick —repetí—. ¿Dónde puedo localizarle?

—Mañana empieza a las ocho. Pásate y hablamos con él.

—¿No podemos llamarle ahora? —insistí.

—¡Ostras! Tengo que irme, tío —dijo de repente apurado mientras miraba la hora en el móvil—. Pierdo el último bus para llegar a casa. —Y se levantó sin que pudiera retenerle.

—Pero... —protesté.

—No te preocupes por la cena, invita la casa. ¡Hasta mañana!

Y se fue. Me quedé ahí, sentado frente al resto de tallarines, desconcertado por la súbita desaparición de Will. Me sentí un poco desolado. Había contado toda mi historia a un desconocido y apenas había recibido nada a cambio. Un nombre, Rick, pero nada más. Esperar al día siguiente se me antojaba eterno. Solo me tranquilizó una cosa: pensar en que en mi juego con Donald, el siguiente movimiento me tocaba a mí. Eso, si las reglas del juego eran las que había imaginado. A falta de saber más, di por buena esa idea. Era lo único a lo que podía agarrarme, lo único que daba un orden.

De camino a casa reflexioné. Mis movimientos hasta entonces habían sido torpes y desesperados. Donald había golpeado y yo, desde la lona, había reaccionado de cualquier manera. Ahora no iba a cometer el mismo error. Investigar qué podía estar pasando me daba un poco de aire. No mucho, pero al menos estaba tomando las riendas de la situación. Si averiguaba algo, por pequeño que fuera, podría empezar a igualar fuerzas con mi adversario. Y si él no sabía por dónde estaba yendo, pronto le alcanzaría.

Con el ánimo renovado, llegué a casa y me acosté. A pesar de que había dormido hasta mediodía, estaba reventado. Mañana sería otro día. Esperaba que el día en el que empezara a ver un poquito de luz en el caos de vida en el que me había instalado.

Antes de las nueve, empezó a sonar mi despertador particular: Kevin. No tengo despertador como tal, ¿para qué, si tengo un *repre* que se encarga de ello?

—Joder, Kevin, ya te vale, que aún es de noche —dije tras abrirle la puerta de mala gana.

—Hace horas que ha amanecido —dijo entrando como una bala y yendo hacia el salón—. Al menos para el resto de los mortales.

—¿No traes desayuno?

—Aquí tienes comida de sobra —dijo olisqueando las tarrinas que habían quedado intactas la noche anterior—. Además, ayer estuvo aquí tu madre. Debes tener a Sahara a tope —dijo refiriéndose a mi nevera.

—Gracias por chivarte, por cierto —le reprendí.

—Madre no hay más que una, Joel. Y no soy yo —respondió como una advertencia—. Tenías que haberte visto después del show.

—Tranquilo, cuando tenga curiosidad por verlo lo busco en Twitter. ¿Algún motivo para honrarme con tu presencia o solo has venido a tocarme las pelotas?

—Lo segundo. Ah, y también porque tengo una noticia que te va a gustar —dijo sonriente.

—Dejas de representarme.

—No tan buena, lo siento. ¡Tienes una oferta! —soltó abriendo mucho los ojos, como si eso fuera increíble.

—¿Y? —pregunté interrogante—. No es la primera que tengo en mi carrera.

—Pero sí después de toda la movida. ¿Ves? La gente olvida rápido. Por suerte —puntualizó aliviado—. Te quieren para el lanzamiento de una marca de refrescos. Suena bien, ¿no?

—Buf —resoplé. No como hacía siempre que me proponían hacer *publi*, lo cual me daba una pereza infinita. Resoplé porque en esos momentos solo pensaba en cazar a Donald.

—¿Buf? —me contestó Kevin de mala leche. Se avecinaba bronquita—. A pesar de todo lo que te ha pasado, y de tus cagadas, que también las has hecho, aún hay gente que quiere trabajar contigo. ¿Eso merece un «buf»?

—Ahora tengo otras prioridades.

—¿Cuáles, hundir más tu carrera?

—No, evitar que eso suceda. Ayer Donald dejó un anónimo en mi pedido de comida, estoy investigando cómo llegó hasta ahí. Además, tengo una melodía que escuché en su llamada, una melodía de violín...

—Para, para... —me interrumpió Kevin—. ¿De qué coño me estás hablando?

—De que voy a por Donald.

—Joel —me dijo conteniendo la ira—, olvídalo. Ya está. Ese tío ya te ha jodido suficiente. La policía está en ello, déjales hacer su trabajo.

—La poli no tiene ningún interés en esto. Ayer estuve ahí y...

—Ya. Harris —me interrumpió de nuevo—. Es un capullo, pero está investigando. —Le miré alucinado—. También me he pasado por ahí, quería saber cómo iba la cosa. Joel, déjate de paranoias y ponte las pilas. Si no reapareces pronto, antes de que te des cuenta serás historia. Solo te recordarán por haber sido el *youtuber* que arruinó su carrera por un vídeo patético.

—Lo que quiere Donald —dije en voz baja.

—Y lo que no queremos ninguno de los dos.

Una hora más tarde entrábamos en un edificio de oficinas frío e impersonal. Se trataba del típico edificio que reunía empresas de todo tipo. El anunciante que quería vernos había alquilado una pequeña zona en la planta doce. Kevin no paraba de hablar, previniéndome sobre las condiciones que podíamos aceptar y las que no. Cuando se abrió la puerta del ascensor, me detuvo antes de salir.

—Y, sobre todo, Joel, cara de póquer. Ninguna mención a lo que ha pasado. Y si el tío nos dice algo, nosotros, como si nada.

—Que sí...

—¿Estás bien?

—Tranquilo —afirmé.

La puerta de la oficina a la que nos dirigíamos estaba al final del pasillo. Al llegar, nos abrió un hombre de unos cuarenta y cinco años vestido de traje y corbata.

—¡Adelante, amigos! —nos recibió con una amabilidad que me sonó totalmente exagerada. Tenía un leve acento extranjero, brasileño o portugués, me pareció.

Solo estaba él. No había ni empleados, ni secretarias.

—Acabo de aterrizar, aún no he incorporado personal —se excusó.

Nos condujo a una pequeña sala de reuniones donde solo había una mesa y varias sillas. La impresión que transmitía todo aquello era de desolación. «Menudo anunciante», pensé. A continuación, miré a Kevin que me contestó con una sonrisa positiva que me quería decir: «Sí, todo es un poco raro, pero ya que estamos aquí, vamos a ver qué pasa».

—¡Aquí lo tienen! —dijo el hombre, que se había presentado como Souza. Y posó unas latas de refresco sobre la mesa—. Esta bebida está arrasando en el cono sur. —Como si arrasaba en la Cochinchina, pensé.

Kevin entabló una rápida conversación con Souza sobre lo que quería, lo que buscaba de mí, términos y condiciones. El acuerdo parecía que iba a ser fácil. Como era habitual, yo me limitaba a escuchar y a apoyar a Kevin en todo lo que decía. Esta vez, sin embargo, mi cabeza desconectaba cada poco y viajaba a lo que de verdad me preocupaba: Donald. Era una buena noticia que me propusieran una *publi*, no había duda. Le demostraría a Donald que seguía con mi vida y que, a pesar de todo lo que había hecho, no había conseguido hundirme.

—¿Estás de acuerdo, Joel? —me preguntó Kevin. Lo miré distraído. No tenía ni idea de qué me preguntaba.

—Sí, claro... —respondí adormilado.

En ese momento sonó el teléfono de Souza. Este miró la pantalla. Al escuchar el tono de la llamada, pegué un bote en el asiento, como si me hubieran despertado echándome un cubo de agua fría en la cabeza: era la melodía de violín.

—¿Quién será...? —dijo para sí arrugando la frente mientras miraba el número.

—¡Deme el teléfono! —grité.

—Joel... —reaccionó Kevin alarmado.

—¿Disculpe? —preguntó Souza. El teléfono seguía sonando en sus manos y me miraba desconcertado.

—¿Quién le llama? ¡Démelo! —me levanté y traté de arrebatarle el aparato, pero Souza lo alejó de mi alcance.

—Joel, tranquilo... —Kevin trataba de contenerme. Me cogió del brazo y me hablaba con suavidad, como si yo fuera un demente. Lo aparté con brusquedad y rodeé la mesa para acercarme a Souza, que se echó para atrás en su silla sin levantarse.

—¡Esa, esa es la melodía del violín! ¡Usted sabe algo! —dije mientras me acercaba a él.

—¿De qué habla? —preguntó Souza a Kevin asustado.

—No lo sé —contestó Kevin. Y me miró como nunca lo había hecho: harto, furioso—. Pero si da un paso más, seré yo quien llame a la policía.

Las palabras de Kevin me pararon en seco. Tenía a Souza a menos de un metro. La melodía cesó en ese momento.

—Era la melodía —dije mirando a Kevin en un tono suplicante—. La de la llamada... ¿Por qué tiene ese tono? —interrogué a Souza.

—Es una melodía clásica..., ¡yo qué sé! —se justificó Souza.

—Joel, ya vale —me ordenó Kevin. Estaba muy cabreado conmigo. No podía contar con él. Bajé la mirada derrotado.

—No... no esperaba que esta reunión terminara así —dijo Souza algo más recuperado de la impresión, pero aún asustado.

—Disculpe a mi cliente, señor Souza. Como sabe, ha pasado unos días de mucho estrés y...

—Creo que lo mejor es que nos tomemos un tiempo para reflexionar sobre nuestra colaboración —dijo Souza al tiempo que se levantaba, se guardaba el teléfono en el bolsillo de la chaqueta y se ajustaba la corbata, sin duda un tic que usaba para sentir que recuperaba el control.

—Por nuestra parte, está claro y queremos seguir adelante con el proyecto —afirmó Kevin que trataba de aferrarse al *business* como fuera.

—Por la nuestra, queremos pensarlo un poquito más —sentenció Souza. Y alargó la mano hacia Kevin para escenificar la despedida. Kevin me miró una décima de segundo y le estrechó la mano.

No nos dirigimos la palabra hasta que salimos a la calle.

—Era la melodía, Kevin... —dije mientras trataba de seguir el ritmo de sus pasos. Casi iba corriendo camino del coche.

—¡¿Y qué importa?! —me respondió. Se detuvo de golpe y se encaró a mí. Tenía mucha rabia acumulada y los dos sabíamos que no iba a conseguir controlarla—. ¿Qué cojones ha sido eso que ha pasado ahí arriba?

—¿No te parece un poco raro? La misma melodía, que no he escuchado en mi vida, de repente aparece por todos lados.

—Una casualidad, Joel. Una puta casualidad.

—No lo creo —negué incrédulo.

—Y si no lo es, ¿qué más da? Ya hemos perdido este curro.

—¿Crees que me importa? Habrá más.

—¿Estás seguro? —respondió desafiante—. Porque como se corra la voz, tu reputación caerá en picado, y no ya solo entre tus seguidores, sino entre los anunciantes y patrocinadores que, por si no lo sabías, son los que te dan de comer.

«Maldito *business*», pensé.

—¡Pues que les den a todos! —Yo también me estaba poniendo nervioso—. No puedo mirar a otro lado, no puedo hacer como si no pasara nada. Hay un tío que me está jodiendo la vida, no puedo quedarme de brazos cruzados esperando a ver qué es lo próximo que se le ocurre para putearme.

—Pues conmigo no cuentes.

Kevin se dio media vuelta y se dirigió a su coche, que estaba aparcado a unos metros. Tardé un instante en reaccionar.

—¿Qué quieres decir? —pregunté.

Kevin no se giró. Se limitó a subirse al coche, arrancar e irse sin mirarme.

7.

Era la primera vez que Kevin reaccionaba así. Al principio me enfadé: era mi representante, ¿a qué venían esos humos? Estuve tentado de llamarle y echarle la bronca, pero desestimé la idea cuando el cabreo dio paso a la preocupación: «es la primera vez que Kevin reacciona así», me repetí. Y eso no podía ser una buena señal. Pasara lo que pasase, y nos habían pasado unas cuantas cosas, siempre me había comprendido. Que se fuera como se había ido me daba la medida de lo que le debía de estar bullendo por dentro. Sabía que no le preocupaba haber perdido un contrato. Vivía de las comisiones de mis trabajos, pero no era tan materialista como para enfadarse por eso. Si se había ido, dejándome tirado en mitad de una zona de oficinas alejada del centro, sin ni siquiera mirarme, era porque estaba dolido de verdad. Dolido conmigo. Pero, ¿qué podía hacer? Por mucho que Kevin se pusiera en mi lugar, no podía entender lo que yo estaba viviendo. Desde que apareció Donald, poco a poco iba perdiendo todo lo que tenía: prestigio, reputación, seguidores... Ahora anunciantes. Esa era mi prioridad: detener la sangría. Y eso era lo que necesitaba de él: que me comprendiera ahora.

Miré hacia el edificio que quedaba a mi espalda. Por un momento pensé que Souza había podido ser testigo de nuestra bronca. Hubiera puesto la guinda al espectáculo. Tenía que salir de ahí.

Una hora más tarde había logrado llegar a mi casa. Nada más cruzar la puerta, sonó mi teléfono fijo. Tardé varios tonos en encontrarlo debajo de un cojín del sofá.

—¿Quién es?

—De la Compañía de Agua. ¿Sabe usted que debe varios recibos y que hemos procedido a cortarle el suministro? —amenazó un hombre al otro lado.

—¿De qué me está hablando? El agua no se corta nunca.

—¿Ah, no? Abra un grifo, verá...

Aunque me sonaba increíble, iba a correr a la cocina a comprobarlo.

—¡Pringao! —escuché por el auricular—. Soy Will, del restaurante.

—¡Joder, tío! —exclamé aliviado—. Lo último que me faltaba es que me cortaran el agua.

—No la cortan nunca, tú lo has dicho. ¿Cómo lo llevas? —Me extrañó su llamada. No nos conocíamos más que de la noche anterior.

—¿Por qué tienes mi número?

—Eres cliente, estás en nuestra base de datos. No te molesta, ¿no? Tengo noticias —me dijo—. De tu «caso». —Rio. No era para tomárselo a broma, la verdad, pero en ese momento me hizo gracia que se refiriera a todo ello como «mi caso»—. He hablado con Rick, el repartidor.

—¿Ah, sí? —pregunté con sorpresa—. ¿No empezaba su turno a las ocho?

—Le he llamado. Ayer te vi tan de bajón que me imaginé que no podías esperar a esta noche.

—¿Y qué te ha dicho? ¿Sabe algo?

—No. Me ha prometido que no fue el quien metió la nota en tu bolsa.

—¿Y qué más da lo que diga? Puede mentir.

—Yo le creo. Es un chavalín, no le veo haciendo ese tipo de cosas.

Hasta yo creía que lo que decía Will era lo más lógico del mundo. Sin embargo, no podía aceptarlo sin más.

—Pero esa nota estaba en mi bolsa. Alguien la tuvo que poner.

—Es un misterio, Sherlock —respondió Will sin abandonar el tono amable.

—¿Crees que Donald pudo abrir la caja de la moto mientras Rick subía otro pedido?

—Por poder... Casi es la única opción que nos queda.

—¡Pues vaya servicio que tenéis! —dije medio en broma con intención de sumarme al tono relajado.

—El peor de la ciudad, ya lo sabes —respondió de coña—. Tengo que dejarte, tío. Suerte con la investigación.

—Gracias por llamar.

No era mucho. No era nada, en realidad. Solo podía pensar que Rick mentía. O que le habían abierto la caja durante su reparto. Tenía que descartar una de las dos. O las dos.

A las ocho de la tarde estaba dentro de mi coche, aparcado a unos metros del restaurante donde podía ver bien la entrada y el movimiento de clientes y trabajadores. Las motos de reparto apuntaban sus ruedas delanteras hacia la calzada, en formación, ordenadas, esperando a que los repartidores las usaran para llevar los pedidos. Poco a poco estos iban llegando. Mientras esperaban, hablaban en corrillo, bromeaban entre ellos. No sabía quién de todos ellos era Rick y no quería recurrir a Will, al que había visto llegar hacía unos minutos, para averiguarlo. Lo que tenía previsto hacer, quería hacerlo solo, con discreción.

Mientras esperaba, miraba mi teléfono cada poco. Esperaba recibir un mensaje de Kevin. No de disculpa —no tenía nada de que disculparse, en realidad, solo por haberme dejado tirado en las afueras—, ni de conciliación —Kevin nunca bajaría la guardia, demasiado orgulloso—; pero sí esperaba que se comunicara conmigo, aunque fuera para informarme de una cita al día siguiente o para echarme la bronca por algo, cualquier tontería. En nuestro código particular eso ya sería suficiente para reconducir las cosas y abandonar el mal rollo. Pero no, esta vez Kevin no daba señales. Estaba disgustado de verdad, como nunca lo había estado antes. Llamarle yo no me parecía buena idea. Era mi representante, no era yo quien tenía que ir detrás. No tenía problema en reconocer mis errores cuando los cometía; tampoco en disculparme cuando la cagaba, lo que sucedía con frecuencia. Pero no era yo quien tenía que suplicarle nada. Éramos amigos, pero ante todo, era mi empleado. No podía perder eso de vista.

Pensé que, en esa situación, solo podía esperar a que las aguas se calmasen.

En la calle, frente a la puerta del restaurante, un grupito de tres repartidores se tomaban el pelo. Desde mi coche me llegaban fragmentos de su conversación.

—Llámala, y si no te lo coge, es que está con otro.

—No te pases —se defendió la víctima de las mofas de los otros dos.

—Es una pendeja, huevón. Y tú un *pichacorta* —se burló el tercero.

—Anda, trae, que la llamo yo —dijo el primero, quitándole el móvil.

—¡Trae *hijoeputa*! —se defendió el segundo, a la vez que iniciaba una persecución por la acera tras el chaval que le había usurpado el móvil—. ¡Te reviento, míster! —¿«Míster»?, eso me sonaba: es como me llamó el repartidor cuando me trajo el pedido a casa la noche anterior. No era una expresión muy frecuente. Abrí un poco más la ventanilla para escuchar mejor.

—No lo coge, ¿ves? Está con el otro. —El chaval saltó sobre él y consiguió recuperar su teléfono. Echó un vistazo a la pantalla.

—No la has llamado, mal parido.

—Pero está con otro —sentenció el «ladrón» sin intención de parar la broma.

—Putos maricas.

—Eh, Rick, sin pasarse.

Ahí lo tenía. Como decía Will, el pobre Rick no tenía pinta de haber metido una nota en mi bolsa. Se apartó unos metros para teclear en su teléfono mientras sus dos compañeros por fin le dejaban tranquilo. Cogí el mío —de paso volví a comprobar que no tenía ningún mensaje de Kevin—, y marqué. Dentro del restaurante, uno de los chicos del mostrador descolgó.

—Quería hacer un pedido —dije—. Tallarines fritos con curry rojo, teppanyaki de pollo y Shao Mai. —Lo de siempre, vamos. ¿Para qué complicarme la vida? Di mi dirección para la entrega y esperé.

Unos minutos más tarde, Rick entraba en el local y recogía, de manos de Will, varias bolsas con sus respectivos pedidos. Una de ellas tenía que ser la mía. Arranqué el coche, esperé a que Rick metiera las bolsas en la caja de su moto y, cuando salió dispuesto a entregarlas, salí tras él.

Nunca había seguido a nadie antes por las calles, menos a una moto, y me pareció una de las cosas más difíciles que había hecho nunca. En las películas se ve sencillo, pero en la vida real, con peatones reales y coches reales, era otra cosa. Rick, como buen repartidor de comida rápida, culebreaba entre los coches, se saltaba señales, apuraba las curvas al máximo. Apenas podía seguirle y en más de un momento temí perderle. Por suerte, los semáforos y el tráfico tranquilo de esas horas jugaban a mi favor y me permitían recuperar la distancia a cada poco. Sin embargo, estaba tan preocupado de no perderle que me olvidé por completo de ser discreto. Ser detective no era lo mío, estaba claro. En un semáforo, al ver la moto de Rick esperando el verde y darme cuenta de que no había ningún coche entre nosotros, frené exagerada-mente lejos de él, dejando entre los dos una distancia totalmente ilógica. Rick debió de darse cuenta de mi maniobra y se giró para mirarme. En un acto reflejo ridículo, agaché la cabeza. Me había delatado. Rick no esperó a que el semáforo se pusiera en verde y aceleró para desaparecer de mi vista.

—¡Maldito! —exclamé en voz alta refiriéndome más a mí que a él.

Una vez descubierto, solo tenía la opción de alcanzarle si quería sacar algo de esa noche. Por eso, en cuanto Rick aceleró, avancé hasta la línea del semáforo, que se puso en verde en ese instante, y metí caña para darle caza. El chico, consciente de que le estaba siguiendo, corría todo lo que su modesta moto le permitía. No me costó darle alcance, pero ahí surgió mi duda: ¿qué hacer? En las pelis las persecuciones son intensas, con toques entre los vehículos, salidas de la carretera, pistolas que asoman por las ventanillas. Aquí todo era más cutre: una moto de reparto de comida y un aprendiz de detective siguiéndose por las calles de la ciudad y tratando de no llamar demasiado la atención y de no atropellar a los viandantes. Rick se atrevió con alguna maniobra arriesgada que me obligó a apurar algún adelantamiento. No sabía qué hacer para detenerle. Por un momento pensé que, si el chico no lograba darme esquinazo, la persecución solo iba a terminar cuando uno de los dos se quedara sin gasolina.

Unas calles más tarde, cuando ya pensaba que todo aquel circo no tenía mucho sentido, Rick aminoró la marcha y, tras subir la moto a una acera, se detuvo. Se bajó de la moto y fue directo hacia mi coche, que había detenido a unos metros, con el candado de la moto.

—¿Qué quieres, mal parido? —me amenazó. Bajé del coche y me quedé junto a él, cerca de la puerta abierta. No pensaba que fuera a pasar nada, pero por si acaso, quería tener una salida.

—Tranquilo, Rick... —dije extendiendo las palmas de mis manos y agitándolas delante de mí como si con eso fuera a disipar el recelo que sentía el repartidor.

—¿Quién eres, cómo sabes mi nombre?

—Soy el de la nota en la bolsa. Sabes, ¿no?

Rick no dijo nada. Solo me miró desconfiado. No sabía de qué iba todo eso, pero al menos conseguí que bajara el candado.

—Yo no sé nada, ya se lo he dicho a Will —se defendió.

—¿Seguro? —insistí—. ¿Nadie te pidió que pusieras esa nota en mi pedido?

—¿Quién? A mí me dan los pedidos, yo los llevo, vuelvo al restaurante... ¡No sé nada!

—Pues la nota no llegó sola. —No podía irme de ahí con las manos vacías—. Alguien aprovechó que subías a entregar otros pedidos para abrir la caja de la moto y meterla dentro.

—Míster, se lo suplico... —El chaval se derrumbó—, no se lo cuente a nadie. Si me echan, me voy al carajo. Mi novia está embarazada y...

—Vale, vale... —le interrumpí. No quería hundirle la vida, solo intentar averiguar algo. Rick podía estar mintiendo, pero si era así, era un excelente actor—. Vamos a hacer una cosa. Yo necesito saber cómo ha llegado la nota a mi bolsa y tú, conservar tu curro. Ahí dentro llevas un pedido para mí. Lo vas a entregar el último. Mientras repartes los otros, yo estaré vigilando la moto desde mi coche. Si alguien quiere dejarme otro mensaje mientras subes a las casas, lo veré.

Rick siguió observándome con desconfianza. Todo aquello le debía de sonar demasiado raro. A mí también me sonaría así si me propusieran lo mismo, pero debió de pensar que en esos momentos la mejor opción que tenía para salir de esa era hacerme caso y aceptó.

—¿De cuánto está tu chica? —le pregunté antes de que arrancara la moto.

—Poco, tres meses.

—¿Lo saben tus compañeros?

—No.

—Pues deberías decírselo. Así dejarían de tomarte el pelo con ella.

Subí al coche sin esperar respuesta. No me hizo falta mirar a Rick para percibir su perplejidad. Lo que le acababa de decir lo pensaba de verdad. Me caía bien el chico. Pero también me servía para darle a entender que sabía más de lo que creía y de que todo eso iba en serio.

Rick repartió los pedidos. Como repartidor no sé, pero como actor era un número uno. Ni una vez miró hacia mí, que le seguía agazapado en mi coche a unos metros. Actuó con total naturalidad sin mostrar el más mínimo gesto de saberse observado. Cada vez que entraba en un portal, yo esperaba, más bien, deseaba, que apareciera Donald, abriera la caja, buscara mi pedido y dejara algo dentro. Según Rick iba dejando pedidos y eso no sucedía, me iba desesperando. Me di cuenta de lo endeble de mi plan. Era improbable que funcionara como había previsto, lo sabía: Donald no iba a utilizar el mismo método dos veces. Pero no podía hacer mucho más. Solo esperar a que la suerte me sonriera por primera vez desde que empezó todo y mi adversario cometiera, por fin, un error.

Tras media hora, Rick callejeó en dirección a mi casa. Era la última bolsa que iba a entregar y no había pasado nada. Nadie se había acercado a la moto, nadie había intentado abrir la caja. No había servido de nada. Al llegar a mi portal, Rick siguió con su actuación y llamó a mi piso. Como era de esperar, no contestó nadie. Antes de salir del coche, miré a todos lados. Esperar a que Donald apareciera en el último momento era lo último que podía hacer. Nada. Salí del coche.

—¡Está bien, Rick!

Rick abandonó su papel y se acercó hacia mí.

—¿Lo ves? Nadie me ha abierto la caja —dijo aún angustiado.

—Sí, tío, tranquilo. Gracias por ayudarme.

—De nada, míster —dijo algo más tranquilo.

Cogí la bolsa de sus manos. Al fin y al cabo, era mi comida y, ya que la cena del día anterior se había quedado sin probar, al menos esta sí podía comérmela. Como acto reflejo, sin saber muy bien por qué, abrí la bolsa. Ahí estaba todo el pedido y...

—¿Qué hace esto aquí? —exclamé. Dentro había una nueva nota. Mire a Rick, que caminaba hacia atrás hacia su moto.

—No sé nada... Se lo juro.

—¡No me jodas, Rick! Solo tú has tocado mi pedido. ¡Lo he visto!

—¡No es verdad! —se defendió—. A mí me las dan cerradas, es Will quien las prepara.

—Un momento, tío... —Mi perspectiva sobre todo cambió de golpe—. ¿Me quieres decir que ha sido Will...?

—No, no... —reaccionó Rick apurado—. No tengo ni idea. Si no me han abierto la caja de la moto, la bolsa solo la maneja él. Es quien mete la comida.

No podía creerlo. ¿Will? Me costaba resituarme con esta nueva idea. Era tan retorcida. Cogí la nota de la bolsa y me dispuse a leerla. Fuera Will o no, Donald atacaba de nuevo y quería saber qué me esperaba. Abrí el papel, era diferente al de la nota anterior. Dentro, un mensaje escrito con bolígrafo: «Vaya susto, ¿eh, Sherlock?». ¿Qué cojones...? No entendía nada. Seguí leyendo: «Esta noche salgo a las 12, si quieres nos tomamos unas birras. Will». Me quedé un buen rato mirando el papelito que sujetaba con las dos manos, como si pesara diez kilos y las necesitara para que no se me cayera al suelo. Lo miraba pero ya no leía lo que contenía. Sentía muchas cosas a la vez y todas trataban de abrirse paso para alzarse con el trono de mis emociones: alivio por no tratarse de un mensaje de Donald; enfado por haber sido víctima de una broma de Will; vergüenza por haber caído en la trampa; ridículo por haberlo hecho delante de Rick; alegría por darme cuenta de que había alguien que pensaba en mí en esos momentos.

—¿Todo bien, míster? —preguntó Rick con curiosidad al ver que no levantaba la mirada del papel.

—Sí, sí... —respondí con una sonrisa forzada para alejar cualquier reflejo de lo que pasaba por mi cabeza delante del repartidor—. Gracias, tío. Te agradezco de verdad que me hayas ayudado.

Rick se quedó quieto, mirando a un lado.

—Si quieres, puedes irte —dije por si necesitaba que le liberara.

—Es que... —Me miró cortado—. Son dieciséis con veinte.

Empecé a reírme. Al final, fue la alegría la que ocupó el lugar principal de mis emociones. Saqué un billete de cincuenta.

—Quédate con el cambio —dije dirigiéndome a la puerta de mi casa—. Y cómprale algo a tu chica.

—¡Gracias, míster! —respondió Rick encantado.

8.

Tras engullir la cena en casa, volví a salir a la calle al encuentro de Will. No estaba para mucha fiesta, pero pensé que me vendría bien despejarme un rato. Podía llamar a Connor, Silvestre y compañía, pero desde que había empezado todo el lío de Donald, sentía ciertos reparos en verles. No sabía muy bien por qué. Demasiada confianza entre nosotros, pensaba. Me iban a tomar el pelo y no me apetecía. No lo iban a hacer con mala intención, todo lo contrario, pero yo estaba muy sensible y tomarme algo con Will, que no sabía ni quién era yo ni estaba al día del mundo *youtuber*, me motivaba más.

Si no llamaba a Kevin era por algo parecido. A esas horas de la noche, además, ya no esperaba ningún mensaje de él. Aún estaba caliente la movida de la mañana a las puertas de la oficina del anunciante. Más allá de eso, podía llamarle para charlar y desahogarme. Lo hacía a veces: cuando me entraba algún bajón porque algún vídeo no había funcionado bien; cuando me agobiaba porque no me salía alguna idea; también cuando estaba eufórico por el éxito de mi última pieza. Le había conocido gracias a sus comentarios sobre mis vídeos y no había nadie que analizara mejor mi trabajo que él. Pero, en esa ocasión, sentía con Kevin lo mismo que con mis amigos: demasiado cerca, demasiada confianza para decirme lo que había hecho bien y lo que había hecho mal; lo que había hecho o lo que había dejado de hacer. En esos momentos, quería alejarme un poco de todos ellos, no sabía si por cobardía, porque tenía miedo a lo que me pudieran decir o porque necesitaba ver las cosas con distancia. Cualquier razón me sonaba a excusa, la verdad, así que elegí hacer lo que me pedía el cuerpo y quedar con Will, que estaba justo donde yo quería estar: lejos de cualquier cosa que me recordara lo que me estaba pasando.

Llegué al restaurante a las doce en punto. Cuando miré la hora en mi móvil me asombré. La puntualidad no era mi fuerte, ni mucho menos. ¿Me estaba cambiando Donald? Sonreí para mis adentros. Algo bueno estaba teniendo todo eso, pensé. Al menos para los demás, que siempre me criticaban que llegara tarde. Vi salir a Rick.

—Hasta luego, «papá» —le dijo uno de los compañeros que le había tomado el pelo hacía unas horas.

—Que os den, mal paridos —respondió Rick en tono de broma. Siguiendo mi consejo había soltado lo de su próxima paternidad y los chistes sobre su novia se habían terminado. Me gustaba saber que esa noche había hecho una buena obra.

—¿Siempre llevas esa cara de panoli cuando nadie te mira? —escuché a mi derecha. Era Will, que arrastraba un cubo lleno de cascos de vidrio.

—Eh... —me quedé cortado. Me había quedado absorto observando la escena de Rick y me imaginaba la cara de bobo que se me había puesto.

—Si tan feliz te hace estar aquí, yo te meto de repartidor. O de friegaplatos.

—No, era por... Nada, una chorrada. ¿Te ayudo?

Acompañé a Will a un contenedor de vidrio que había al otro lado de la acera. Una a una fuimos vaciando el cubo de botellas.

—Menudo susto me has dado con la notita —dije con tono reprobatorio, como el profe que regaña al alumno díscolo aunque sin ánimo de castigarle.

—Sabía que te iba a gustar —respondió.

—No estés tan seguro. Por un momento he pensado que estabas compinchado con Donald.

—Ja, ja... —Río con ganas—. Eres bueno, tío. ¿Has pensado en abrir un canal de YouTube?

Reí con él. Me asombraba que, después de su jornada laboral, donde no paraba ni un minuto, aún tuviera energía para estar de buen humor.

—Eso mejor hazlo tú, que eres el que tiene talento.

Unos minutos más tarde, caminábamos por las calles casi desiertas. Le había propuesto ir a algún garito a tomar algo, pero Will me dijo que prefería pasear. Ya había estado unas cuantas horas metido en un «garito». Me gustó la idea: me vendría bien estirar un poco las piernas, sobre todo cuando ya me había saltado varios entrenamientos y un partido de mi equipo.

—... En resumen, que se ha enfadado y no me dirige la palabra —dije para terminar el relato de mi discusión con Kevin.

—En cuanto vea que vuelves a producir vídeos y todo vuelve a la normalidad, se le pasará.

—Ya —respondí lacónico.

—Ese «ya» ha sonado de pena.

—Desde que empezó todo esto no he colgado nada nuevo en mi canal. Lo único que se ha sabido de mí es lo que ha querido Donald.

—Éxito ha tenido —dijo con ironía.

—Mucho, no me puedo quejar —dije siguiendo la coña—. Mi canal ha pegado un subidón de seguidores de la leche. Todos para ver si pueden reírse de mí —dije con amargura.

—Eh, tío... —dijo Will para animarme—. No te vengas abajo.

—¿Y qué quieres que haga? La he cagado con mis seguidores, la he cagado con mis anunciantes... Y, lo peor, no se me ocurre nada, ni un vídeo, ni una idea.

—¿No tienes alguno en la recámara? Es lo que hacéis los creadores, ¿no? Tener un fondo de armario de ideas para estas emergencias.

—Sí, tengo cosas, pero el problema no es ese —dije sin ser capaz de seguir. Will me miró interrogante.

—¿Cuál es? —dijo al cabo de un rato para ver si así arrancaba.

—Tengo pánico a mi canal.

Will se detuvo y me miró con una cara mezcla de asombro y de preocupación.

—¿Nos sentamos? —y señaló un banco a la entrada de un parque que teníamos a unos metros.

Will se sentó en el respaldo, poniendo los pies en el asiento. Yo me senté a su lado, normal, como se sentaría cualquiera. Nos quedamos un rato en silencio, comiendo pipas que habíamos comprado en una tienda de chinos. Un hombre paseaba a su perro por el parque. De vez en cuando, el perro se acercaba al banco y olisqueaba mis pies.

—Explícame eso —dijo Will en el momento exacto antes de que el silencio fuera demasiado largo y pudiera convertirse en algo dramático, o bien en algo aburrido—. Si te apetece, claro.

—Es eso, tío —dije. Claro que me apetecía. A veces es más fácil sincerarse con alguien a quien conoces poco—. Siento que mi canal ya no me pertenece. Desde que Donald lo ha *hackeado*, es como si no fuera mío. ¿Te imaginas que un día llegas a casa y te encuentras a un pavo en tu habitación con tu pijama y tus zapatillas?

—No uso pijama —dijo para relajar—. Pero vamos, sí, me lo imagino.

—Aunque luego lo eches, o se vaya, el tío ha estado ahí, ha usado tus cosas... Te ha robado tu espacio, tu lugar más íntimo.

—¿También se ha puesto tus gayumbos, quieres decir?

Sonreí.

—Y se ha acostado con tu novia, ¿no te jode?

Reímos los dos.

—Te entiendo, tío —dijo Will comprensivo. Que metiera alguna coña de vez en cuando no quería decir que no me estuviera escuchando—. Es una mierda.

—Por eso siento rechazo por mi canal. Me da miedo entrar y no saber qué me voy a encontrar.

—Pero es tuyo, no puedes abandonarlo en la puerta de una iglesia, como se hacía hace un siglo con los bebés. Además, tu canal ya no es un bebé, llevas con él un montón de tiempo.

—Más bien es como un adolescente que se ha vuelto rebelde y no deja de dar por saco —dije continuando la metáfora.

—Pues a los adolescentes sobrados hay que atarles en corto. Un par de...

—Eh, eh... Sin violencia —dije.

—... un par de buenos consejos, quería decir.

—Qué huevos tienes —sonreí.

Volvimos a quedarnos callados unos instantes. Un silencio solo roto por el crujir de las pipas y las carreras del perro por el parque. De fondo llegaba el rumor del motor de algún coche que pasaba cerca. Un momento tranquilo y agradable. Al menos por fuera. Dentro de mí solo había ruido y agitación.

—Esto es como cuando a un equipo de fútbol el máximo rival le quita a su mejor estrella —soltó Will convencido. Alcé la cabeza interrogante, al estar sentado en el respaldo, me obligaba a torcer el cuello para mirarle—. La afición se lleva un disgusto, se enfadan, silban al presidente... Parece que se acaba el mundo. ¡El equipo rival de toda la vida ha entrado en tu casa y se ha llevado a tu estrella! ¿Y qué hace el presidente?

—Fichar a otro —dije como una verdad aplastante. Lo era.

—Eso. Fichar a una nueva estrella. Luego mete tres goles en el primer partido y ya nadie se acuerda del rebote que se pillaron con el presidente por dejarse robar a su jugador más importante.

—¿Quieres decirme que tengo que fichar a alguien? —Entendía solo a medias lo que Will quería decirme con la «parábola de los futbolistas y los presidentes».

—Bueno, si me quieres fichar a mí...

—Uf... —respondí—. No das el perfil. Para tener un personaje friki para reírme, a lo mejor.

—Lo que te quiero decir es que hagas algo más grande. Que no te escondas, que salgas.

—¿Hacer cómo si nada? —respondí con recelo; era lo que había hecho en el show y no me había salido bien, precisamente.

—No. Hacer como si «todo» —dijo convencido.

Me levanté y me puse de pie frente a él. Me estaba cansando de torcer el cuerpo para mirarle a la cara. También de no estar a la misma altura.

—Menos adivinanzas, tío. Suéltalo —le apremié.

—No sé... —dudó—. Cómo hacerlo es cosa tuya. Pero no hacer nada o hacer como si nada, que es lo mismo que no hacer nada, no es lo suyo. Yo haría «todo». Es decir, salir ahí y explicar lo que te ha pasado, que la gente lo entienda, que vean que lo has pasado mal, que eres humano, como ellos. Salir y decir: aquí estoy yo, Joel Graham, me han puteado, me han *hackeado*, han intentado hundirme... Ha sido una mierda. ¿Y qué? —Will se levantó y siguió hablando como si tuviera a una numerosa audiencia delante—. Sigo siendo un *youtuber* de la leche. No me escondo, al contrario, doblo la apuesta y vais a flipar con lo que vais a ver a partir de ahora. Si os gustaba lo que hacía antes, más os va a gustar lo que voy a hacer ahora. ¿Entendido?

Will se quedó callado. Hasta el perro, que no había parado de corretear hasta entonces, se había sentado frente a él y le miraba con la cabeza torcida y la lengua fuera. Los dos lo miramos y luego nos miramos entre nosotros. Al segundo, estallamos en una carcajada. El perro salió corriendo de nuevo consciente de que el espectáculo había terminado.

—Deberías dedicarte a la política —dije cuando me hube repuesto del ataque de risa—. O a vender sartenes antiadherentes en los programas de teletienda de la noche.

—Me he venido un poco arriba, ¿no? —preguntó algo cortado.

—¡Qué va! Me ha encantado todo lo que me has dicho.

—¿En serio?

—Voy a salir ahí y explicarlo todo. Si no eres tú quien cuenta tu historia, serán otros los que la cuenten por ti.

—¿Ves? —dijo admirado—. Esa frase no se me hubiera ocurrido a mí nunca. Se nota que te dedicas a esto.

—Y esto —dije ajeno a su comentario—, es lo que está sucediendo ahora: todo el mundo está contando lo que me ha pasado menos yo.

—Y la bola se hace cada vez más grande.

—Pero lo voy a cortar de raíz.

—¿Cómo? —Quiso saber Will con curiosidad.

—Para saberlo, vas a tener que suscribirte a mi canal —respondí enigmático.

Al día siguiente empecé a moverme por mis redes sociales desde primera hora. Quería que todo el mundo se enterara: «Joel Graham, vuelve». Programé una emisión en directo en mi canal para hablar con mis seguidores, para explicarles todo lo que me había sucedido, para dar mi versión de los hechos. No quería dar pena, ni que me compadecieran. Solo que me comprendieran. Que me escucharan. A mí, a la víctima de todo aquello. Mi última aparición pública fue en el show y mi imagen no había quedado lo que se dice bien parada. Es cierto que habían pasado ya varios días y los comentarios sobre mí iban a menos. Es lo que tiene internet: lo que no está pasando en ese momento, no tiene valor.

Aun así, «hacer un Joel Graham», es decir, hacer el ridículo más espantoso, todavía circulaba como meme en la red. Eso era lo de menos para mí. De hecho, uno de los motivos que usé en redes sociales fue ese: «Joel Graham hace un Joel Graham» impresionado sobre una imagen mía pataleando en el aire mientras dos seguratas me sacaban del escenario donde iba a realizar el show. Me parecía que empezar riéndome de mí mismo era mejor que ponerme serio y a la defensiva. Era un guiño para mis seguidores, pero también para Donald. El enfado, la rabia, la frustración, se combaten fácilmente. El humor, solo puede combatirse con humor, y Donald no tenía recursos para ello. Solo para la burla y la destrucción. Nunca podría responderme con un chiste. Ahí, al menos, sabía que yo era superior.

Hubo expectación desde el principio. Los «me gusta» de Instagram, retuits y comentarios de Facebook fueron inmediatos. Desde horas antes de la emisión en directo la gente empezó a volcarse en mí. No era lo que buscaba, no tan pronto, pero haber cambiado el tono, aparecer sereno y positivo había creado un clima mucho más relajado; como antes, como siempre: una comunidad de gente que solo quería divertirse con mis vídeos y que no quería malos rollos.

El resto del día me lo pasé pensando en lo que iba a decir en la emisión, ensayando un poco, preparándome para el momento. Las emisiones en directo me encantan. Son como los *Meet and Greet* que hago después de los shows, pero con mucha más gente y de todos los rincones del mundo. Hacía una cada cierto tiempo y todas habían salido bien. Esta era especial pero no por eso tenía que ser diferente. Solo echaba de menos una cosa: a Kevin. Él solía estar conmigo cuando estaba en directo. Me filtraba las preguntas que me llegaban por chat, me pasaba alguna nota cuando me quedaba en blanco, me daba ideas para respuestas. No salía en la emisión, claro, estaba fuera de plano. Era, digamos, mi ayudante, mi «pinche» de cocina. No solo me ayudaba él, alguna vez me ayudó Connor, pero su ayuda era más caótica que otra cosa. Prefería a Kevin: él entendía mejor la filosofía de mi canal y sabía que, para serme útil, debía pensar como yo, estar a mi servicio, cosa que Connor era incapaz de hacer. Traté de no pensar mucho en su ausencia. Aún no se había comunicado conmigo y no dejaba de resultarme molesto. Seguro que había leído mis mensajes en las redes sociales. No entendía por qué estaba haciéndose el interesante. Pensé que ya había desaparecido una vez, al principio, antes de conocerle personalmente. Temí que volviera a hacerlo.

Al mismo tiempo pensaba en Donald. ¿Cómo se iba a tomar una cosa así? La emisión en directo iba de él. No pensaba atacarle, ni ponerle verde. Humor, era la clave. Explicarme, reconciliarme con mis fans. Él no pintaba nada más en ese asunto que haber sido el instigador, el que lo empezó todo. Quería que su papel estuviera muy bien delimitado y no tuviera más protagonismo que ese. Pero no dudaba de que estaba al tanto de lo que iba a hacer esa tarde. ¿Qué mecha iba a prender con mi reaparición? Si lo nuestro era un diálogo, como creía, el turno era mío. Su última palabra fue en la conversación que tuvimos por videoconferencia y ahí aseguró que su objetivo era acabar conmigo. Desde entonces había estado muy calladito. Sin duda me estaba esperando. Y esa tarde yo iba a hablar. Y lo quisiera o no, también para él.

A la hora indicada, me senté frente a la cámara, respiré hondo, puse mi cara de bienvenida y empecé la emisión. En pocos segundos, ya había miles de personas viéndome. No me enrollé demasiado al principio.

—... es, lo que se dice, una putada —dije para terminar mis explicaciones sobre lo que había pasado—. ¿Qué haríais vosotros si os pasara algo así, sin poder defenderos de un tramposo? Creo que lo mínimo que puedes hacer es hundirte como el Titanic. Lo único bueno es que yo no soy un barco y el cuerpo humano, como sabéis, flota. Y eso es lo que estoy haciendo: flotar. Y nadar para volver a la orilla y seguir estando con vosotros, que sé que me estáis esperando.

Las preguntas en mi *timeline* de Twitter saltaban a decenas. Era imposible atenderlas todas.

—Ya voy, ya voy... —dije para no impacientar a mis seguidores—. Me estáis acribillando a preguntas. A ver... —Me detuve a leer algunas—. Anda, mira, un troll. «Lo que te pasa es que no eres capaz de reconocer que los vídeos de Donald son mejores que los tuyos». —Miré a cámara—. ¿Qué hacemos con él? Mira, chincheta, que es lo que eres, si te gustan más los vídeos de... ya sabes, vete a su canal a verlos. Ah, que no tiene canal, que solo sabe meterse en el canal de otros para mostrar sus obras de arte. Qué pena... —dije con falsa tristeza—. Eso es lo que me diferencia a mí de él, y también de ti: que unos damos la cara y otros solo habláis si estáis escondidos. Cobardes... Seguro que en el cole eras de los que daba una colleja y luego se escondía detrás de la profe.

Más preguntas... —leí al azar, había cientos—. «¿Qué le harías si te lo encontraras en la cola del súper?». Esta es buena, *poker99* —así firmaba mi seguidor o seguidora—, es difícil que eso suceda. Primero, porque no suelo ir al súper. Ya conocéis mi nevera, ¿no? Os la presenté un día —era verdad: en una ocasión, salió en uno de mis vídeos—, Sahara, ¿recordáis? Pues si se llama así es porque nunca hay nada. Para llenarla tendría que ir a la compra y... ¡me da una pereza! Adelantando a las señoras con carrito, peleándome por la última cebolla... Pero vale, pongamos que alguna vez fuera a comprar..., no sé, pilas para el mando a distancia. ¿Cómo sabría quién es el tipo en cuestión? —seguía resistiéndome a decir el nombre de Donald—. A no ser que fuera disfrazado de Trump, no sabría cómo reconocerle. Pero ya, haciendo un esfuerzo superlativo e imaginando que voy al súper, que me encuentro con el susodicho y le reconozco..., ¿qué le haría? Lo tengo claro: le cantaría una jotica aragonesa, ¿no te jo...? Eso. En serio, me colaría delante de él en la caja. Así, a lo bruto. Se iba a enterar de quién es Joel Graham —dije con sorna. Humor, me repetía mentalmente.

—Otra pregunta... —Leí en la pantalla—. «¿Cuándo vas a volver a hacer un show?». Pues mira, *fuckingalondra*... ¡Joder, vaya nick! —Me reí—. ¿Qué te han hecho a ti las alondras? ¿Te han quitado a la novia? O al novio, que a las alondras les va la carne y el pescado, según me han dicho. A lo que íbamos. Creo que el próximo show lo voy a hacer desde un plasma, como los políticos. —Reí—. En serio... Estoy ensayando un nuevo número que os va a encantar: yo, cogido por dos gorilas de seguridad, dando volteretas en el aire y haciendo el *Dirty Dancing* al final. Sabéis, ¿no? Volando, solo sujetado por los brazos de los seguratas. —Hice la parodia de la peli mientras tarareaba la melodía de la película—. Va a quedar de bonico...

Me estaba divirtiendo. Todo el miedo que había sentido por volver a ponerme delante de la cámara me parecía ahora una chorrada, un terror infantil sin pies ni cabeza. Ese era mi sitio y esa mi gente. El cerdo de Donald me lo quería arrebatar y yo no iba a permitírselo. En una décima de segundo, mientras seguía charlando con mis seguidores, pensé que lo que me estaba pasando era como cuando te diagnostican una enfermedad que va a ser difícil de curar. Sigues tu vida, tu rutina, pero llevas el peso del virus encima, como una mochila que sabes que no vas a poder quitarte hasta que el tratamiento haga efecto. La irrupción de Donald en mi vida era algo así: un virus que estaba dentro de mí y que no dejaba de amenazarme. Algo que iba a costar eliminar. El tratamiento que había elegido hasta entonces —perder los nervios, desesperarme—, había hecho al virus más fuerte. El antídoto que estaba usando esa tarde —mis seguidores—, en cambio, parecía provocar un efecto más positivo. Al menos en mi organismo.

—... Más preguntas. A ver... —el *timeline* de Twitter bullía como nunca—. Hombre, uno con la foto de Trump en su perfil. Me gusta tu rollo, tío. A ver qué dices, *justicieroTrump*. —Su nick, y ya no me hizo tanta gracia—. «¿Qué opinan de lo que te ha pasado las amigas de tu madre en el club de lectura?».

Me quedé en silencio. Mi madre iba a un club de lectura del barrio. Pero podía ser una casualidad: «madre» y «club de lectura» es lo mismo que «madre» y «croquetas», es decir, una combinación de palabras que funciona para hacer chistes de marujas.

—¿Te interesa lo que opinen las amigas de mi madre? Eso si tengo madre y, si la tuviera, si tiene amigas y fuera a un club de lectura —solté para jugar al despiste—. Si de mi vida privada no hablo, de la vida privada de las amigas de mi madre, ni te cuento —dije con intención de zanjar el asunto. Cómo echaba de menos a Kevin, esa pregunta no habría pasado su filtro—. ¡Siguiente!

Buceé en el *timeline* buscando alguna pregunta interesante, pero volví a toparme con *justicieroTrump*. Insistía: «Sí que va a un club de lectura. Todos los jueves. Tus últimos shows deben de ser la comidilla del grupo». La idea de que detrás de ese nick estaba Donald cobraba cuerpo. Tenía que asegurarme.

—Perdonad, chicos —dije serio a cámara—, pero *justicieroTrump* está tocándome un poco... las partes nobles. Para él, y para todos, os advierto de que mi vida, es mi vida. Y mi familia es parte de ella. Esto —y señalé a mi alrededor—, es mi trabajo. Lo que está fuera de estas cuatro paredes no es parte del show. Y, o estoy medio ciego, o aquí dentro no está ni mi madre, ni mi padre ni la Virgen Santísima. Conclusión: si no están aquí, no existen para vosotros. *Capici?*

Trataba de que el tono no se me fuera y de que pareciera que aún me lo tomaba con humor. Pero era consciente de que no resultaba muy convincente. Me disponía a reanudar la charla, pero un nuevo mensaje de *justicieroTrump* saltó en la pantalla: «Y tu hermana Grette, ¿lo ha comentado ya en el patio del colegio?». Me levanté de la silla y grité furioso a la pantalla.

—¡Deja a mi hermana en paz, hijo de puta!

¿La había cagado? ¿Otra vez? Miré a mi imagen en la pantalla del ordenador, la misma imagen que se estaba viendo en todo el planeta en ese momento: yo, de pie, en un gesto congelado, amenazando con el dedo a un enemigo imaginario. Sí, la había cagado.

—Lo siento, chicos —dije tratando de recuperar la compostura—. Dejad a mi gente en paz, os lo suplico.

Pero ya era tarde. La pregunta de *justicieroTrump*, o sea, de Donald, y mi reacción ya habían prendido la mecha de nuevo. Aunque yo no la hubiera leído en voz alta, el *timeline* es público. Las preguntas y la charla tranquila dio paso a comentarios hirientes: «¿Tienes una hermana? ¡Preséntanosla!»; «Qué calladito te lo tenías...». Y no solo eso. Mi reacción de rabia también había desatado la creatividad de la gente que estaba viendo la emisión: «¡Ataca, Joel, ataca!»; «Cuidado, que viene el rottweiler»; «¡Llamad a los de seguridad!».

—A ver, por favor... —Quería mantener la calma, pero me estaba costando—. Olvidemos todo esto, ¿vale? Perdonad, pero soy muy celoso de mi intimidad y no tolero que se hable de gente cercana que no tiene nada que ver con...

Mientras hablaba, mi mirada se posó en un nuevo mensaje de *justicieroTrump*: «Es adorable. Me encanta ver cómo juega con sus amigas en el parque».

—¡Hijo de la gran...!

Me levanté de la silla y salí corriendo del estudio sin detener la emisión. Estaba ante un psicópata y temí que fuera capaz de acabar conmigo y los míos.

9.

Corrí. Mejor dicho, volé a casa de mi madre. Podía haber llamado, pero no se me pasó por la cabeza. El último mensaje de Donald (estaba seguro de que era él), me había hecho saltar de mi silla y me había empujado con una fuerza desconocida hacia mi coche. Conduje sin pensar y aún hoy me asombra que llegara vivo a la calle donde vivían mi madre y Grette. No se tarda más de media hora en recorrer la distancia que hay entre mi casa y la suya. Esa tarde no sé en cuánto lo hice. En menos, seguro. Como me pasó en mitad del show, perdí la noción del tiempo. Las amenazas de Donald me estaban trastornando. Era capaz de hacerme perder el control y eso era lo que hacía que mi acosador siempre fuera por delante. No servía de nada que me mentalizara, que me preparara, que intentara adivinar su siguiente paso. Hiciera lo que hiciera, Donald siempre ganaba la batalla.

—¿Estáis bien? —pregunté a mi madre jadeando cuando me abrió la puerta.

—Joel, hijo, ¿qué te pasa? —respondió preocupada.

—Solo dime que estáis bien, por favor.

—Claro. ¿No lo ves?

—¿Y Grette?

—Dando su clase de violín —me tranquilizó—. Estamos perfectamente. ¿Y tú?

Miré a mi madre desolado. Fue en ese momento cuando tuve la sensación de que recobraba la razón desde que salí de mi estudio.

—Pasa, hijo. —Me agarró del brazo y me hizo entrar.

No podía disimular mi estado, menos ante mi madre. Tienen un radar, un sexto sentido para saber lo que les pasa a sus hijos. La última vez que vino a mi casa aún pude salir del paso y darle largas. Pero esta vez, viendo cómo había llegado, era imposible disimular.

—No estás bien, Joel. Necesitas ayuda.

—Sí, ¿pero cuál? Ese tío... —No sabía qué sabía mi madre y qué no. Supongo que todo. En su club de lectura los chismes corrían como la pólvora.

—A ese «tío» ya le está buscando la policía. ¿Por qué no dejas que hagan su trabajo y le cojan?

—Si fuera tan sencillo...

—Haces todo lo que puedes, hijo. No te presiones de más.

Eran palabras que no servían de mucho, pero dichas por mi madre, me reconfortaron. Sentado en el sofá, me apoyé en su pecho y estuve un rato así, con la mirada perdida en las líneas del parqué que tantas veces había mirado de niño. Su respiración y su mano acariciándome el pelo me llevaron a un estado de paz y somnolencia que hacía tiempo que no experimentaba. Si el ser humano pudiera elegir vivir así, apoyado en el pecho generoso de su madre, sin duda no haría otra cosa.

—Todo se arreglará, Joel —susurró.

Afirmé con la cabeza. Me lo creí. En esos momentos, cualquier cosa que me dijera la iba a creer. Todo me pareció pequeño y fugaz: mi carrera de *youtuber*, mis vídeos, el acoso de Donald y cómo me estaba hundiendo la vida. Todo me parecía lejano y sin importancia. Después de la tormenta venía una calma infinita. Quería cerrar los ojos e instalarme en el sueño, donde todo era más fácil. Todo era perfecto: mi madre abrazándome, Grette estudiando en su habitación. Todo ello representaba el orden, las líneas bien dibujadas, el plan de vuelo diseñado con esmero y luego cumplido. Me dejé ir y cerré los ojos.

Las notas torpes de Grette al violín se confundían con el aclarado de la lavadora que sonaba de fondo. Mi hermanita repetía una y otra vez el mismo compás. Una melodía interrumpida desde su inicio. Después de varios intentos, por fin logró arrancar y, desde las puertas del sueño en el que me hallaba, imaginé las notas que salían de su violín escalando una pendiente, luchando por abrirse paso en el pentagrama y cumplir su función de armar la melodía que Grette amenazaba con disolver a cada inclinación de arco. Tras unos segundos, la melodía cobró forma y por fin tomó cuerpo. Sonreí. Sabía que lo conseguiría, sabía que Grette lo haría. Pero la sonrisa se apagó en seguida. No porque Grette se confundiera otra vez. Al contrario, había cogido carrerilla y podía escuchar la melodía con total nitidez. Era esa. La melodía de los vídeos de Donald.

—¿Quién está con Grette? —dije tras incorporarme de un bote. Mi madre me miró desconcertada y con un leve gesto de enfado. Creo que empezaba a estar un poco harta de mis altibajos.

—Su profesor de violín —dijo con la máxima paciencia—. ¿Qué problema hay ahora?

Como respuesta, salí corriendo por el pasillo hacia la habitación de Grette. ¿Era Donald quien estaba ahí? Era una idea absurda, pero, ¿no era todo lo que me estaba sucediendo una auténtica locura? Abrí la puerta de golpe.

—¿Quién coño eres? —pregunté al chico que estaba con Grette.

—Hola, Joel —saludó mi hermana deteniendo su interpretación y bajando el violín de su barbilla—. ¿Qué te pasa?

—Di, ¿quién eres? —insistí mientras me encaraba con el chico. No debía de tener más de veinte años y por la cara de susto con la que me miraba, no debía de estar entendiendo nada.

—Yo..., el profe de...

—¡Dilo, joder!

—Joel... —gimoteó Grette que, asustada había retrocedido dos pasos y buscaba protección apoyándose en la pared.

—¿Por qué tocas esa canción? ¿Quién te lo ha pedido? —insistí. El chico estaba cada vez más bloqueado.

—Es... del programa.

—¿Te envía Donald? —preguntaba sin escuchar sus respuestas. No las quería, en realidad. Solo deseaba que él fuera Donald. Pero no. No lo era.

—¡Deja al chico! —Escuché a mi espalda. Era mi madre—. ¡Déjalo ahora mismo!

Me giré y al verla en la puerta me costó reconocerla. Nunca la había visto tan enfadada.

—Mamá... —supliqué como un crío—. Es la melodía... —dije como si todos los presentes supieran de qué estaba hablando.

—Perdona, Bernnie —dijo mi madre dirigiéndose al profesor de mi hermana. Avanzó hacia él y le pasó el brazo por el hombro para alejarlo de mí. Por un momento me vi desplazado, sustituido como destinatario del afecto que mi madre me había dado en exclusiva hacía unos segundos, cuando estábamos en el sofá.

—Está loco... —respondió el chico aún impactado.

—¿Por... por qué tocaba esa melodía? —pregunté con sensación de haber hecho el ridículo. A esas alturas ya era consciente de que todo había sido un malentendido.

—Es lo que se estudia en primero de violín, ¿yo qué sé? Se la mandan en el conservatorio.

Miré a Grette, que aguantaba las ganas de llorar, apoyada contra la pared y abrazando su violín, como si el instrumento fuera a protegerla de mí. Luego miré a mi madre, que me observaba severa, los brazos separados del cuerpo, en posición de alerta. Luego posé mi mirada en Bernnie, que no quitaba sus ojos de mí, aún enojado y dispuesto a actuar si se reproducía el brote que me había llevado a irrumpir ahí e interrumpir su clase.

—¿Es eso verdad? —pregunté a Grette.

—Joel, Bernnie estudia último curso de violín. Da clases a Grette para sacarse un dinero —aclaró mi madre.

—¿Conoces a Donald? —Me miró perplejo. No sabía de qué le hablaba—. ¿Das clases en su casa? —preguntaba sin rumbo. Estaba naufragando.

—Solo doy clases a Grette. —Empezó a recoger sus cosas—. Es mejor que me vaya. —Y salió sin decir nada.

—Espera... —dije tratando de retenerle, pero mi madre me detuvo agarrándome del brazo. No insistí.

—No estás bien, Joel.

No, no lo estaba.

«Perder», esa era la única palabra que tenía en mi cabeza cuando llegué a casa. «Perder» escrito en mayúsculas, en letras de neón, culminando el edifico más alto de la ciudad, parpadeando... Escrita en cualquier formato pero omnipresente en mi mente. Eso era lo que me estaba sucediendo: PERDER. No el juego con Donald. Ningún juego se pierde o se gana hasta que se termina, y el juego en el que estaba participando no parecía que hubiera llegado todavía a su fin. Mi sensación era que, desde que hice el maldito vídeo de la llamada, lo único que había hecho era perder: a mis amigos, a quienes había dejado de lado; a Kevin, que se había cansado de mis ataques de nervios —que yo aún consideraba justificados—; a mi madre y a Grette, que habían sido testigos de mi agresividad con el pobre chaval que daba clases de violín. Perder seguidores, perder prestigio como *youtuber*, fama o éxito, era irrelevante al lado de perder a la gente que me rodeaba. Y de eso no podía culpar a Donald, lo había hecho yo solito. Él había trazado una senda y yo me había perdido en ella. ¿Era eso a lo que se refería cuando me advirtió de que no iba a parar hasta que acabara conmigo? Perder a mi gente era mucho peor que perder mi canal. Si lo que buscaba era acabar conmigo, lo estaba consiguiendo. Lo había conseguido. Estaba solo.

En silencio, derrumbado en el sofá, escuché el zumbido de mi móvil. Como una señal, justo cuando llegué a la conclusión de que estaba solo, sonaba mi teléfono. Tal vez no estaba todo perdido. Como un crío que busca por toda la casa los juguetes de los Reyes Magos, recorrí cada rincón tratando de encontrar mi teléfono antes de que se cortara la llamada. ¿Por qué siempre lo tengo en silencio?, me reproché. ¡¿Por qué siempre lo dejo tirado en cualquier sitio?!, me maldije. La llamada se cortó antes de que lo encontrara. Mierda. Inmóvil, en mitad del salón, esperé unos segundos. Como deseaba, el móvil volvió a sonar. Solo podía ser Kevin. Esta vez tuve más suerte y lo encontré debajo del sofá. No es extraño, muchas veces lo dejo en el suelo, sobre la alfombra, cuando estoy tirado viendo la tele. La pantalla parpadeaba iluminada.

—¡Kevin! —exclamé como si se tratara de un primo que hace décadas que no veía—. No te lo vas a creer, pero me alegro de escucharte.

—¡Corta la emisión! —dijo Kevin al otro lado atacado.

—¿Cómo? —No entendía a qué se refería.

—Llevas más de tres horas emitiendo en tu canal. ¡Córtalo!

¡La emisión! Había salido corriendo de casa cuando Donald apareció en el chat de mi directo y no me había preocupado de cortar la emisión. Me quedé paralizado, con el móvil en la oreja.

—¡Espabila! —insistió Kevin.

Sin responder ni cortar la llamada, tiré el móvil en el sofá y salí corriendo hacia mi estudio. Sin embargo, antes de entrar, frené en seco. Mi dignidad ya importaba poco, mucho menos mi dignidad como *youtuber*, pero una cosa era ser el hazmerreír de la comunidad, y otra entrar como un poseso en mi estudio para cortar la emisión y que todo el mundo —porque no dudaba de que había miles de personas esperando ese momento— lo viera. Retrocedí sigilosamente, una reacción absurda porque ahí, en el pasillo, nadie me veía. Entré de nuevo en el salón y apagué el *router*. Se acabó el *wifi*, se acabó la emisión. Por si acaso, fui junto a la puerta de la entrada y bajé los plomos. Un fundido a negro, un apagón. Como en mi propia vida.

Al regresar al salón, escuché la voz metálica y apagada que salía del móvil.

—¡Joel! ¡Coge el puto móvil! —gritaba Kevin.

Rescaté el teléfono del sofá y me lo llevé a la oreja, esta vez sin el entusiasmo que había experimentado hacía unos segundos, cuando descolgué.

—Joder... —dije.

—Eso digo yo: jo-der. ¿Qué tienes en la cabeza, tío?

—¿Has visto todo lo que ha pasado? —pregunté para que los hechos hablaran por sí solos y no tuviera que dar ninguna explicación.

—Más o menos —respondió Kevin—. Sí, vamos.

—Pues eso. Donald insinuó que seguía a mi hermana y salí pitando.

—Ya —dijo Kevin sin más. No era una respuesta muy conciliadora, pero, al menos parecía que había enterrado el hacha de guerra.

—Otra cagada, ¿no?

—Gorda.

Me quedé en silencio. Kevin también. Parecíamos dos viejos amigos dándose el pésame por la muerte del pariente de uno de ellos.

—¿Qué más da una más? —dije con convencimiento.

—Visto así, nada.

—¿Hay otra manera de verlo?

—No. Supongo.

Volvimos a quedarnos callados. Ni una bronca, ni un «ánimo, Joel», ni un «Ya te vale». Nada. Kevin no era capaz de decirme nada.

—¿Necesitas algo? —me preguntó. A esas alturas ya no tenía ninguna duda de que Kevin seguía enfadado. Por lo del anunciante, por lo de la emisión, porque todo se había ido a la mierda.

—No. Supongo.

—Ya hablaremos en otro momento, ¿vale?

—Claro. —No quería presionarle para hablar. Tampoco tenía ganas de reprocharle haber desaparecido esos días. Ya habría tiempo para eso.

—Borra el vídeo.

—¿Cómo?

—El vídeo del directo, que lo borres. Casi todo el tiempo es tu silla vacía. A no ser que quieras pasarte al videoarte, no tiene interés.

—Ya.

—Chao —respondió. Y colgó.

Volví a subir los plomos y a encender el *router*. Como un sonámbulo, entré en mi estudio y encendí mi ordenador. Inicié mi sesión en la plataforma y eliminé el vídeo de mi directo. No me molesté en mirar el número de visitas ni las estadísticas. Tampoco los comentarios. Lo borré sin más. Tuve la sensación de que, con ese gesto, se cerraba una etapa de mi vida. Suena exagerado, pero sentí que, al hacerlo, me quitaba un peso de encima.

Regresé camino del salón. Quería tumbarme en el sofá y cambiar de canal en la televisión hasta borrar los números del mando a distancia. No tenía ganas de otra cosa. Pero antes de sentarme, sonó el timbre de la puerta. No pensaba abrir. Ni de broma. Si era mi madre, estaba lo suficiente avergonzado como para verla. Además, ella podía llamar, pero si no contestaba, no tendría reparo en abrir con su llave. Podía ser Kevin. Algo así era típico de él: llamarme desde el portal y luego subir. Pero no, la conversación había terminado de forma seca y no parecía que mi representante tuviera ganas de verme en ese momento. ¿Quién podía ser? El timbre volvió a sonar. Seguí sin moverme, no quería que, quienquiera que fuese, pensara que estaba en casa. Llamaron una vez más.

—Abre, Joel, sabemos que estás ahí —dijo Connor al otro lado.

Mis amigos. Había regresado a casa esa tarde con la palabra «perder» en la cabeza. Y puede que fuera así, pero al menos en ese momento había olvidado la palabra. Fui a la puerta y abrí.

—¿Qué hacéis aquí?

—Evitar que acabes convirtiéndote en un capullo —dijo Connor entrando sin preguntar.

—Y no te plantes en medio, que vamos a entrar te pongas como te pongas —me advirtió Silvestre pasando delante de mí.

—Os lo dije. Se le convence con pizzas, no con pelis frikis —dijo Jan que entró cargado con varias cajas de pizzas—. Hemos traído una de anchoas y piña.

—Esa tan asquerosa que solo te gusta a ti —dijo Silvestre.

Antes de que pudiera decir nada, mis amigos ya habían entrado en el salón. En la puerta solo quedaba Flavia, la única que parecía dispuesta a pedir permiso para entrar. La miré interrogante.

—¿Puedo ir al baño? —preguntó cortada.

10.

—¿Esperas a alguien más o vienes antes de que Connor se coma todas las pizzas? —dijo Silvestre desde el salón.

Entré en el salón y me encontré a mis amigos abriendo las cajas y repartiendo refrescos. Era una imagen habitual en mi vida: después del videoclub de Silvestre, mi casa era nuestro segundo lugar de reunión.

—Esta es la de Joel —dijo Jan señalando una pizza donde las anchoas surcaban los trozos amarillos de la piña.

—No sé cómo puedes comértela —dijo Silvestre—. Aunque solo sea por su aspecto dan ganas de echarse cuerpo a tierra.

—A mí me gusta, ¿qué pasa? —me defendí al tiempo que me hacía hueco para sentarme en el sofá. Era fácil estar con ellos, me sentía a gusto—. Y es la más sana: fruta y pescado.

—Si la llevamos a analizar, seguro que sale que es tóxica —resumió Connor.

—Flavia, ¿una porción de *pepperoni*? —preguntó Jan a su novia, que acababa de entrar.

Flavia se sentó en el suelo y empezó a engullir la pizza mientras nos miraba a todos con los ojos muy abiertos. No hablaba mucho, pero nunca tenías la sensación de que estaba ausente.

—¿Qué tal los entrenamientos? —pregunté—. He estado un poco liado estos días, pero espero volver ya.

—¿Liado? —preguntó Connor incrédulo.

—Tío... —le reprendió Jan—. Connor quiere decir que lo entendemos y que...

—Se te ha ido la olla, tío —dijo Connor. No se cortaba un pelo y eso era parte de su encanto, aunque escociera.

—¡Que espero volver a jugar esta semana! —me defendí—. Tampoco soy tan importante, ¿no? Porque estamos los justos para el equipo titular, que si no, iba a chupar más banquillo...

—No, si el fútbol es lo de menos.

—Ya —dije. Lo había entendido desde el primer momento, pero deseaba con todas mis fuerzas que se estuviera refiriendo a la liguilla y no al caos en el que se había convertido mi vida. Se me había ido la olla, sí, y Connor tenía todo el derecho a recordármelo.

—Pues no está tan mal —dijo Jan con la boca llena después de dar un bocado a mi pizza. No soportaba el mal rollo.

—Sí, se me ha ido —dije ignorando su intento por cambiar de tema—. Pero ya está. Se acabó.

—¿El qué? —preguntó Silvestre alarmado.

—Todo —respondí—. Bueno, menos el fútbol.

—¿Vas a dedicarte al fútbol en exclusiva? —preguntó Flavia—. Pero si acabas de decir que...

—¿Qué es lo que se acabó? —insistió Silvestre interrumpiéndola.

—Ni de coña —dijo Connor. Todos sabían a qué me refería, pero solo Connor se atrevía a admitirlo.

—Se me ha ido la olla, tú lo has dicho —me expliqué—. Y esto ya no lo remonto. Es mejor dejarlo y dedicarme a otra cosa.

—Pero, tío... —protestó Silvestre—. No puedes abandonar.

—Va a cerrar su canal —le explicó Jan a Flavia, que se había quedado con la boca abierta a medio masticar un trozo de pizza—. Eso es lo que dice que se acabó.

—Ah —respondió Flavia y siguió masticando—. ¡¿Cómo?! —Reaccionó un segundo después, cuando su cerebro procesó la información.

—Se te está yendo la olla otra vez —dijo Connor—. Y mucho.

—Pero, ¿qué queréis que haga? Cada vez que abro la boca, la cago. No sé qué hacer, qué pasos dar, cómo arreglar esto. A lo mejor todo esto ha pasado porque tenía que pasar y era el momento de dejarlo.

—Pues menuda mierda —dijo Silvestre.

—Con lo que molaba tener un colega famoso —dijo Jan.

Nos quedamos en silencio. Solo Flavia comía. Los demás mirábamos a cualquier sitio con la mirada perdida. Parecía un funeral. Y en cierto modo lo era. Estábamos ahí reunidos para celebrar el fin de mi carrera como *youtuber*. No había ataúd, ni lápidas, ni nadie con traje negro, pero el silencio que nos envolvía en ese momento era idéntico al que se escucha cuando se ha ido alguien para siempre. Uno siempre fantasea sobre quién irá o no a su entierro. Y se imagina que ahí estarán sus seres más queridos. Que todos le recordarán con cariño y contarán anécdotas brillantes de su vida. Es una fantasía, nadie estará ahí para verlo. En esos momentos, sin embargo, me sentí un privilegiado por poder estar presente en el momento en el que una parte de mi vida se iba para siempre. No iba a volver a ser *youtuber* y en la despedida me gustaba estar rodeado de mis amigos.

—Cobarde.

Fue Connor quien rompió el silencio. Todos le miramos. Jan con pánico. Nadie le contestó, mucho menos yo. Aunque escocía.

—¿Vas a dejar que gane? —insistió.

Tampoco dije nada. El resto me miraron fugazmente pero luego bajaron la mirada al suelo cortados.

—Pues yo no —dijo Connor levantándose con energía.

—Ni yo —dijo Silvestre—. Vamos, ni lo pienses.

—¿Cómo? —pregunté desconcertado. Me podía esperar cualquier cosa de mis amigos, pero esta me había descolocado por completo.

—Que tú no te rindes —dijo Jan sumándose a los otros dos.

—Pero... ¿qué vais a hacer? —pregunté aún conmocionado por lo que estaba pasando.

—No tenemos ni idea —reconoció Connor, que se había situado de pie frente a mí para dirigir la rebelión—. ¿Por qué no nos lo dices tú?

—¿Yo? —respondí incrédulo—. Lo he intentado todo: dar la cara, explicarme...

—¿Y la poli? —preguntó Jan.

—¿La poli? —dije con desdén—. Supongo que investigarán el caso dentro de diez años, cuando resuelvan los setecientos crímenes que hay por delante. He investigado por mi cuenta, pero no soy Sherlock Holmes. —Y me acordé de Will, que me había llamado así hacía unos días—. No doy más de mí.

—¿Qué has investigado? —quiso saber Silvestre.

Les conté que había aparecido un mensaje en mi pedido de comida, que había hablado con Donald por videoconferencia, que había seguido a Rick, el repartidor. También les hablé de la melodía de violín, del ridículo que había hecho esa misma tarde con el profesor de Grette. Eran las únicas pistas que creía que me acercaban a Donald, pero ninguna había tenido éxito.

—Hay que encontrarle —dijo Flavia, que había seguido comiendo sin perderse ni una línea de mi relato. Todos la miramos confundidos.

—Obvio —respondió Connor.

—Es lo que llevo intentando hacer desde hace días, ya os lo he dicho —le aclaré con paciencia.

—El problema es que el cabrón está bien escondido —dijo Silvestre.

—Y sabe lo que hace —afirmó Jan con cara de resignación.

—A Donald, no —dijo Flavia. Todos volvimos a mirarla desconcertados—. Al profesor de violín. La melodía es la única pista que tenemos. Gracias al profesor de Grette, sabemos que es una pieza que se estudia en primero de violín, ¿no? Pues ya está.

—¿Cómo no se te había ocurrido antes, Joel? —me preguntó Connor con ironía—. Gracias, Flavia, el Cuerpo Nacional de Policía se ha perdido a una gran investigadora.

—No te pases —dijo Jan molesto.

—Perdona, pero, ¿en qué nos ayuda eso? —se disculpó Connor—. ¿Vamos a las casas de todos los chavales que estudian violín en la ciudad? Qué digo..., ¡en el país entero! Que tampoco sabemos dónde vive Donald.

—Niños que estudien violín puede que haya muchos, pero profesores que den clases particulares... —dijo Flavia.

—Eso sí —dijo Silvestre consciente de que el razonamiento de Flavia tenía futuro. Cuando estaba inspirada, estaba inspirada, había que reconocerlo.

—Ya, pero, ¡que no sabemos si es de aquí! —insistió Connor. No le gustaba no tener razón y se agarraba a cualquier cosa con tal de mantenerla.

—Y viene a la ciudad para dejar notitas en las bolsas de pedidos de comida rápida, ¿no? —le replicó Jan burlón como venganza por haberse metido antes con su chica.

Connor se calló. No tenía más argumentos. Todos nos quedamos callados. Me sentía desubicado. Hacía tan solo unos minutos quería extender el certificado de defunción de mi canal y, con él, el de mi carrera como *youtuber*. Ahora, mis amigos insistían en seguir luchando. Pero la idea de Flavia se me antojaba inabarcable.

—¿A qué estamos esperando? —dijo Connor.

Al instante todos, incluida Flavia, se pusieron en marcha. Solo yo me quedé sentado en el sofá.

—Pero, ¿cómo vamos a dar con él? —pregunté sin saber qué hacer.

—Ni idea, pero si no está en Google, no existe —respondió Jan—. No te importa, ¿no? —dijo tecleando en mi portátil.

—¿Conservatorio de música? —preguntaba Silvestre por su teléfono—. Mi hijo necesita una profesor particular de violín, ¿podría aconsejarme alguno?

—Qué crack —sonrió Connor—. Su hijo...

—Yo... —empecé a decir. Estaba emocionado con la reacción de mis amigos.

—Menos discursitos y más currar. Busca tiendas de instrumentos. Ahí seguro que saben quién puede dar clases.

—¿... Que qué edad tiene mi hijo? —decía Silvestre al teléfono—. No sé... ¿Cuatro años?

—¿No sabe la edad de su hijo? —preguntó Flavia a Jan mientras anotaba en una libreta los teléfonos que su novio iba encontrando en internet.

—Normal. No tiene —respondió Connor.

—¿Cuántos años tiene tu hermana, Joel? —me preguntó Silvestre tapando el auricular.

—Nueve —respondí en voz baja mientras buscaba tiendas de instrumentos en mi *tablet*.

—Nueve, nueve años... —dijo Silvestre al teléfono—. Claro que sé la edad de mi hijo. Cuatro tiene el pequeño, que estudia clarinete.

—No, si va a tener familia numerosa, al final —se mofó Connor—. ¿Me vais dando teléfonos?

Había traído una pizarra que tenía en mi estudio y la había apoyado sobre la mesa. Jan y Flavia le fueron dando números. Yo conseguí otros en las tiendas de música. Silvestre, tras hablar de sus hijos un buen rato, consiguió otros tantos. En total, reunimos los números de diecisiete profesores particulares de violín.

—Muchos me parecen —dijo Silvestre.

—En la vida me hubiera imaginado que hubiera tantos padres interesados en que sus hijos les destrozaran los tímpanos —reflexionó Connor—. Este mundo está loco.

—¿Qué hacemos ahora? —preguntó Jan—. Seguir a los diecisiete todos los días hasta todas las casas donde van a dar clases nos va a llevar la tira.

—Bueno... —pensaba Silvestre—. Somos cinco. Si cada uno se encarga de tres...

—Podemos eternizarnos —sentenció Connor.

Nos quedamos mirando la pizarra en silencio, como si entre nombres y números de teléfono fuéramos a encontrar la solución.

—Un momento —dije sin apartar la mirada del jeroglífico de la pizarra—. Las dos veces que me he comunicado con Donald ha sonado la melodía, pero la primera vez sonaba mejor que la segunda.

Mis amigos me miraron interrogantes. No sabían a dónde quería llegar.

—Es un profesor al revés, ¿es lo que quieres decir? —preguntó Connor con sorna.

—¿Al revés? ¿Bocabajo? —dijo Flavia desconcertada.

—Es un chiste de Connor —le explicó Jan— para decir que en lugar de enseñar...

—... «Desenseña» —aclaró Silvestre—. Típica chorrada de Connor.

—Ah —respondió Flavia, que tenía cara de no haber entendido la gracia.

—Es raro, sí —dijo Connor serio—. Ningún alumno toca peor con el tiempo. Como mínimo, sigue tocando igual de mal.

—Es eso —proseguí—, o... —y me quedé callado, tratando de hilar lo que de verdad quería decir.

—¿O...?

—No es un profesor que va a domicilio. —Les miré uno a uno antes de terminar—. Es uno que recibe a domicilio.

Todos me miraron asombrados, como si fuera imposible que no hubiéramos llegado antes a una obviedad como esa. No solo era un gran descubrimiento, también nos facilitaba mucho la búsqueda.

—Entonces... —dijo Flavia—, Donald es vecino del profesor.

—O es el propio profesor —añadió Connor entusiasmado.

Como cuando les revelé mi descubrimiento, todos miramos esta vez a Connor. Pero nuestras caras no eran de asombro, más bien eran de incredulidad.

—¿Qué dices, tío? —preguntó Silvestre sin dar crédito.

—¡Pensadlo! ¡Es profesor de violín! ¡Todo cuadra! —insistió.

—Y acosa a Joel mientras un mocoso le destroza los oídos en la habitación de al lado, ¿no? —dijo Jan con ironía.

—Ya, visto así... —Se rindió Connor.

—Pues entonces, ya sabemos qué tenemos que hacer, ¿no? —les apremié.

—Sí, perdona —dijo Flavia, que se puso a recoger los restos de la cena.

—No, cariño —la interrumpió Jan—. Se refiere a la búsqueda del profesor.

—Ah... —Sonrío Flavia avergonzada.

Al mismo tiempo, todos cogimos nuestros móviles dispuestos a llamar uno a uno a los profesores de la lista para saber quién daba clases en su casa y quién no. Cuando iba a marcar el primer número, sonó el timbre de casa. Nadie se inmutó, solo yo parecía que lo había escuchado. Sin ánimo de entretener la tarea de mis amigos, me levanté y fui a abrir. No pensé en quién podía ser. Mi madre, tal vez. Dudaba que fuera Kevin. Era Will.

—¡Hola, tío! —le saludé efusivo. Me parecía una gran noticia que hubiera aparecido. Estaba deseando presentárselo a mis amigos.

—¿Qué pasa, Sherlock? —llamarme así ya se había convertido en una costumbre— ¿Cómo lo llevas?

—Bien, bien... —Y era como me sentía en esos momentos—. Pasa, que estoy con mis colegas.

—Ah —dijo cortado. Me eché a un lado para que pasara, pero se quedó clavado en la puerta. Me sorprendió, no le tenía por una persona tímida.

—¿Pasa algo?

—No, ¡qué va! —dijo tratando de recuperar el tono amigable—. Es que solo pasaba para pedirte disculpas.

—¿Disculpas?

—¡Bingo! —se escuchó decir a Silvestre desde el salón.

—¿Estáis jugando al...? —preguntó Will sorprendido.

—¿Eh? Ah... No, no, no estamos jugando al bingo. Es que estamos buscando a un profesor de violín, por lo de la melodía, ¿te acuerdas?

—¿Un profesor?

—Sí, creemos que Donald vive al lado de uno y... ¿por qué no pasas y te lo cuento?

—No, tío, de verdad. Además, me tengo que ir a currar, que llego tarde. Solo pasaba para pedirte disculpas por haberte metido en el embolado del directo.

—¿Es por eso? —Sonreí. Me sorprendió que estuviera preocupado por algo de lo que no tenía la culpa.

—Sí, yo te di la idea y ya me he enterado de cómo ha terminado. Lo siento, tío.

—No te preocupes. Que yo sepa, no me has puesto una pistola en la sien para hacerlo. Tu idea era cojonuda, solo que se torció. O la torcí yo, más bien. ¿Seguro que no quieres pasar? Me encantaría que conocieras a mis colegas.

—Joel... —dijo Connor asomándose al pasillo—. Ah... Hola —saludó al ver a Will.

—Este es Connor —le dije a Will—. Un capullo, pero buen tío. Te presento a Will, un colega.

—Encantado —saludó Connor. Luego se dirigió a mí—. ¿Vienes? Hemos acotado la lista un huevo. Solo hay cuatro que den clase en su casa.

—¡Cojonudo! —exclamé.

—Os dejo —se despidió Will—. Otro día me cuentas qué tal la investigación.

—¡Claro!

Cerré la puerta y me dispuse a entrar en el salón, pero Connor seguía ahí. Mirando hacia la puerta cerrada.

—¿Qué te pasa?

—Ese tío... ¿De qué le conoces?

—Trabaja en el restaurante donde pido comida a veces. Nos hemos hecho colegas. Es un crack.

—En el restaurante —repitió Connor.

—Sí —afirmé interrogante y algo impaciente.

—De donde salió la bolsa que tenía la nota de Donald.

—¿A dónde quieres llegar, Connor? —Su sospecha me estaba molestando.

—Blanco y en botella, Joel. Tu verás —dijo antes de darse la vuelta y meterse de nuevo en el salón.

Me quedé en la entrada pensando en lo que había querido insinuar Connor y mirando hacia la puerta cerrada, como si mirar hacia donde se había ido Will fuera darme alguna respuesta. ¿Will compinchado con Donald? No podía creerlo. No quería.

11.

No, no podía creerlo. No podía creer que Will hubiera sido cómplice de un personaje tan siniestro como Donald. Era, además, demasiado evidente. Despreciaba a Donald con toda mi alma, pero le reconocía bastante habilidad para hacerme daño. Acercarse a mí a través de Will me parecía burdo, muy lejos de su nivel de maldad.

No volví a hablar del tema el resto de la velada. Tampoco Connor, que, tras dejar la semilla de la sospecha, no había vuelto a mencionar a Will. Por un momento pensé que todo respondía a un ataque de celos. Connor era mi mejor amigo y ver cómo otro colega aparecía en mi vida podía haberle puesto en alerta. Me parecía una idea absurda, Connor era un tío generoso, pero quería agarrarme a ella, a cualquiera, antes de pensar que Will me había traicionado. Al mismo tiempo, ¿qué sabía de él? Nada. Apenas nos habíamos visto tres veces pero, por algún motivo, me había hecho sentir cómodo. Habíamos cogido confianza muy deprisa, era cierto, pero, ¿hay que conocerse profundamente para pasar un par de buenos ratos con alguien? ¡Como si fuera una novia! No, no podía ser, me repetía. Pero, ¿y si era?

Mis amigos se fueron casi a medianoche. Se había hecho tarde para intentar cualquier avance sobre el tema de los profesores, así que nos pasamos el resto del tiempo hablando de las chorradas habituales. Agradecí que así fuera, necesitaba sentir que, al menos, había algo que seguía como siempre. Pero mi cabeza se iba una y otra vez a la sospecha que me había presentado Connor. Cuando se hizo tarde, empecé a bostezar y, argumentando agotamiento, les invité a irse. Deseaba quedarme con mis pensamientos, para saborear a solas el mal trago. Los malos tragos, en realidad.

Una vez solo, retomé la idea de abandonar mi canal. Mis amigos me habían animado a no rendirme y gracias a ellos aparqué la idea. Pero solo la había aparcado. En cuanto se fueron volví a pensar en ello y otra vez, como hacía unas horas, cuando eliminé el vídeo del directo, me sentí más ligero, como si me hubiera quitado un peso de encima. Había muchas señales que apuntaban a esa decisión. No me refería a los ridículos repetidos que había cometido delante de mis seguidores gracias a Donald; eran, más bien, las sensaciones que había tenido en los últimos días: la fuerza interior que me impedía entrar en mi estudio tras los primeros ataques, la liberación que sentí cuando eliminé el vídeo. Advertencias que mi cabeza me mandaba de forma subliminal esperando a que yo me diera cuenta. No tenía que ver con lo mental, tenía que ver con lo físico. Una de ellas, de miedo; la otra, de libertad. Como les dije a mis amigos, a lo mejor todo esto estaba pasando porque tenía que pasar. A veces hacemos cosas de manera inconsciente que, sin darnos cuenta, nos llevan a donde queríamos ir. Un día nos encontramos en el pico de una montaña y nos preguntamos cómo hemos llegado hasta ahí. Si en ese momento hiciéramos el recorrido inverso, nos daríamos cuenta de que siempre habíamos deseado hacer eso: un día compramos unas botas de *treking* que no necesitábamos pero estaban de oferta; otro, empezamos a salir a caminar por puro placer; otro, nos apuntamos a un club de senderismo; otro, acompañamos a un amigo a hacer escalada urbana a un rocódromo... Y al final, acabas en la cima de una montaña y no dudas de que eso era exactamente lo que siempre habías querido hacer.

Con mi canal me estaba sucediendo algo parecido. O eso creía. Hacer esa llamada suicida a Donald, no hacer caso a sus provocaciones, apostar con él a ver quién era más listo, participar de su juego sin conocer las reglas... Comportamientos irracionales que me llevaron a ese punto: considerar la idea de dejarlo todo y dedicarme a otra cosa. Tal vez lo deseaba muy dentro de mí, aunque, siendo sincero, me costaba creerlo.

En la cama, mirando al techo iluminado por la luz que entraba de la calle, traté de imaginar mi vida sin YouTube. Había estudiado Comunicación Audiovisual, pero no había trabajado nunca en la televisión ni en el cine. Muy pronto me metí en la plataforma y al poco se convirtió en mi dedicación exclusiva. Era lo que sabía hacer: vídeos para mi canal. Sabía otras muchas cosas que había aprendido en la Universidad, pero nunca las había puesto en práctica. Me gustaba mucho el cine. Podía ser crítico, pero diferente, haciendo críticas en YouTube... No, eso significaba tener otro canal.

Podía probar con los juegos, era bastante bueno en la *Play*. Luego me podía grabar jugando y... Otra vez la idea terminaba conmigo en internet. Todas las ideas terminaban ahí. ¿Es que no sabía hacer nada más que compartir lo que fuera que hiciera en la red? Al final, Kevin tenía razón con aquello que me dijo cuando le conocí: si no vemos las cosas en una pantalla, no las entendemos. Sonreí. Por la gran verdad que me había dicho y por acordarme de sus burradas. Kevin. Había estado raro esa tarde. Muy raro.

Cuando desperté, a la mañana siguiente, me sentí extraño. «El primer día post-YouTube», me dije. Y me levanté ligero, sin la necesidad de ir a mi canal a ver las estadísticas casi antes de ir al baño, como hacía la mayor parte de los días. Una tarea menos que hacer. Fui a la cocina a desayunar y me vi pensando en qué me apetecía y en todo el tiempo que tenía para pensar en ello, sin tener la cabeza dividida entre la cafetera y el guion de mi siguiente vídeo. Otra tarea menos. Me duché, me vestí, y ahí también me puse cualquier cosa. No iba a salir más en pantalla, daba igual lo que me pusiera. Tampoco es que cuidara mi estilismo al límite, pero siempre dedicaba un rato, por pequeño que fuera, a escoger esta u otra camiseta. La vida sin YouTube me ofrecía un montón de ventajas, parecía. Pero cuando terminé todo lo que tenía que hacer y aún me quedaba un día entero por delante, recapacité y cambié de opinión.

—Chorradas —dije en voz alta. ¿Qué necesidad tenía de engañarme de esa manera? Podía decirme una y mil veces que sin YouTube se vivía mejor, pero la mentira no iba a durar mucho tiempo.

Salí de casa en dirección al videoclub. Habíamos quedado ahí para empezar la búsqueda del profesor que nos habría de llevar a Donald. Al llegar, me encontré a Silvestre subiendo el cierre metálico de la entrada.

—¿Abres ahora?

—Son las diez —me respondió Silvestre sorprendido—. ¿A qué hora crees que vienen los frikis a por su dosis de pelis raras?

No respondí. Me había levantado y me había comportado como un autómata sin fijarme en la hora que era y sin pensar que, además de mí, había un mundo alrededor que tenía su propio ritmo. Me sentí como un jubilado que no tiene nada que hacer y para quien ir al ambulatorio a por recetas es la única ocupación en toda la semana. El día que tiene que ir está en la sala de espera una hora antes, impaciente ante lo que va a ser el mayor acontecimiento en días.

Estuve ayudando a Silvestre a colocar las películas que sus clientes habían devuelto el día anterior. Más bien, estuve siguiéndole como un perrito por entre las estanterías del local mientras mi amigo iba de un lado para otro colocando las cajas. Lo hacía a una velocidad sorprendente y, a falta de comprobarlo, en su sitio justo. Aunque, como dije al principio, siempre pensé que las ponía al azar.

—Vas a salir de esta, tío, ya verás —me dijo mientras reordenaba las películas en la sección de *Anime*.

—No sé, Sil... No estoy tan seguro. Sigo pensando en cerrar mi canal.

—Estás ofuscado, no sabes lo que dices.

—Lo sé de sobra. Ocurra lo que ocurra con Donald, creo que ha llegado el momento de pasar página.

Silvestre se dio la vuelta y me miró sosteniendo dos pilas de películas en sus brazos.

—¿Y qué vas a hacer, venir todos los días a la hora de abrir a comentar conmigo el programa de la tele de la noche anterior?

—¿La tele? ¿Qué era eso? —dije de broma. Era cierto. Pocas veces usaba la televisión para ver un programa que se estuviera emitiendo. Qué lejos quedaba mi infancia, cuando me sentaba con mis padres en el sofá para ver qué «echaban».

—Pues como cierres tu canal, así es como te veo.

—Un jubilado prematuro —reflexioné en voz alta.

—Y yo te agradezco que vengas a hacerme compañía de vez en cuando, pero vamos, todos los días...

—Desagradecido... Como si estar aquí todo el día encerrado fuera lo más estimulante que pudieras hacer en la vida.

—Se conoce gente, no te creas.

—¿A los seres que pasan por aquí les consideras «gente»?

—Les gusta el cine laosiano, ¿qué le van a hacer?

—¿Laosiano? —pregunté perplejo—. ¿Se hacen películas en Laos?

—Sí, Joel —dijo con resignación—. Se hacen películas hasta en Bostwana.

—Eso ya flipa. Pero flipa más que haya gente aquí que esté interesada en verlas.

—Cuanto más friki, más demandada —resumió Silvestre—. ¿De qué si no, crees que vive este videoclub? —Una explicación más que convincente.

Al cabo de una hora, ya habíamos terminado todo lo que Silvestre tenía que hacer, salvo, claro está, atender a la clientela. Pero una mañana entre semana como esa no parecía tener una gran afluencia de público.

—¿Y ahora, qué hacemos? —pregunté.

—Nada —dijo Silvestre con una sonrisa sentado en la banqueta tras el mostrador.

Admiré su temple. Así eran sus días, uno detrás de otro: iguales, repetidos, sin sobresaltos ni sorpresas. Me pregunté si yo sería capaz de llevar ese ritmo.

—Pues nada —respondí. Me acodé en el mostrador del otro lado. Estaba dispuesto a dejarme llevar por la placidez de la inactividad que me ofrecía Silvestre. Quería demostrarme que podía. Pero a los treinta segundos no aguanté más.

—¡Tío, esto es un coñazo!

—¿Qué? —preguntó extrañado. Por suerte, en ese momento entraron Connor, Jan y Flavia.

—¡Por fin! —exclamé. Todos me miraron extrañados excepto Connor.

—¿Qué? Son duras las mañanas en el templo del cine bizarro, ¿eh?

—Son insoportables —dije.

—Gracias, hombre —respondió Silvestre molesto.

—Yo no podría ser tú, Sil, lo siento —me justifiqué.

—El tema es que Sil tampoco puede ser Sil. Es una paradoja —dijo Connor, siempre dado a soltar la frase más enrevesada.

—¿Si Sil no es Sil..., entonces quién es? —preguntó Flavia a destiempo.

—Un ectoplasma —dije. Todos estallamos en una carcajada.

—Cabrones —dijo Silvestre sin evitar secundar la risa.

—¿Estamos listos? —preguntó Jan. Sacó su portátil de la mochila—. Traigo todo lo que necesitamos para cazar a nuestro hombre.

Me gustó que Donald pasara de ser *mi* acosador a ser *nuestro* hombre. Me hacía sentir menos solo. Los problemas, mejor en compañía.

—Pues vamos allá —dijo Silvestre con brío saltando por encima del mostrador.

—¿Y el videoclub? —pregunté desconcertado—. ¿Vas a dejarlo solo?

—¿Has visto entrar a alguien desde que he abierto? Nadie va a notar que está cerrado. —Y sin más se dirigió a la entrada. Nada que objetar. Le seguimos sin hacer más preguntas.

Un poco más tarde estábamos en mi coche rumbo a la primera dirección que habíamos elegido para empezar nuestra búsqueda.

—Porque sería patético —dijo Connor—, pero esto se presta a unos cuantos chistes sobre «los cinco» —que éramos los que estábamos ahí.

—¿Los de los libros? —preguntó Flavia.

—Solo nos falta el perro —insistió Connor.

—Y la cerveza. ¿Alguien entendió alguna vez por qué los niños de *Los Cinco* bebían cerveza? —pregunté.

—Para soportarse unos a otros —sonrió Connor.

El GPS del móvil de Jan —el encargado de toda la infraestructura técnica— nos llevó hasta las afueras de la ciudad. Recorrimos unas cuantas calles residenciales y desembocamos en una zona de chalés. La dirección que buscábamos era una casa unifamiliar rodeada de jardín por sus cuatro costados.

—O los niños que vienen a estudiar aquí tocan con amplificador, o es imposible que se escuche nada en la casa de al lado —dije. Las casas que la rodeaban estaban, por lo menos a diez metros.

—Aquí no es —dijo Silvestre.

Continuamos la ruta. La siguiente dirección era en un barrio del centro, en un bloque de viviendas. Subimos al piso y nos recibió un tipo de unos cuarenta años, despeinado y con gafas: el prototipo de músico atormentado. Nos enseñó la sala donde daba clase y donde tocaba él. Estaba totalmente insonorizada. De ahí no se escapaba ni una nota. Descartado.

Solo quedaban dos direcciones que comprobar. Poco a poco las conversaciones dentro del coche se habían ido apagando. Se percibía que la inquietud iba creciendo. Una de las dos podía ser la que nos condujera a Donald y ser conscientes de eso aumentaba la inquietud.

—¿Nadie ha pensado qué vamos a hacer si le encontramos? —preguntó Jan. Nadie respondió.

—Primero, hay que encontrarle —respondió Connor—. Como decía Hannibal Lecter: «vamos por partes».

Sonreí, pero era consciente de que, como los demás, estaba esquivando la decisión de qué hacer si encontrábamos a Donald. No quise agobiarme con eso entonces, aunque no me sentía cómodo con la idea de que, llegado el momento, tuviéramos que improvisar.

—Cara a cara, Donald seguro que pierde —dijo Flavia.

—No lo sabemos, igual mide dos metros —apuntó Silvestre.

—Digo que es muy valiente en la sombra. Pero en la realidad seguro que es un *cagao* —insistió Flavia—. Así son los ciberacosadores.

Todos la miramos sorprendidos.

—Ahí la has dado —dijo Silvestre.

—Pero si mide dos metros, mejor estar preparados —sentenció Connor.

Al llegar a la tercera dirección y detener el coche, nos quedamos callados sin decidirnos a salir. Había un cincuenta por ciento de posibilidades de que fuera ahí donde estaba Donald.

—Al toro, ¿no? —dije.

Nos abrió la puerta una mujer de unos sesenta años. Connor y yo —los encargados de subir— nos miramos. Algo nos decía que no era ese el lugar que buscábamos. Lo confirmamos cuando la venerable maestra nos dijo que acababa de regresar de una gira que la había llevado a varios países de Sudamérica.

—¿Cuándo regresó? —preguntó Connor.

—¿Están interesados en recibir clases o no? —preguntó la señora suspicaz.

—Sí, sí... —respondí—. Es que queríamos empezar ahora mismo y si está usted con el *jet lag*, pues como que no.

—Regresé anoche, pero estoy perfectamente —replicó la señora a quien todo ese teatro la estaba poniendo nerviosa. Si había estado fuera hasta la noche anterior, no era la vecina de Donald—. Podemos empezar, si quieren. ¿Traen el instrumento?

Connor y yo volvimos a mirarnos y, como era de esperar, se nos escapó la risa. Sin más, la señora nos cerró la puerta en las narices. Bajamos a la calle tronchándonos. No había sido tan gracioso, pero fue la forma que encontramos de liberar la tensión. Los dos éramos conscientes de que la siguiente visita que hiciéramos sería la definitiva.

Al llegar al coche, más tranquilos, Jan, Silvestre y Flavia nos miraron desconcertados.

—¿Estáis bien? —preguntó Jan.

—Tenéis los ojos empapados. ¿Os ha hecho llorar? —preguntó Flavia preocupada. Connor y yo volvimos a estallar en una carcajada.

—Lloran del descojone —dijo Silvestre—. Anda, vamos...

Subimos al coche y reanudamos la marcha. Las risas dieron paso al silencio. Un silencio tenso. Ahora sí, sabíamos que el enfrentamiento con Donald era inminente.

—Para —dijo Jan—. Es aquí.

Estábamos en una calle apacible, en un barrio como cualquier otro. Era mediodía y el ambiente estaba tranquilo. Aparqué el coche a unos metros del portal donde se suponía que vivía el profesor.

—Bueno, a lo mejor no le encontramos —dijo Silvestre. Era una posibilidad, claro, pero también lo era dar con él.

—Le vamos a encontrar, no os caguéis ahora —dijo Connor.

—Es puro cálculo de probabilidades —insistió Silvestre.

—Deja de ver pelis de Tom Cruise, tío —dijo Jan—. Ese tío está ahí y vamos a acabar con esto de una vez.

—¿Cómo hacemos? —pregunté. Habíamos visitado tres domicilios de profesores y no nos habíamos hecho esa pregunta, tal vez intuyendo que no eran nuestro destino. Pero ahora, en el momento de la verdad, sabíamos que esto iba en serio y que no podíamos subir a lo loco.

—Sabe *hackear* cuentas de YouTube, no luchar contra cinco adversarios —apuntó Flavia. Todos la miramos interrogantes—. Bueno, cuatro. Yo soy la que va a pedir ayuda.

—Pero, ¿vamos a luchar? —preguntó Silvestre, el que se mostraba más preocupado de todos.

—Haremos lo que haya que hacer —dijo Connor.

—A ver. —Intenté poner orden—. Esto no es un capítulo de *Narcos*. Esto es una charla entre adultos. No va a pasar nada, solo vamos a pillarle, llamar a la policía y arreglar esto como personas civilizadas.

—No, si civilizados somos —dijo Silvestre—. Pero él, no sabemos.

—Solo lo averiguaremos si nos lanzamos a la piscina —dije—. Es la única manera de saber si dentro hay agua.

Como en las visitas anteriores, decidimos que fuéramos Connor y yo quienes subiéramos al piso. Esta vez, sin embargo, el resto asumió un papel más relevante. Sabíamos que si había una posibilidad de dar con Donald, era esta y no queríamos correr ningún riesgo. Jan se pegó a la fachada del edificio con su portátil y empezó a buscar las redes *wifi* disponibles. La idea era localizar la de Donald y tratar de meterse en ella. No era *hacker* ni mucho menos, pero Jan sabía moverse bastante bien por el mundo cibernético. Flavia se puso los auriculares de su móvil y llamó a Connor, que llevaba los suyos, para estar en contacto permanente. Silvestre se sentó al volante de mi coche y lo puso en marcha, dispuesto a salir pitando en caso de que la cosa se pusiera fea.

—¿Estamos listos? —pregunté. Todos me miraron y, al segundo, estallamos en una carcajada.

—¿Qué somos, el puto Equipo A? —dijo Connor.

—Pero en guapos —dijo Jan.

—Vaya panda... —dije. La fantasmada que estábamos preparando la íbamos a recordar hasta el fin de nuestros días. Al final, los grupos de amigos necesitan de estas cosas para tener su propio pasado. Si no, ¿qué anécdotas íbamos a contar cuando fuéramos mayores?

Después del ataque de risa, volvimos a ponernos serios. Había estado bien para relajar, pero ya tocaba ponerse en marcha.

—Suerte —nos dijimos a la vez.

—Hoy empieza el día de tu libertad —sentenció Silvestre. Amaba las frases épicas, aunque no tuvieran sentido.

—Ni que estuviera en el corredor de la muerte —dijo Flavia.

Cuando entramos en el portal, Connor fue directo a los buzones para fotografiar todos los nombres. Uno de ellos podría ser el de Donald. Mientras, yo llamaba al ascensor. El piso en el que vivía el profesor era el tercero y pensábamos que Donald debía de vivir en el mismo piso, justo al lado. Aunque podía vivir encima o debajo. Para empezar, pensamos que ir al piso donde daba clase el profesor era lo mejor.

—Date prisa, Connor —le apremié cuando vi que el ascensor estaba llegando. Él debía subir en él y yo andando, para que no diera la casualidad de que nos cruzáramos con Donald. No sabíamos qué cara tenía, pero no dudábamos de que, si me veía a mí, de alguna manera se notaría—. ¡Va!

—Espera tío... —respondió Connor.

—¿Qué te pasa? No entendía por qué no venía.

—Deberías ver esto.

Miré hacia donde estaba Connor, frente a los buzones. Le vi con la mirada fija en uno de ellos. Me acerqué nervioso y desconcertado. Esperaba que no fuera una de sus bromas. No era momento de jugar.

—Connor, tío, como sea una de tus...

—Lee. —Y me señaló el letrero del buzón que correspondía al tercero B. Me acerqué y lo que leí me golpeó como una bola de hierro en la cara: «Joel Graham», ponía.

—¿Qué significa...? —dije mirando a Connor.

—Sabe que estamos aquí.

Sin pensarlo, corrí escaleras arriba. No me preocupé de esperar a Connor, que se quedó rezagado, hablando con Flavia por el teléfono.

—... no lo sabemos. —Alcancé a escuchar antes de desaparecer por las escaleras—. Creo que nos estaba esperando. Estad prevenidos.

Ya no escuché nada más. Subía los peldaños de tres en tres, ansioso por llegar al tercer piso. Hacía unos minutos, en la acera, había dicho a mis amigos que no se preocuparan, que el cara a cara con Donald iba a ser una charla entre adultos. Que, en cualquier caso, pasara lo que pasara, iba a quedar en manos de la policía. De alguna manera, esperaba que Donald, al verse descubierto, aceptaría las reglas del juego —ese que solo él conocía—, y firmaría la derrota. Le había pillado, no había nada más que hacer. Confiar en que el otro tiene la misma decencia que uno mismo es el gran error de la gente bien pensante, como yo. Al final, uno siempre está dispuesto a tender la mano cuando cree que las cosas están claras. Pero el adversario suele tener otros planes y aceptar la derrota no suele estar entre ellos.

No habría charla entre adultos, de eso estaba seguro. Donald sabía —¿cómo?, ¿por qué?— que estaba tras él. Por eso había puesto mi nombre en el buzón que correspondía a su piso. Era su manera de decirme que corría decenas de metros por delante de mí. Y corría al trote, sin esforzarse, dedicando tiempo a darse la vuelta y reírse de mí al verme desfondado, con la lengua fuera, esprintando para que la distancia no fuera cada vez más inabarcable. Poner mi nombre en el buzón era, además, una burla. Un gesto que me anulaba, me desposeía de mí mismo y me señalaba que no tenía el control, no ya de la situación sino de mi propia identidad. ¿Habría también cartas a mi nombre en el buzón? ¿Estaría yo, sin saberlo, viviendo una doble vida? Donald me había robado mi canal. ¿Me había robado también mi vida? No iba a ser una charla entre adultos, no. Iba a pelear hasta que no me quedaran fuerzas en los puños.

Al llegar al tercero, localicé la letra B y me dirigí hacia la puerta. Sin embargo, antes me detuvo algo. Tras la puerta contigua, se escuchaba la melodía de violín que me había llevado hasta ahí. Algún mocoso luchaba contra ella a las órdenes de su profesor y un metrónomo. Escucharla me dio un poco de pausa. Respiré hondo y con esa precaria y desafinada banda sonora de fondo, me dirigí a la puerta del piso de Donald.

—¡Joel, espera! —escuché por el hueco de la escalera. Connor subía a mi encuentro, pero en ningún momento me planteé esperarle. Era yo, Joel Graham, el mismo que figuraba en el buzón del portal, quien tenía que enfrentarse solo a lo que pudiera pasar desde ese momento en adelante.

La puerta estaba entreabierta. Con cautela, la empujé y esta dio paso a un largo pasillo en penumbra. No se escuchaba ningún ruido, tampoco se percibían señales de que ahí hubiera alguien. Si la puerta estaba abierta era por algún motivo; tratándose de Donald, tenía que querer decirme algo. No podía perder el tiempo en hipótesis. Tenía que enfrentarme a lo que fuera que pasara ahí y en ese momento deseaba con todas mis fuerzas que fuera a Donald a quien me encontrara.

Avancé lentamente. A ambos lados del pasillo había puertas que daban a habitaciones también en penumbra y vacías. Al final del pasillo me encontré con la única puerta cerrada. Era ahí donde iba a suceder todo.

—Joel... —Escuché a mi espalda. Era Connor quien, jadeante, había llegado a la puerta de la casa—. Espérame...

Giré un poco la cabeza sin llegar a mirarle y, al tiempo que volvía a mirar al frente, giraba el pomo de la puerta.

—Ten cuidado, tío... —dijo Connor, cuyos pasos escuchaba tras de mí.

Sin hacerle caso, abrí la puerta, despacio, apretando los puños, dispuesto a abalanzarme sobre Donald sin preguntar si era él quién me estaba esperando. Pero al abrir aún no pude resolver esa duda. Frente a mí, un sillón de despacho me daba la espalda. Era un sillón alto que no dejaba ver quién estaba sentado en él.

—¿Quién eres? —pregunté. No quería avanzar y ponerme delante. Esperaba que el inquilino de esa estancia diera el primer paso—. ¡Date la vuelta, cabrón!

Nadie contestó. Antes de decidirme a avanzar hasta la silla, miré de reojo la habitación. Nada más abrir la puerta, tuve la sensación de estar en un lugar conocido. En esos momentos, mientras decidía qué hacer, pude comprobar por qué: la mesa, el ordenador, los pósteres... Eran los mismos que tenía en mi estudio. ¡Estaba en mi propia casa! Una reproducción exacta de mi lugar de trabajo. Una broma macabra, un juego siniestro.

—Joder... —dijo Connor detrás de mí—. ¿Has visto esto?

Miré de nuevo hacia la silla. Quienquiera que fuera quien estaba ahí seguía inmóvil.

—¡Da la cara! —grité. Y sin esperar acción alguna, avancé hasta la silla y le di la vuelta. Lo que vi sobrepasaba cualquier expectativa que pudiera tener. Era yo quien estaba sentado. Yo, Joel Graham, un muñeco a escala natural, pésimamente hecho, desde luego, pero al que se reconocía con claridad. Donald había puesto mi nombre en el buzón, había reproducido mi estudio y me había calcado a mí. Sabía que iba a ir y su intención era que, al llegar, me cazara a mí mismo, convirtiendo el laberinto en el que me había metido en un lugar más y más enrevesado. Al verme, al reconocerme en el muñeco, algo en mi cerebro dejó de encajar. Era yo quien estaba en los dos lados del espejo. Era yo quien luchaba contra mí mismo. Era yo, solo yo, quien me tenía de adversario. Una puesta en escena perfecta para decirme que yo era mi enemigo.

—¡Para, Joel! —dijo Connor.

Sentí sus brazos agarrándome, tratando de detenerme. Me había echado sobre el muñeco —sobre mí mismo—, y había empezado a destrozarlo, a rasgar sus costuras y vaciarlo de su relleno, como si quisiera ajusticiarme a mí mismo, abofetearme, descargar contra mí mi frustración, mi incapacidad para salir del lugar donde Donald me había metido. Qué frágil es la mente humana. Qué frágiles son los hilos que nos sujetan. Solo hace falta rasgar uno para que el equilibrio se rompa y el títere que somos y que tanto tiempo dedicamos a mover por el mundo todos los días, empiece a cojear hasta enredarse en su propia estructura y caer desarmado. Donald bien lo sabía.

—¡Para, joder!

Connor logró separarme del muñeco cuando este ya solo era un amasijo de retales y gomaespuma.

—Mira —y me señaló a la mesa donde, como en mi estudio, estaba el ordenador y, como en mi estudio, estaba emitiendo para mi canal. Otro espectáculo en directo para todo el planeta. Más carnaza para la comunidad *youtuber*.

No me alteré. Al contrario, la agitación que me había poseído hasta ese momento, desapareció de golpe. Supe de inmediato lo que tenía que hacer. Fui al rincón donde en mi estudio tenía mi bate de beisbol —y ahí estaba—, lo empuñé y, de un golpe, destrocé la cámara, el disco duro y el monitor.

Fin.

Expediente 09/000317
Asunto: Ciberacoso.
Agente encargado: Inspector Lionel Harris.
Comisaría: Distrito Este.

Informe de hechos:

Tras denuncia realizada por Joel Graham por ciberacoso reiterado e intromisión ilegítima (hackeo de cuenta privada de la plataforma YouTube), con agravante de amenazas y exhibición pública de los hechos aquí relatados (se adjuntan pruebas p-001, p-002, p-003), el denunciante aporta nueva documentación a través de su representante, Kevin Albright. Dicha documentación relata la existencia de un inmueble desde el que, presuntamente, el denunciado como acosador —que responde al nombre en clave de Donald Collins—, ha realizado su última acción, consistente en reproducir el set de grabación de Joel Graham así como una reproducción a escala de su cuerpo y fisonomía. Dicho ardid tenía como finalidad, según el representante del denunciante, humillar públicamente al Sr. Graham y ser esta humillación retransmitida en directo por la susodicha plataforma.

Tras proceder al registro del inmueble y prestar declaración a los testigos (anexos d-001, d-001b, d-002, d-003, d003b, c y d), se inicia trámite de solicitud de documentación al Registro Municipal de la Propiedad para conocer la titularidad del inmueble. Se recibe respuesta favorable y se remite a esta oficina el expediente núm. Reg. 073/0017, donde figura como titular del inmueble una sociedad de capital de riesgo —Inverting, Ltd—. Al requerir a esta sociedad informe de alquiler del piso donde se han desarrollado los hechos denunciados, esta ha informado —aportando documentación: d-004— que el piso se hallaba desocupado desde hacía 11 meses.

Conclusiones:

Una vez recabada la información y los testimonios, se deduce que el denunciado se sirvió del inmueble de manera ilícita para llevar a cabo sus acciones de acoso al denunciante. Este inspector afirma que el denunciado —a la luz de las evidencias que así lo demuestran— no vivió en el inmueble ni realizó actividades domésticas más allá de las básicas.

Por alguna razón, el denunciante, por boca de su representante, el señor Albright, sospecha que el denunciado supo de su visita con anterioridad y preparó el escenario que reproducía su estudio privado con el fin de continuar con el acoso que lleva sufriendo desde hace un tiempo. Se apuntan en este sentido tres líneas de investigación que se encuentran abiertas en el momento de redactar este informe:

(1). Espionaje y seguimiento de Joel Graham por parte del denunciado.

En un primer barrido, se descarta la presencia de micrófonos o cámaras en el domicilio del denunciante. Pendiente de analizar sus dispositivos móviles de comunicación para descartar asimismo pinchazos telefónicos por parte del denunciado.

(2). Filtraciones desde su entorno: amigos personales y representante.

Tras interrogarlos y comprobar sus coartadas, se descarta su implicación con el denunciado.

(3). William Foster. Conocido como «Will», encargado del restaurante Asian Fusion, amigo del denunciante.

Línea de investigación abierta.

A la espera de resultados, este inspector muestra su preocupación por la reciente desaparición del denunciante, Joel Graham que, tras el incidente relatado en el piso que, presuntamente, utilizó Donald Collins, se halla en paradero desconocido. A pesar de tener la sospecha de tratarse de una desaparición voluntaria, remito al departamento correspondiente copia del informe para iniciar las investigaciones pertinentes.

Mientras tanto, este inspector y su departamento continúan la investigación del caso, actualmente en punto muerto al no tener pistas sobre la identidad del denunciado que responde al nombre de «Donald Collins», ni resultar posible seguir el rastro de su huella digital.

Sin otro particular,
Inspector Lionel Harris, comisaría Distrito Este.

12.

—¡No sé nada, os lo juro! —Will se defendía de las acusaciones de Kevin y Connor, que habían ido a verle al restaurante antes de que empezara su turno.

—Pues eres el sospechoso número uno —replicó Connor.

—¿De dónde vino la nota en el pedido de comida? De aquí. ¿Quién más, aparte de nosotros, sabía que Joel estaba buscando al profesor de violín? Tú. Demasiadas casualidades, ¿no crees?

—Ya hablé con el policía. Todo lo que tengo que decir ya lo he dicho. Y si encuentran pruebas, que me detengan.

—Deja a la policía en paz, ellos van a otro ritmo —advirtió Kevin—. Esto es entre nosotros.

—¿Me estáis amenazando?

—Sabemos que eres tú. No es una amenaza, es una realidad.

—Demostradlo.

Dicho esto, Will se dio media vuelta y dejó a Kevin y a Connor plantados en la ventanilla por donde entregaba los pedidos. Conscientes de que poco más podían hacer, salieron a la calle.

—Es como cuando encuentras un billete de cincuenta en el suelo pero cuando lo vas a coger el aire se lo lleva —dijo Connor al salir.

—¿Y si no es él, si Will de verdad no sabe nada?

—Entonces estamos jodidos.

Kevin y Connor echaron a andar decaídos. Después de la visita al piso donde Donald había puesto en escena la última humillación a Joel, este se había esfumado. El inspector Harris, acompañado de dos agentes, había acudido a registrar el lugar, pero no había encontrado nada que les llevara a Donald. Interrogó a Connor, a Silvestre, a Jan y a Flavia, así como a los vecinos y al profesor de violín. Nadie sabía nada, nadie recordaba haber visto a nadie. Era un fantasma. Donald no existía.

Sin que nadie se diera cuenta, Joel salió de la casa y desde entonces no se había vuelto a saber de él. Alertado por Connor, Kevin le buscó por todos los sitios donde creía que podía encontrarle, pero ni su madre ni nadie pudo dar fe de su paradero. Tenía el teléfono apagado y había eliminado sus cuentas de correo. El canal de YouTube estaba inactivo y, según informó la plataforma tras requerimiento judicial de Harris, no se había producido ningún acceso a la cuenta desde hacía varios días. Al principio todos pensaron que quería estar solo, aislarse unas horas, pero tras comprobar que no estaba en casa ni daba señales, no dudaron de que Joel había decidido desaparecer.

—¿Y si no ha sido voluntario? —preguntó Flavia cuando todos tuvieron la certeza de que Joel no se había ido solo a dar una vuelta.

—La policía lo descarta —aclaró Silvestre—. No hay evidencias de secuestro.

—¿Y cómo lo saben? —preguntó Jan.

—Tienen su manual, ¿yo qué sé? —replicó Connor molesto. Era el que peor lo estaba pasando. Se sentía responsable en cierto modo. Creía que no había apoyado a Joel lo suficiente.

—Por el perfil de Donald, la poli cree que si él le hubiera secuestrado, buscaría la manera de hacerlo público —aclaró Silvestre—. Es un exhibicionista, todo lo hace para darse notoriedad.

—Pues se ha quedado sin víctima —dijo Flavia.

—A lo mejor por eso se ha evaporado —resumió Connor.

Desde ese día, se pusieron en marcha para hacer su investigación paralela. Kevin y Connor habían ido a ver a Will varias veces, al principio simulando preocupación y buscando su complicidad. Luego, ya con las caretas quitadas, acusándole de estar del lado de Donald. Ninguna de las dos estrategias había dado resultado. Esa tarde habían ido a verle al restaurante a la desesperada y, con ello, habían abortado cualquier posibilidad de lograr sacarle nada a Will.

Caminaban en silencio, derrotados. Hacía casi una semana que no sabían nada de Joel. Tampoco de Donald que, tras su último numerito, parecía darse por satisfecho y no había vuelto a manifestarse. Ya había acabado con el niñato, debía de pensar.

—Eh, compadres —escucharon a su espalda.

Kevin y Connor se dieron la vuelta y vieron a Rick, el repartidor, acercándose a ellos por la calzada con la moto al ralentí.

—Síganme —aceleró la moto y se alejó unos metros. Más adelante, se subió a la acera y se escondió en un callejón.

Connor y Kevin observaron la manobra de Rick con extrañeza. A continuación, se miraron y, sin decirse nada, aceleraron el paso para encontrarse con él. En el callejón, entre cubos de basura, estaba Rick, que se había quitado el casco.

—Son amigos del *youtuber*, ¿no? —preguntó Rick.

—¿Quién eres? —preguntó Connor receloso.

—Un amigo —sonrió.

—No nos toques los cojones —amenazó Kevin—. ¿Por qué quieres hablar con nosotros?

—Tengo un mensaje de Joel.

—¿Qué han dicho? —Estaba impaciente por las noticias de Rick. Sabía que mis amigos estaban preocupados por mí y no quería que sufrieran más de la cuenta.

—No se lo han creído —respondió Rick—. Te lo dije, míster.

—Sí, sí se lo han creído. —Sabía que iban a desconfiar delante de él, no le conocían de nada, pero a solas seguro que daban mi mensaje como verdadero. Y, en cualquier caso, no tenían otro remedio, era lo único que sabían de mí desde hacía una semana. No podían agarrarse a nada más—. ¿Cómo está Melly?

—Engordando. Bien —Melly era su novia—. Le encantó la ropa de embarazada que le compré con tus cincuenta pavos.

—Me alegro.

Cuando decidí desaparecer, solo se me ocurrió recurrir a Rick. Era un riesgo, podía haber sido él quien metió la nota en mi bolsa a cambio de dinero o amenazado por Donald. Pero algo me decía que no, que Rick era de fiar. Y después de la propina que le di cuando me ayudó el día que le seguí durante su reparto, él también confiaba en mí.

—¿Qué hacemos ahora, míster? —preguntó.

—Esperar. ¿Quieres tomar algo? Sírvete.

Me había instalado en un apartamento turístico de la ciudad, en un barrio de las afueras. Lo había alquilado por internet desde un locutorio (no quería usar ninguno de mis dispositivos) y había pagado en efectivo. Después de la última jugada de Donald, no sabía hasta dónde había llegado en el acoso al que me estaba sometiendo. Sonaba a fantasmada, pero temía que conociera mis contraseñas o pudiera rastrear mis tarjetas. Por si acaso, pensé. Apagué mi teléfono y le quité la SIM y la batería. Compré otro de prepago aunque no había llamado a nadie en todos esos días salvo a Rick. A mi madre le mandé por mi nuevo aliado un mensaje escrito para que no se preocupara. Rick me contó que, tras leerlo, solo dijo:

—Este se cree que está en una película de espías. —Señal de que no estaba preocupada por mí en absoluto. Y le dio varios *tuppers* con comida.

Todo sucedió muy rápido. Tras destrozar la cámara y el ordenador en el falso set de grabación que Donald había construido recreando el mío, me quedé en un estado de letargo que, ni mis amigos, ni el inspector Harris, ni Kevin, que apareció un poco después, lograron disipar. Les escuchaba hablar, hacer hipótesis, especular sobre si había pasado esto o lo otro. Sentado en el suelo, solo podía responder con monosílabos. Al cabo de un rato, me di cuenta de que todo el mundo estaba más preocupado por encontrar algún indicio o relatar una y otra vez lo que había sucedido que por saber cómo estaba yo. Cuando me levanté del suelo y me dirigí a la puerta, nadie reparó en mí. Salí a la calle y me puse a andar sin rumbo. Me sentía traicionado. No tenía duda de que alguien había dado el soplo a Donald, si no, ¿cómo había podido preparar todo eso en tan poco tiempo? Todos me parecían sospechosos y, al mismo tiempo, inocentes. ¿Connor, mi mejor amigo, ácido pero incapaz de romper un plato? ¿Jan, el más puro y transparente de todos ellos? ¿Flavia, todo bondad e inocencia? ¿Silvestre, colega de la infancia, mi compañero fiel pase lo que pase? ¿Will? Solo podía ser él, pero seguía sin querer creérmelo.

Caminando por las calles se me hizo de noche. No quería volver a casa, pensé que a lo mejor había micros escondidos. No quería llamar a nadie ni conectarme a internet. Llegué al límite de la ciudad que marcaba una carretera de circunvalación. Más allá, no podía continuar caminando. El ruido de los coches pasando a gran velocidad era insoportable, pero gracias a él, al tener bloqueados los sentidos del oído y la vista (solo veía coches pasar a la luz de las farolas), pude encontrar la solución dentro de mí. Recordé una anécdota de Cruyff que había leído no sabía dónde. Ante un partido importante, preguntó a sus jugadores cuál era la mejor habilidad del delantero rival más peligroso. Alguien levantó la mano y dijo que su mayor talento era desmarcarse de los defensas. Cruyff preguntó qué podían hacer ante esa circunstancia. Nadie se atrevió a responder al maestro. Al cabo de unos segundos, el entrenador dio la solución: «si la mejor cualidad del delantero rival es desmarcarse, que no le marque nadie, así no podrá hacer lo que mejor sabe». Y eso decidí hacer: si la mayor habilidad de Donald era cazarme, iba a dejar de ponerme a tiro. Era la única manera de dejar a Donald sin nada que hacer.

—Esta tarta está padre —dijo Rick mientras engullía una porción de tarta de queso que había comprado en una pastelería dos calles más abajo.

—Llévate la que queda, si quieres.

—No, míster, que Melly está que se lo come todo y no puede coger peso.

—Toda para ti, ¿eh, mamón?

Rick rió y se sirvió otro trozo. En la semana que llevaba en el apartamento, solo salía para comprar víveres. Haber desaparecido no significaba que me rindiera. Al contrario. Empezaba la remontada. Y ese partido lo iba a ganar.

—¿Qué demonios significa esto? —preguntó Silvestre mirando el papelito encima del mostrador.

—Shhhh... —advirtió Kevin. Un cliente había entrado en el videoclub y Kevin no quería correr riesgos.

—Tranquilo, es Alan, es de toda la vida. ¿Qué pasa, Alan? —dijo Silvestre saludando a un chico de unos veinte años, desaliñado y con pinta de no haberse lavado el pelo en los últimos diez años. Alan desvió la mirada asustado y se perdió por los pasillos de estantes.

—Demasiado cine asiático —puntualizó Connor.

—Sed discretos, igualmente, no sabemos quién puede oírnos —insistió Kevin.

Los cinco miraban el papelito como si fuera un jeroglífico imposible de resolver. Y en cierto modo lo era.

—¿Y decís que os lo ha dado el repartidor del restaurante? —preguntó Jan.

—Sí, de parte de Joel.

—Y no ha dicho nada más.

—No significa nada —apuntó Flavia—. Es para decirnos que está bien y que está tramando algo.

—«Solo sigo deseando que hubiera una manera de demostrarle que no le pertenezco, que soy más que una pieza en su juego» —leyó Silvestre.

—Es de *Los juegos del hambre* —dijo Flavia. Todos la miraron sorprendidos—. No quiere decir más que eso: que sigue luchando, que no se ha rendido.

—Menudo gilipollas —dijo Kevin.

—Eh... —respondió Jan molesto—. ¿Por qué dices eso? Ha tenido el detalle de comunicarse con nosotros.

—¿Para qué? Llevamos una semana buscándole por todos lados, acosando a Will, dando el coñazo a Harris... Y lo único que hace es mandarnos una frasecita de una peli.

—Es del libro —puntualizó Flavia. Kevin la miró con recelo—. Pero vamos, que seguro que sale en la peli, también —corrigió Flavia intimidada por la reacción de Kevin.

—Dice que «desea que hubiera una manera» —dijo Silvestre—. Nos quiere decir que aún no sabe cómo.

—No creo que haya que tomárselo de manera literal —dijo Connor—. Si es una frase de la peli..., del libro —corrigió—, viene así.

—Si ha contactado con nosotros es porque ya sabe qué va a hacer —apuntó Kevin.

—O porque necesita ayuda —sugirió Flavia. Kevin se abstuvo de mirarla, no quería intimidarla otra vez.

—Pero, ¿cómo podemos ayudarle?

—Esperando a que vuelva a dar señales de vida —respondió Jan—. ¿Qué otra cosa podemos hacer?

—¿Qué os ha dicho Will? —preguntó Silvestre cambiando de tema.

—Lo de siempre, que no sabe nada.

—¿Le creéis?

—Yo qué sé —respondió Kevin de mala gana.

—No —negó rotundo Connor—. Pero esto es como lo de los políticos, mientras no se pueda demostrar, puedes pasarte la vida negándolo todo.

Alan se acercó al mostrador con varias carátulas en sus manos, pero se detuvo a unos pasos. Silvestre levantó la cabeza.

—Acércate, Alan, son colegas.

—Yo... Yo... —tartamudeó—. Vu-vuelvo otro día. —Y se dispuso a dejar las películas e irse sin ellas. Silvestre salió de detrás del mostrador antes de que se diera media vuelta.

—Tranqui, Alan. Te las apunto aquí. —Le cogió las películas, había por lo menos diez—. Te vas a poner morado, ¿eh?

—Ya... Ya las he vi-visto.

—Lo tuyo sí que es vocación. —Terminó de apuntar las referencias en un papel.

—Es po-por los detalles.

—Tráelas cuando quieras, sin prisa.

—Gra... Gra... gracias, Si... Sil... vestre —respondió Alan con una gran sonrisa de felicidad, como si poder devolver las películas fuera de plazo fuera la mejor noticia que iba a escuchar ese día.

—¿Y se va sin pagar? —preguntó Kevin extrañado.

—Tiene bono anual. Es cliente VIP —dijo Silvestre regresando tras el mostrador.

—Más bien cliente «psych» —puntualizó Connor.

—Gracias a tíos como él, tengo trabajo, un respeto.

—¿Quién es Souza? —preguntó Flavia sin venir a cuento.

—¿Perdón? —respondió Connor molesto. Había veces que no podía con las salidas de su amiga.

—¿A alguien le suena ese nombre? —insistió.

—No, cariño —respondió Jan— ¿Verdad? —preguntó a todos con cara de «no entiendo nada».

—¿Por qué lo preguntas? —preguntó Kevin. No quería mostrar interés antes de saber por qué Flavia preguntaba por ese nombre.

—Bah, una tontería, seguro.

—Vaya noticia —dijo Connor con ironía.

—No, Flavia, seguro que no lo es —insistió Kevin—. ¿De dónde te ha venido ese nombre?

—Seguro que no es nada. Pero estaba mirando la nota de Joel y esas letras están un poco más marcadas.

Los cinco bajaron la mirada hacia el papelito al instante. Como había dicho Flavia, algunas letras estaban ligeramente más oscuras: «Solo sigo deseando que hubiera una manera de demostrarle que no le pertenezco, que soy más que una pieza en su juego». Era muy sutil, pero no podía ser casualidad que se marcaran precisamente esas letras.

—Pero que igual es el boli que ha usado, que a veces sueltan más tinta —trató de quitarse méritos Flavia.

—Eres una genio —dijo Kevin con una sonrisa que seguramente hacía semanas que no usaba. Era también una manera de recuperar la confianza que había perdido con Flavia hacía unos minutos.

—¿Ahora te das cuenta? —le replicó Connor con ironía.

—¿Qué pasa, Kevin, por qué sonríes? —preguntó Jan.

—Así es como Joel nos está pidiendo ayuda. Quiere que formemos parte de su plan.

—¿Sabes qué significa eso de «Souza»? —preguntó Silvestre desconcertado.

—¿Tenéis algo que hacer ahora? —preguntó Kevin. Los cuatro lo miraron interrogantes.

Kevin condujo en silencio pero con una sonrisa. Connor, Jan, Silvestre y Flavia se apretaron en su coche sin hacer demasiadas preguntas pero con la curiosidad a flor de piel.

—Es mejor que seamos discretos, no sabemos quién puede estar escuchando —repitió Kevin antes de salir del videoclub. Y con ese tono de misterio emprendieron la marcha.

Al cabo de unos minutos, llegaron a la zona de oficinas donde Kevin y Joel se habían encontrado con Souza, el comercial que quería contratarle para lanzar una marca de refrescos hacía unos días. Kevin aparcó el coche en una calle lateral al edificio donde estaba la oficina de Souza.

—Subid vosotros —dijo Kevin señalando a Connor y Silvestre—. Es ese edificio, planta doce. La oficina que buscáis está al final del pasillo.

—Pero, ¿a qué vamos? —quiso saber Silvestre, al que tanto suspense le estaba sacando de sus casillas.

—Preguntad por Souza. Si está, decís que os habéis equivocado. Inventaros cualquier excusa y os vais.

—¿Y si no está? —preguntó Connor.

—Entonces el plan de Joel sigue adelante.

—¡¿Qué plan?! —dijo Silvestre atacado.

—Es mejor que subas tú —le dijo Kevin a Jan—. Sil está demasiado nervioso.

—Ni de coña —protestó Silvestre—. Subo yo.

—Aunque podrías darnos un poco más de información —dijo Jan.

—Luego. Ahora es mejor ser cautos. Seguro que así es como quiere Joel que lo hagamos.

Connor y Silvestre salieron del coche y doblaron la esquina camino al edificio donde se suponía que estaba la oficina de Souza. Kevin no se movió de su asiento y empezó a tamborilear en el volante.

—¿Podemos hacer algo nosotros? —preguntó Jan.

—Esperar.

Connor y Silvestre entraron en el edificio y pasaron delante de un mostrador donde un guardia de seguridad apenas levantó la vista de su periódico deportivo. El trasiego de personas en ese vestíbulo era continuo. En el directorio figuraban más de treinta empresas. Connor se detuvo frente a él.

—No hay ningún cartel en la planta doce —miró a Silvestre—. O no hay ninguna empresa o no ha tenido el detalle de anunciarse aquí abajo.

—Subamos —respondió Silvestre nervioso mientras se dirigía al ascensor.

Compartieron viaje con varias personas que fueron bajándose en los pisos intermedios. El último trayecto, desde el piso noveno, lo hicieron acompañados de una señora cargada de carpetas. Iba a la planta catorce, el único número iluminado en el panel, además del doce.

—¿Van a alquilar? —preguntó la señora suspicaz.

—¿Cómo? —respondió Silvestre.

—La planta doce está vacía, se alquila entera o por partes. ¿Van a alquilar?

—Sí. Entera —respondió Connor con rostro imperturbable.

—Ya... —respondió la señora desconfiada. No creía que Connor y Silvestre tuvieran pinta de alquilar una planta entera de un edificio de oficinas como ese.

—El garaje donde hemos creado Apple se nos ha quedado pequeño —aclaró Connor con sarcasmo antes de bajar del ascensor—. Tenga un buen día.

Salieron al pasillo sin tiempo de ver cómo la señora arrugaba la frente sin entender nada.

—¿Tenías que meterte con ella? —protestó Silvestre.

—Era una cotilla, que se meta en sus asuntos. Vamos.

Como les había dicho la señora, la planta estaba desierta. Recorrieron el pasillo con paso decidido pero sin perder detalle. A ambos lados se abrían puertas que daban a despachos o a salas de tamaño considerable que, paneladas, podían convertirse en oficinas independientes. La única puerta cerrada era la del fondo, a donde se dirigían.

—Aquí no curra nadie —dijo Silvestre.

—A no ser que busquemos a un *okupa*.

—No me gusta ir a ciegas sin saber qué buscamos ni qué nos vamos a encontrar. A mí, ese tío... —dijo Silvestre refiriéndose a Kevin.

—Olvídate de Kevin. Ahora ya estamos aquí. Solo prepárate para salir corriendo —dijo Connor con gravedad.

—¿Crees que puede ser peligroso?

—Pringado... —dijo Connor riéndose de su amigo.

Al llegar al final del pasillo, se detuvieron en la puerta. Acercaron la oreja pero, como supusieron, no escucharon ningún ruido dentro. Silvestre llamó con los nudillos.

—¿Qué haces?

—Ver si hay alguien.

—Así les damos tiempo a reaccionar, ¿no? No podemos darles ventaja —dijo Connor girando el picaporte decidido.

—¿A quién?

—A quién sea.

Empujó la puerta y entraron. Nada.

—Entonces se supone que el plan de Joel va como estaba previsto —dijo Silvestre.

—Eso parece. Aquí no trabaja ningún Souza. Ni trabaja nadie, vamos.

—¡Ahí los tiene!

Connor y Silvestre se dieron la vuelta y vieron a la señora del ascensor al inicio del pasillo. Junto a ella, el guardia de seguridad que vieron en la puerta de abajo. Al verlos, emprendió la marcha hacia ellos caminando deprisa y moviendo los brazos a ritmo.

—¡Chicos!

Connor y Silvestre se miraron y salieron a la vez de la oficina. Huir por el pasillo iba a ser imposible, tenían al guardia delante. Tenían que encontrar una alternativa.

—¡Por los despachos!

Connor y Silvestre entraron por una de las puertas del pasillo y empezaron a correr entre mesas vacías y sillas descolocadas. Los despachos estaban comunicados entre sí y solo tuvieron que esquivar el mobiliario en desuso para avanzar. Como era de esperar, al guardia se le ocurrió lo mismo y entró en la zona por otra puerta más adelante y fue en su contra.

—¡Crucemos!

Cuando ya tenían al guardia encima, salieron de nuevo al pasillo, no sin que antes Connor empujara una silla hacia él.

—¡Salta, Salta!

La silla golpeó en las rodillas del guardia y eso les permitió lograr una ligera ventaja que aprovecharon para correr por el pasillo en dirección al vestíbulo de la planta.

—¡Deténgales! —gritó el guardia a la señora, que observaba la persecución desde la puerta del ascensor con un gesto de pánico.

—No se moleste, señora —le dijo Silvestre.

—Vamos a contratar a gente. Si quiere, déjenos su currículum para el puesto de chivata —le dijo Connor al pasar frente a ella. Abrieron la puerta que daba a las escaleras y desaparecieron.

—¿Por qué no les ha retenido? —preguntó el guardia a la señora cuando llegó a su altura desfondado.

—Eran dos y más fuertes —dijo la señora asustada.

Connor y Silvestre bajaron los doce pisos quemando los escalones de cuatro en cuatro. Al llegar a la planta baja, trataron de disimular su urgencia por salir cruzando el vestíbulo con paso firme pero ligero. En la puerta de salida vieron a otro guardia de seguridad que hablaba por un *walkie*, sin duda con el guardia que les había perseguido arriba. Antes de arriesgarse a ser vistos, sin siquiera mirarse entre ellos, Connor y Silvestre salieron corriendo a la calle.

—¡Eh, vosotros! —escucharon gritar al guardia de seguridad.

Sin mirar atrás, corrieron en dirección al coche de Kevin que, al verles, arrancó el motor y avanzó hacia ellos. Frenó cuando los tuvo a su altura.

—¡Dale! —le apremió Connor tras entrar y cerrar la puerta del asiento del acompañante. En ese instante doblaban la esquina tres guardias de seguridad.

—¿De dónde demonios han salido? —preguntó Silvestre tirándose, literalmente, sobre Jan y Flavia.

—¿Qué habéis hecho? —preguntó Kevin desconcertado.

—Lo que nos has dicho. ¡Acelera! —dijo Connor.

Kevin aceleró, pero los guardias salieron a la calzada para bloquearle el paso. Frenó, dio un trompo y salió en dirección contraria. Sus cuatro acompañantes le miraron alucinados.

—Soy de barrio, qué queréis —dijo Kevin con una sonrisa.

13.

—Joel insistía en que era un montaje. Yo no lo creí, pero tenía razón —reconoció Kevin un poco avergonzado.

Habían regresado al videoclub y Kevin les había contado toda la historia del anunciante que se presentó como Souza. También que, debido a lo que sucedió durante la entrevista que mantuvieron con él, se había distanciado de Joel.

—¿Ibas a dejar de representarle? —preguntó Silvestre incrédulo. Kevin no contestó—. Qué fuerte.

—No, no iba a hacerlo, pero quería tomarme un tiempo. Todo esto no solo le ha afectado a Joel.

Nadie contestó. Kevin había dado en el clavo: lo que llevaba sucediendo desde hacía unas semanas les había dejado a todos tocados. Un grupo de amigos es como un organismo, un ser vivo: cuando a uno de sus miembros le pasa algo, el resto del cuerpo se resiente. Esa era la amistad verdadera, aunque ser consciente de ello significara asumir mayores responsabilidades con tus colegas.

—Es muy fuerte, de todas maneras —resumió Silvestre.

—Ahora ya no sirve de nada juzgar a Kevin —intercedió Connor—. Lo importante es ver qué hacemos con lo que hemos averiguado.

—Sabemos que el anunciante era falso, como siempre sospechó Joel —empezó a decir Jan para ordenar las ideas—. Llevaba la melodía de violín en su teléfono...

—Eso ya era motivo suficiente como para creer a Joel —insistió Silvestre.

—Déjalo estar, tío —le reprendió Connor.

—Con lo cual —prosiguió Jan—, podemos asegurar que el tal Souza trabaja con Donald.

—O es el mismo Donald —apuntó Flavia.

—O es el mismo... —Jan se calló de golpe—. ¿Podría serlo?

—¿Quién sabe? —respondió Kevin—. Si era Donald, imitaba perfectamente el acento portugués.

—¿Podrías hacer una descripción de su fisonomía?

—¿Qué quieres, hacer un retrato robot? —se mofó Connor de Silvestre, que había dejado de lado el resentimiento por Kevin y había vuelto a subirse al carro de la investigación en su modalidad peliculera.

—Tampoco iba a servir de mucho —aseguró Kevin—. Creo que sería mejor investigar en la oficina. Tuvo que alquilarla alguien.

—Como el piso —respondió Silvestre resignado haciendo referencia al inmueble donde Donald había perpetrado la última humillación a Joel y que resultó estar a nombre de una sociedad de capital riesgo.

—Joel no quiere salir de donde está y espera que el trabajo de investigar lo hagamos nosotros. Tiene sus motivos, cada vez que ha hecho algún movimiento, Donald lo ha adivinado y ha respondido con una fuerza mayor. Si tenéis alguna idea mejor que investigar quién alquiló la oficina, estamos deseando escucharla.

Nadie dijo nada.

—Creo que pueden hacerlo Connor y Silvestre. Seguro que son muy bien recibidos en el edifico de oficinas —dijo Jan riéndose.

Rick terminó de subirse la cremallera de su anorak y se dispuso a irse. Había vaciado la nevera de mi apartamento convirtiéndola en nuevo desierto. Sonreí con ironía ante su esfuerzo por hacerme sentir como en casa.

—Gobi —dije.

—¿Qué dices, míster?

—No me salía el nombre. La llamaré Gobi. Sáhara ya está pillado. La nevera, digo.

—Tienes que salir a que te dé el aire, empiezas a decir cosas sin sentido —dijo antes de salir.

—Espera. —Rick se dio la vuelta—. Cuando dejes el último pedido, pasa por aquí antes de volver al restaurante, ¿vale?

—¿Por?

—Tú pasa.

Rick se encogió de hombros y se fue. Tenía razón: tenía que salir un poco. Llevaba una semana encerrado y, aunque estaba bien, empezaba a dejar más espacio a mi cabeza que otra cosa. Y a la cabeza hay que darle margen, pero no dedicarle todo el tiempo: llega un momento en que acaba construyendo una realidad paralela que termina por devorarte. Pero tenía que aguantar, un poco más. Solo un poco.

Trataba de ponerme en el lugar de Donald: qué estaría pensando, qué esperaba que hiciera. ¿Imaginaba mi situación? Era probable. Había demostrado tener una mente aguda y perspicaz. O, simplemente, yo había actuado de manera tan previsible que le había resultado muy fácil adelantarse a mis movimientos. El mérito de mi hundimiento también era mío, pensé, y me colgué una medalla por mi incompetencia. Pero no estaba para machacarme en esos momentos. Tenía que reconocer mis errores si quería avanzar, pero una cosa era eso y otra regodearme en mi desgracia. Desde mi encierro había podido ver las cosas de otra manera. Parar, detener la batalla, eso era lo que necesitaba. Y después de hacerlo, me sentía con fuerzas, seguro de mí mismo. No tenía claro qué iba a suceder, ni si era un buen camino, pero, al menos, creía estar haciendo algo. Y eso, sabiendo cómo habían ido las cosas hasta entonces, era un paso de gigante.

Esperaba que mis amigos hubieran pillado el mensaje de *Los juegos del hambre*. Era una peli que nos gustaba a todos. Marcar en la frase las letras que formaban el nombre de Souza no solo era una manera de hacerles llegar el mensaje de forma secreta —no podía fiarme de nadie, ni de Rick—, también sabía que les iba a gustar. Les estaba pidiendo ayuda, pero también les estaba invitando a jugar. Era nuestro código, era un detalle por mi parte hacerlo un poco más divertido.

Souza era la única pista que vi posible. Tras quemar la vía del profesor y ver que la nota en la bolsa del pedido solo conducía a Will, recordé el incidente con el anunciante. Parecía descabellado, como dijo Kevin en su momento, podía ser una casualidad. Pero no tenía otra. Yo nunca creí que ese anunciante fuera real pero haber sido el origen de mi conflicto con Kevin lo había dejado en segundo término. Encerrado en ese apartamento, quité las capas que no me dejaban ver el mapa completo. Souza era un elemento aparentemente anecdótico pero importante. Había que tirar de ese hilo.

Me alegré cuando Rick me contó que Kevin estaba preocupado. Le había visto por el restaurante acompañado del «grandullón», es decir, Connor. No sabía qué pensaba de todo esto, ni si creía en mí de nuevo, pero me gustó que volviera a implicarse. Si luchar contra Donald había sido duro, hacerlo sin Kevin lo había hecho más difícil. No sabía qué iba a pasar en el futuro. Tampoco si iba a seguir con mi canal. Si dejaba YouTube no tenía sentido tener representante. Seguramente nuestros caminos se alejarían. También, incluso, si seguía haciendo vídeos. Donald había llegado a mi vida para cerrar muchas etapas. Kevin podía ser una de ellas.

Según se fue acercando la noche, empecé a ponerme nervioso. Me había acostumbrado a la tranquilidad anodina de no hacer nada y ser consciente de que esa noche me iba a poner en marcha me resultaba incómodo, como cuando te pones un jersey de lana antes de que haga el frío suficiente y te provoca picor en todo el cuerpo. Tenía que moverme, no podía esperar más. Era arriesgado, tenía la desventaja de no saber dónde estaba mi adversario. Pero, esta vez, Donald tampoco sabía dónde estaba yo. Salir de mi escondite podía volver a situarme en el centro de la diana y esa era, justo, la consecuencia que perseguía.

Poco antes de medianoche, Rick llamó a la puerta con los tres toques largos y tres cortos que habíamos establecido como contraseña.

—Hoy no puedo quedarme, míster, Melly lleva toda la tarde vomitando.

Rick se quedaba a veces un poco conmigo, solo por pasar el rato. No hablábamos mucho, pero me vaciaba la nevera y me hacía compañía.

—Tranquilo, no te voy a entretener. Quítate la ropa.

—Eh, eh...

Rick se echó para atrás y puso las manos entre él y yo, creando una barrera imaginaria que pretendía infranqueable en caso de que me atreviera a sobrepasarla.

—¿Estás de coña? —le dije—. Solo quiero tu uniforme de repartidor.

—¿Para?

—No lo necesitas, has terminado ya tu jornada, ¿no?

—¿Y mañana?

—Mañana pasas por aquí antes de ir a currar y te lo pones. También quiero las llaves de la moto.

—¡¿Qué dices, míster?! Tú sueñas.

—Necesito ser tú unas horas, nadie se va a dar cuenta.

—La moto es del restaurante.

—La dejaré ahí, tranquilo —afirmé—. Venga, tío...

Rick me miró desconfiado. Estaba seguro de que pensaba en Melly, en no perder el curro, en lo descabellado que sonaba todo. Pensó unos segundos sin dejar de mirarme y empezó a quitarse el anorak. En su balanza mental debió pesar más la seguridad que yo le transmitía que el riesgo que suponía dejarme su uniforme y su moto.

—¿Y cómo vuelvo a casa?

—En taxi, yo te doy pasta.

Eso terminó de convencerle y se quitó el pantalón de motorista que llevaba por encima del suyo. Tal cual se desprendía de las prendas, yo me las iba poniendo. Al final, solo me quedaba el casco.

—¿Qué tal? —pregunté. Con el uniforme, que difuminaba las formas del cuerpo, podía pasar por él sin problemas. Era importante que no se me reconociera. No podía salir tal cual, como Joel, y exponerme a que Donald me encontrara. No aún.

—¿Sabes conducir una moto?

—No, pero si lo haces tú no debe de ser tan difícil.

—*Hijueputa.*

Nos despedimos en la calle. Rick esperó a que arrancara la moto y saliera. Para hacerle temblar, simulé que perdía el equilibrio, pero en seguida aceleré y me alejé sin mirar atrás. Me imaginaba su cara de pavor. Podía hacerle perder el trabajo, era una posibilidad. Pensaba ayudarle a encontrar otro si eso sucedía. No iba a dejarle tirado.

Conduje por las calles casi desiertas hasta aproximarme al restaurante. Cuando estaba a un par de manzanas, aminoré la marcha, no quería llegar apresurado. Como había previsto, cuando tuve el restaurante delante, comprobé que todas las motos estaban ya aparcadas y que apenas había actividad. «Un pedido que se ha retrasado en la entrega», pensé como excusa para mí, metido de lleno en el papel de repartidor.

—¡Hasta luego, Rick! —escuché a mi izquierda. Me giré sobresaltado y vi a una pareja de compañeros de Rick alejándose por la calle. Saludé con la mano y deseé con todas mis fuerzas que no se les ocurriera interactuar conmigo. Bajo el casco y con el uniforme podía pasar por Rick, pero imitar su acento y sus bromas, eso ya era inalcanzable para mí. Por suerte, continuaron su camino sin prestarme atención.

Paré el motor y recorrí los últimos metros arrastrando la moto por el manillar. Cuando iba a dejar la moto en su sitio, junto a las otras, Will se asomó. Como había previsto.

—¡Joder, Rick! —dijo autoritario.

—Un pedido que se ha retrasado en la entrega —dije reproduciendo la excusa que había inventado hacía unos segundos. Mi voz sonó apagada dentro del casco. Will me miró extrañado. Algo no le cuadraba.

—¿Ha habido queja del cliente? —preguntó Will como rutina, aunque olía que algo no iba como esperaba.

Como respuesta, aparqué la moto y abrí la caja para sacar la funda térmica donde Rick llevaba sus pedidos para que no se enfriaran. Aunque no le estaba mirando, sabía que Will me observaba desconcertado.

—No, todo bien —respondí. Me acerqué a Will y me quité el casco—. De puta madre, vamos.

Will me miró como si acabara de ver a alguien al que despidió en un aeropuerto para siempre y esperaba no volver a ver jamás.

—¿De qué vas, Joel?

—De Rick, ¿no lo has notado?

—No hacía falta que te pusieras su ropa para venir a verme.

—Si vengo tal cual, a lo mejor sales corriendo.

—Tú flipas... —respondió. Se dio media vuelta y se dispuso a regresar al restaurante.

—Fuiste tú, ¿no? —pregunté antes de que cruzara la puerta.

—¿También lo crees?

Le miré a los ojos sin decir nada. Quería que fuera él quien se contestara.

—Da igual lo que diga, no me vas a creer. Igual que tus amigos —y volvió a encaminarse al interior.

—No, no te creo —dije. Will se dio la vuelta de nuevo.

—Entonces, ¿por qué no me dejáis en paz?

—Porque solo pudiste ser tú.

Will me miró en silencio. Le vi como el falso culpable que teme auto inculparse diga lo que diga. O el culpable que calcula su margen de error para no perder la confianza que acababa de mostrarle.

—¿Por qué? —Quería saber qué pensaba yo y eso le señalaba. No era su mejor respuesta, pensé.

—Nadie más pudo avisar a Donald.

—¿Has pensado que, tal vez, no le avisó nadie?

—Sí. Por eso estoy aquí.

Volvimos a quedarnos callados. Toda la confianza y camaradería que nos habíamos mostrado hacía unos días se había convertido en distancia y recelo.

—Creo que ninguno de los dos podrá demostrarlo —dije—. Hasta que termine todo.

Seguí mirándole a los ojos en busca de cualquier signo que me desvelara que anunciar el final de Donald significaba anunciar el suyo. Pero mantuvo la misma expresión, sin apartar los ojos de los míos.

—¿Y dónde nos deja esto? —Era la cuarta vez que me respondía con una pregunta. No quería manifestarse, no quería darme un solo centímetro de ventaja.

—¿Me lo dices tú? —respondí preguntando también. Podíamos estar así hasta la mañana siguiente.

—Déjalo, tío. —Y se metió dentro.

Me alejé del restaurante con una sensación extraña. No estaba seguro de que Will me hubiera traicionado y eso no me dejaba definir mis sentimientos. Podía odiarle y también podía sentir confianza. Podía todo mientras no supiera si me la había jugado o no. Esa noche no supe si había sido Will. Tampoco esperaba averiguarlo. Siempre cabía la posibilidad de que se derrumbara, claro, pero nunca entró en mis planes que lo hiciera. La visita tenía otra finalidad y para ello había que esperar.

Kevin había ido al registro de la propiedad, había merodeado por el edificio de oficinas, había, incluso, subido a la planta catorce en busca de la señora que había delatado a

Connor y a Silvestre el día anterior. Sacó sus dotes de periodista y enlazando una historia con otra, consiguió que la mujer largara de todo y terminara hablando hasta de sus hijos.

—Tiene uno de veintisiete que trabaja en Stuttgart, ingeniero aeronáutico —les explicó apoyado en el mostrador del videoclub.

—¿Y el otro? —preguntó Flavia con curiosidad. Era irrelevante para la investigación, pero no podía quedarse sin saber el desenlace de la historia familiar de la señora.

—Una chica. Tiene veinte, se ha operado las tetas y quiere ser *tronista* —dijo con cierto desprecio.

—¿Para qué va a estudiar, si enseñando culo gana lo mismo? O más —dijo Silvestre también despectivo.

—Qué juventud —sentenció Connor.

—Y de Souza, ¿qué? —preguntó Jan impaciente.

Kevin les contó que, tras escuchar las penas de la señora —su marido se había quedado en paro con cincuenta y siete años y estaba pendiente de una operación de vesícula—, se fue con la certeza de que la oficina de la planta doce, la que supuestamente alquiló Souza, llevaba vacía más de seis meses.

—La última empresa que estuvo ahí fue una empresa de venta de yogurt helado por internet. Según la señora, fracasó, nunca llegaban en buen estado al cliente.

—Vender helados *online*. Hacía tiempo que no escuchaba una tontería semejante —renegó Connor.

—Así que la «okupó» —dijo Jan desanimado—. Sin registro, sin contrato...

—Pero vosotros le visteis ahí, alguien más pudo verlo —insistió Silvestre.

—La señora, no. Y se sabe los cotilleos de todo el edificio. El contable de la planta tercera tiene un lío con la secretaria de la séptima —dijo Kevin impostando voz de cotilleo televisivo.

—Cualquiera puede entrar ahí. Pudimos hasta Sil y yo... —dijo Connor.

—La reunión no duró ni quince minutos. En cuanto nos fuimos, Souza salió... y aquí no ha pasado nada —explicó Kevin.

—¿Qué haces? —preguntó Silvestre a Jan, que tecleaba en su móvil.

—*Googleo* «Souza».

—Seguro que sale —respondió Connor.

—¿Se te ocurre algo mejor?

La búsqueda de Jan, como era de esperar, no dio ningún resultado. No se molestó ni en anunciarlo. Los cinco se habían quedado callados, mirando a ninguna parte, desanimados.

—Lo peor de todo es que seguimos sin poder ayudar a Joel —resumió Jan.

—¿Creéis que está esperando nuestra respuesta? —preguntó Silvestre.

—No tiene otra cosa —dijo Kevin.

—Ni tiene a nadie más —añadió Connor.

—Menudo montaje —sentenció Silvestre—. Hay que tener imaginación para colarse en una oficina y montar ahí una reunión. Con el riesgo de que te pillen, que a tu amiga, la señora, no se le escapa una.

—¿Será guionista? ¿Escritor?

—O eso, o ve muchas películas.

—Actor —dijo Flavia.

—¿Actor? —preguntó Connor—. ¿De dónde deduces que Donald es actor? Ha hecho de todo menos actuar.

—Donald, no. Souza.

No hicieron falta más explicaciones. Los cuatro estiraron la espalda y levantaron la cabeza, señal de que el desánimo que les había invadido quedaba atrás. La deducción de Flavia era sorprendente, como todas las suyas, pero esta vez, no sabían si porque estaban desesperados o porque había dado en el clavo, nadie la cuestionó.

—¡Lo contrató Donald para hacer ese papel! —dijo Silvestre como una gran revelación.

—¿Estáis seguros? —preguntó Connor—. ¿Qué clase de actor aceptaría hacer algo así?

—La profesión está complicada, Connor. Y todo lo que sea ganar un dinero... —le explicó Kevin.

—Actor y portugués.

—O brasileño.

—No debe de ser muy difícil de encontrar.

14.

A media tarde, escuché los pies de Rick arrastrándose por el pasillo del rellano del apartamento. Antes de que tocara la puerta con nuestra contraseña, abrí.

—No he llamado, míster —me advirtió Rick sorprendido, como si necesitara que me lo recordara.

—Sabía que eras tú.

—¿Y si te llegas a equivocar? —Rick cerró la puerta preocupado. Parecía que era a él a quien no debían encontrar. Se había metido en el papel hasta el fondo.

—Tienes una forma de andar que se escucha desde la calle. Tú como espía ibas a durar cinco minutos.

El comentario debió de dolerle porque se quedó clavado en mitad del saloncito del apartamento sin hacer su viaje habitual a la nevera.

—Puedes visitar a Gobi, me acaban de subir la compra.

—¿A quién? —Seguía sin entender el paralelismo de mis neveras con la geografía. A pesar de eso, se dirigió a la nevera y buceó entre los estantes a ver qué podía pillar.

—¿Quién está embarazado, tú o Melly?

—Es que la ansiedad me da hambre, míster. Este juguecito me tiene atacado.

—Ya... —dije intentando transmitirle compasión. Su papel estaba llegando a su fin. Me dio pena, me había acostumbrado a sus visitas—. He comprado los batidos esos que te gustan.

—¡Guau! —cogió todo el pack y lo metió en su mochila. Al ver mi cara de sorpresa, se sintió obligado a justificarse—. Es que a mi Melly le encantan.

—Así está luego, vomitando toda la tarde.

Sin hacer caso de mi advertencia, cerró la cremallera y echó un vistazo a la estancia.

—¿El uniforme? Tengo que ir al curro.

—Ahí lo tienes —señalé una silla—. La moto está en el restaurante.

—¿Me vas a explicar por qué todo ese lío ayer? —dijo mientras se ponía los pantalones sobre los suyos.

—No. —Y reí—. Mejor que no sepas nada.

—Soy un agente sonámbulo, ¿eh? —dijo divertido.

—Más bien zombi. Va más contigo.

—Mal parido... —Terminó de ponerse el anorak y cargó su mochila a la espalda—. ¿Vengo luego?

—No. Ya no.

Su sonrisa se desdibujó. Entendió que nuestra colaboración estaba terminando. Bajó la mirada sin saber qué decir. Esperando a que hablara yo, me imagino.

—Solo una cosa —dije. Rick levantó la cabeza esperanzado—. Hace tiempo que no sé nada de Will y me da pena. Es buen tío. Si pregunta por mí, ¿le dirás dónde estoy?

—¡Pero, míster! ¿No te escondías de él también?

—No, él no tiene nada que ver. Estoy seguro —afirmé con rotundidad—. No quiero llamarle, ya sabes, por si acaso. Pero me gustaría verle.

—Como quieras.

—Gracias por todo, tío.

—De nada, míster. Estás un poco *zumbao*, pero molas.

Sonreí y nos quedamos uno frente al otro sin saber cómo despedirnos. Darnos la mano me parecía demasiado formal; un abrazo, demasiado cercano.

—¿Puedo? —preguntó Rick.

Agradecí que fuera él quien resolviera mis dudas y esperé a que diera el primer paso. Sin embargo, en cuanto afirmé con la cabeza, Rick se dio media vuelta y se dirigió a la nevera mientras se descolgaba la mochila y abría la cremallera. Sin cortarse, la empezó a llenar de todo lo que pudo.

—¡Gracias, Míster!

Sonreí de nuevo. Sí, dejarme saquear la nevera era la mejor manera que teníamos de despedirnos.

Podía parecer sencillo. Un actor de mediana edad que supiera hablar portugués y cuyo rostro Kevin conocía. Solo había que buscar en las webs de agentes y en las guías de actores. Todo lo más, ir a algunas agencias de casting. Pero no. Después de estar buscando todo el día, no habían conseguido dar con él.

—A lo mejor se lo trajo de Portugal —sugirió Jan.

—A ver, que Donald es muy listo, pero traerse un actor de fuera... Como si esto fuera una superproducción —respondió Connor.

—Es una superproducción —dijo Silvestre—. No de pasta, pero sí de puesta en escena. Ha *hackeado* cuentas, ha fabricado muñecos, ha montado escenarios...

—Después de esto le fichan en Hollywood, fijo —dijo Connor con ironía.

—Tiene que aparecer —insistió Kevin, que no estaba dispuesto a rendirse—. Puede que no sea actor.

—Entonces, lo llevamos crudo —dijo Silvestre.

—Actor, vendedor, comercial, empresario... —recitó Flavia. Se calló cuando comprobó que todos la miraban—. Es todo lo que sabemos de él.

—Un vendedor es una especie de actor —sugirió Jan—. Tiene que convencer a los demás de que lo que te ofrece es mejor que lo que ofrece el otro.

—Un charlatán —dijo Kevin—. Eso es, alguien que no vive de actuar aunque no deja de actuar en todo el día. No le hizo falta contratar a un actor. Jan, busca empresas portuguesas que estén en el país. Pero no las importantes. Las cutres, si puede ser.

Jan se puso a ello. A su alrededor, los otros cuatro se quedaron mirando la pantalla de su móvil como si de ahí fuera a salir el propio Souza.

—Si me miráis, me bloqueo —protestó. Su impaciencia era tal que, si no miraban a Jan no sabían qué hacer—. ¿No tenéis móvil vosotros?

Todos a la vez, sacaron sus teléfonos y empezaron a buscar. El terreno a explorar era grande y no había un término de búsqueda claro: «empresas portuguesas», «comerciales portugueses», «vendedores callejeros»... Era difícil filtrar la búsqueda y, al mismo tiempo, discriminar los resultados útiles de los que no sumaban nada. Absortos en sus pantallas, Connor, Kevin, Silvestre, Jan y Flavia no abrieron la boca en un buen rato. Eran cinco seres con las cervicales dobladas a cuarenta y cinco grados ajenos a cualquier realidad que no fuera el rectángulo vertical de su pantalla. Nadie se preocupó en anunciar presuntas pistas buenas ni en maldecir los callejones sin salida a los que les conducía la navegación. Al final fue Jan quien rompió el silencio.

—No sé esto... ¿Puedes mirar? —preguntó a Kevin, que se acercó veloz junto a Jan—. Vienen fotos de los miembros de la plantilla.

Kevin estuvo viendo las fotos una a una.

—Joder... No le reconozco en ninguna. Entre lo pequeño que se ve y que el día que le conocí debía de estar caracterizado...

—Aquí hay una noticia sobre un despido... —dijo Connor leyendo en su pantalla— ...de un empleado de nacionalidad portuguesa. Trabajaba en una empresa de aquí, pero era portugués.

—¿Y? —preguntó Silvestre sin entender.

—Pues que es trabajador y portugués, ¿yo qué sé?

—Aquí nada, Jan. Gracias —dijo Kevin mientras le devolvía su móvil.

—Mira a ver, Kevin —le dijo Connor tendiéndole su teléfono. Kevin lo cogió, pero no miró la pantalla de inmediato.

—A lo mejor podríamos apuntar los sitios donde estamos buscando. Seguro que hemos mirado las mismas webs sin saberlo —dijo. Bajó la mirada al teléfono de Connor—. ¡Es este!

Todos levantaron la cabeza. Era la noticia que esperaban, pero escuchar que había llegado, les dejó paralizados. Kevin deslizaba su dedo índice por la pantalla.

—Fernando Oliveira —dijo—. Se llama Fernando Oliveira.

—Y le echaron hace cuatro meses por reducción de plantilla junto a otros cincuenta trabajadores. Por eso fue a juicio —explicó Connor.

—¿Y por qué salió en prensa? —preguntó Silvestre.

—Parece que fue contratado en su país y luego traslado aquí y consideraba que se le debía aplicar la ley portuguesa. Un lío de la leche.

—¿Y al final? —pregunto Flavia.

—Se fue a la calle, como está mandado. ¿O es que alguna vez se le da la razón al trabajador? —respondió Connor.

—¿Qué empresa era? —quiso saber Silvestre.

—Una de informática —dijo Connor—. Lo típico: echan a los trabajadores mayores y contratan a jóvenes para pagarles la mitad. El mundo funciona de puta madre.

—¿Dejamos de quejarnos y buscamos al tal Oliveira? —apremió Kevin.

—Ya lo tengo —dijo Jan sonriente.

—Eres un crack —le felicitó Silvestre.

—Bueno, sale en la guía telefónica, tampoco tiene tanto mérito —respondió Jan, no tanto por humildad como por señalar la poca sagacidad de sus amigos.

—Recordadme que mañana vaya a ponerle una vela a san Google —dijo Connor.

—¡¿A qué estamos esperando, entonces?! —dijo Silvestre. Todos se pusieron en disposición de salir pitando.

—Vamos Connor y yo —dijo Kevin. El resto lo miraron desconcertados—. Hay que sonsacarle, mejor ser discretos.

Nadie discutió la decisión. Kevin había demostrado con la señora del edificio de oficinas que sus dotes de persuasión eran infalibles. No tenía por qué ser de otra manera esta vez.

Una hora más tarde, Kevin aparcaba su coche frente a un edificio de viviendas del centro.

—Subo contigo, ¿no? —preguntó Connor.

—Mejor quédate aquí. Él me conoce a mí y en cuanto me vea sabrá a qué vengo. Si me ve contigo se pondrá en guardia. Es mejor que vaya solo.

—Sí, no tienes pinta de que le vayas a hacer nada.

—Practico kickboxing, por si no lo sabías.

—¿Tú? —preguntó Connor incrédulo. El físico de Kevin no invitaba a pensar que pudiera practicar cualquier arte marcial.

—¿Quieres comprobarlo?

—Mejor no —respondió Connor por si acaso.

—Solo estate atento, por si pasa algo.

Salió del coche y entró en el portal. Connor se sentó al volante. Era lo único que podía aportar en el plan: estar preparado por si Kevin salía de ahí corriendo.

Dentro del edificio, Kevin subió en el ascensor hasta la planta donde Jan había descubierto que vivía Oliveira. Al llegar, se dirigió a la puerta del piso. Respiró hondo. Por un instante regresó a sus tiempos de estudiante, cuando estuvo un tiempo trabajando como comercial de aspiradores sin bolsa para pagarse los estudios. Era el mejor de su equipo: ama de casa que le dejaba pronunciar la segunda frase cuando le abrían, ama de casa que le compraba un aspirador. La empresa quiso contratarle como vendedor fijo, pero Kevin tenía metas más altas y, aunque pasó por el ingrato mundo del periodismo *online*, vistos los resultados, la decisión de seguir su camino no había sido desacertada. Hasta ahora. Como Joel, no sabía qué iba a suceder con su trabajo cuando todo eso terminara. Porque iba a terminar, no le cabía duda. Llamó al timbre.

Al abrir, Oliveira echó el cuerpo hacia detrás y achinó los ojos, como si necesitara enfocar el rostro de Kevin, bien para verle mejor, bien para recordar quién era. Iba sin gomina, lo cual aumentaba el volumen de su pelo. Llevaba unos vaqueros viejos y una camiseta de propaganda, muy lejos de la imagen que conoció de él en la oficina.

—Ah —dijo al fin Oliveira—. Tengo algo para ti.

Sin más explicaciones, entornó la puerta y dejó a Kevin de pie en el felpudo sin haber abierto la boca, algo incomprensible en él. Desconcertado, empujó la puerta unos centímetros y asomó la cabeza. Solo pudo ver un recibidor minúsculo en penumbra. Dio un bote cuando Oliveira abrió la puerta con energía.

—Es para ti —y le entregó un pequeño sobre.

—¿Qué significa esto? —dijo Kevin sin cogerlo.

—Yo no sé nada. Solo sé que, cuando tú o tu amigo el *youtuber* vinierais, os tenía que dar esto. —El acento portugués seguía igual de marcado que la primera vez que lo vio como Souza.

—¿Quién se lo dio?

—¿Lo coges? Porque a mí me la trae floja.

Mantuvo el sobre en el aire entre él y Kevin durante unos segundos durante los cuales, no desviaron los ojos el uno del otro. Oliveira hizo gesto de retirar el sobre del alcance de Kevin.

—Como quieras.

—Espere —Kevin no cogió el sobre, pero puso el pie dentro del recibidor para evitar que cerrara la puerta—. ¿Quién es Donald?

—Yo solo estoy aquí para darte esto. Si lo coges, bien. Si no, lo tiro a la basura.

Kevin cogió el sobre. Quería saber más, pero prefería amarrar lo que ya tenía seguro. No apartó el pie aún.

—No sé si sabe —dijo.

—No, no sé.

—Su amigo está en búsqueda y captura por la policía. No va a salirse con la suya.

—¿Mi amigo? —Y soltó el aire por la nariz para subrayar lo cómica que le parecía esa idea. Señaló el pie de Kevin—. ¿Me permites?

—Usted puede ayudarme a acabar con esto de una vez. Es lo mejor que puede hacer. Cuando pillemos a Donald, usted tendrá que explicar qué hacía en ese edificio de oficinas vendiéndonos una marca de refrescos.

—¿Estás seguro de que yo estuve ahí? —dijo con aplastante tranquilidad. Era cierto, nadie podría demostrarlo.

—¿Por qué le ayuda?

—Yo solo me ayudo a mí mismo.

A continuación empujó la puerta sin encontrar la oposición de Kevin, que retiró su pie. Escuchó cómo Oliveira se alejaba de la puerta hacia el interior de su piso. Sobre el felpudo, sintió el corazón latiendo fuerte y profundo, pero lento. Había estado cerca, pero cerca, ¿de qué? Del mal, pensó. El corazón respondía a la sensación de haber atravesado el pánico de un extremo a otro, como si este fuera un espacio cerrado y abarcable. No era Oliveira quien lo inspiraba, pero sí era él el que sugería la presencia de la mano de Donald manejando los hilos de esa situación. Unos hilos invisibles. El desconcierto de no saber, de no prever, de estar a merced de esa mano, era la definición del miedo que sentía Kevin en ese momento y que, comprendió, debía de haber sentido Joel las últimas semanas. Bajó la mirada al sobre y se descubrió temblando.

—¿Y si Donald estaba ahí? —preguntó Connor cambiándose de nuevo al asiento del copiloto mientras Kevin entraba.

—¿Y qué iba a hacer, meterme hasta la cocina?

—Déjame verlo —dijo pidiéndole el sobre.

—No, espera.

—¿No quieres saber qué mensaje hay dentro?

—Sí, pero no aquí.

Se guardó el sobre y arrancó. Connor no dijo nada. Se puso el cinturón y miró hacia el frente.

De nuevo en el videoclub, los cinco miraban el papelito en silencio. Habían abierto el sobre con toda la ceremonia que merecía, con cuidado, tratando de rasgarlo lo menos posible.

—Son unas coordenadas de GPS —dijo Jan.

—Ya.

El mensaje no escondía mucho misterio. Solo lo que podía haber ahí, en el lugar que indicaban dichas coordenadas.

—Está a las afueras. Parece que es un parque —completó Jan, que había buscado las coordenadas en su móvil.

—¿Deberíamos ir? —preguntó Flavia.

—Es un mensaje para Joel —dijo Kevin, que volvió a meter el papel en el sobre.

—Sí, pero deberíamos saber por qué ese lugar, qué pretende Donald hacer ahí.

—O qué hay.

—El portugués dijo que era para ti o para Joel, ¿no? —preguntó Connor.

—Para quien fuera a recogerlo. Donald se imaginaba que Joel llegaría en algún momento a la casa de Oliveira, pero cabía la posibilidad de que fuera yo. Yo no tengo nada que ver en esto, solo soy el representante —dijo con un punto de amargura.

—¿Y si no hubiéramos descubierto a Oliveira? —preguntó Silvestre, preocupado por los detalles del juego.

—Hubiera buscado una manera de seguir jugando. Es un ludópata —respondió Connor.

—Un ludópata siniestro —apostilló Jan.

—No, no puede seguir jugando. Para que el juego continúe necesita otro jugador —siguió Kevin—. Y desde que Joel desapareció, se ha quedado solo, necesita que vuelva.

—Y Joel, ¿querrá volver?

Nadie respondió. Eran conscientes de que enfrentarse a Donald era peligroso y que, por lo visto hasta entonces, no había muchas garantías de que fuera a salir bien. Pero ningún jugador se levanta de la mesa hasta que el juego ha terminado.

—Sí, seguro que sí —sentenció Kevin—. Si no, ¿por qué nos ha pedido ayuda?

—Lo que me preocupa es cómo podemos seguir ayudándole ahora.

—No podemos. Esto es entre Joel y Donald —dijo Connor.

—¿Cómo vamos a darle el mensaje? —preguntó Flavia.

Esa tarde fue la más desesperante de todas desde que me había escondido en el apartamento. Tenía la sensación de que había culminado una fase de mi estrategia y la espera hasta empezar la siguiente se me estaba haciendo eterna. Influía el hecho de saber que estaba solo, que Rick no iba a volver a aparecer para saquearme la nevera. También el no poder saber si mis amigos habían averiguado algo acerca de Souza. Estaba a ciegas, tras haber repartido las cartas, y sin saber cómo iba la partida.

Según iba anocheciendo, mi ánimo también se fue apagando. Todos los movimientos que había hecho, y que había meditado hasta sus últimos detalles, me parecían inútiles. A falta de respuestas, solo dudaba de ellos. Podían fracasar y nada hubiera servido. Lo peor era que no tenía un plan B. Si no funcionaba lo que había previsto, tenía que volver a empezar de nuevo y, encerrado y solo, pensar en ello se me hacía un mundo. Me tumbé en el sofá con las luces apagadas. Tenía que esperar, solo eso. Unas horas. Tener la calma y la tenacidad de mi adversario. La paciencia necesaria para que fueran los otros los que arriesgaran con una respuesta. Si me precipitaba alteraría el orden de las cosas. El orden. Las cosas. El precipicio.

Me despertaron los golpes en la puerta. Me había quedado dormido en el sofá y no sabía qué hora era. Me puse de pie de un salto y me quedé inmóvil, recuperando la consciencia. ¿Habían llamado o lo había soñado?

—Míster... —Escuché un susurro al otro lado. Si era Rick, había llamado de manera azarosa, sin respetar nuestra contraseña—. Abre, míster —insistió.

Traté de acercarme con sigilo a la puerta, pero dormido como estaba, tropecé con varios muebles por el camino. Si quería dar a entender que no había nadie en casa, había fracasado estrepitosamente. Aun así, al llegar a la puerta miré por la mirilla. Rick no pintaba nada ahí, menos después de habernos despedido esa tarde. Era sospechoso, pero comprobé que venía solo. Abrí y entró como un rayo.

—¿Qué haces aquí, tío?

—Buf... —resopló—. Creía que no estabas.

—¿Qué hora es?

—Las doce o así. No he podido venir hasta el último reparto. Hoy había fútbol en la tele y la gente se ha puesto a pedir comida como loca.

—Rick, relaja, me estás poniendo de los nervios. —Estaba acelerado y sudoroso, no era tranquilizador que hubiera aparecido así a esas horas—. ¿Qué cojones haces aquí?

—Te traigo algo —y empezó a buscar en los bolsillos, lo cual le llevó unos segundos.

—¿Qué es? —pregunté al límite de mi paciencia.

—Ya lo ves tú. Joder... —no daba con ello—. Aquí.

Rick sacó un pequeño sobre y me lo entregó. Lo cogí temeroso.

—¿Quién te lo ha dado?

—El gafitas y el grandullón —dijo refiriéndose a Kevin y a Connor—. Qué misterio, míster. Han hecho un pedido que he tenido que llevar a tomar por saco. Ahí me lo han dado.

Respiré un poco más tranquilo. Habían actuado con cautela y me gustaba. «A tomar por saco» era la casa de Kevin, que vivía en el campo, a unos diez kilómetros de la ciudad. También respiré al saber que el mensaje era de ellos. Pero antes debía comprobarlo. Abrí el sobre que observé que ya había sido abierto. Dentro encontré dos papeles. El primero era el que yo les había hecho llegar con la frase de *Los juegos del hambre* donde se marcaban las iniciales de Souza. Bien, lo habían pillado. El segundo era uno con unas coordenadas de GPS escritas.

—¿Todo bien, míster? —preguntó Rick desde la nevera. Era incorregible.

—Sí, sí...

Solo podía significar una cosa: habían investigado la pista de Souza y habían llegado a esas coordenadas. ¿Cómo? Lo ignoraba, pero era un paso gigantesco. Una de las líneas que había abierto daba sus frutos. No sabía qué quería decir, pero pronto lo averiguaría.

—Me tengo que ir, tengo que llevar la pasta de las últimas entregas para que cierren la caja —dijo Rick masticando.

—Claro. Muchas gracias, tío.

—¡Nos vemos!

Salió por la puerta a toda velocidad al tiempo que engullía un pedazo de sándwich. Me asombraba la velocidad con la que se preparaba la comida este chico.

—¡Rick! —grité unos segundos más tarde. Había olvidado preguntarle algo. Corrí hacia la puerta y me asomé al rellano. Ni rastro. Al poco escuché la moto de reparto en la calle. Corrí hacia la ventana y vi cómo se alejaba—. Mierda.

Aún no había soltado la nota de mis manos. Me senté en el sofá y volví a mirarla. Souza me había llevado a unas coordenadas. ¿Qué querría decir? Las introduje en mi móvil y comprobé que eran de un parque a las afueras. Había estado alguna vez. Era uno de esos parques de césped y hormigón, caprichos de urbanistas con aires de grandeza. Pero, ¿qué tenía que suceder ahí? ¿Tenía que ir? ¿Cuándo? Sonó el teléfono del apartamento. El fijo. No había sonado ni una sola vez desde que me había instalado ahí. Sorprendido, lo busqué.

—Ve —escuché al otro lado de la línea.

—¿Donald?

—Ve. Mañana, a las nueve de la noche. Solo, por supuesto. —Opté por no decir nada.

Bienvenido de nuevo, Joel.

Y colgó. Dejé el teléfono en su base y estiré las piernas. Sonreí. Donald me citaba al día siguiente en el lugar que marcaban las coordenadas. Los dos caminos se unían por fin. Por eso, a pesar de que mis expectativas se habían cumplido, mi sonrisa era amarga. Tenía que ver con la razón por la que me había llamado Donald, eso que olvidé preguntarle a Rick, que no era otra cosa que saber si Will había preguntado por mí. Ya sabía la respuesta. Sí, lo había hecho. Y Rick le había dicho dónde estaba. Y Will se lo había dicho a Donald.

Bingo.

15.

El tono de Donald al teléfono me había sonado sombrío. Me había recordado más al Donald de la primera llamada, ese oscuro vendedor de muñecos fabricados a mano, que al Donald eufórico y seguro de sí mismo que había conocido después. Mi retirada del tablero le había afectado, llegué a pensar. Un jugador sin adversario, un delantero sin defensa del que desmarcarse. Pero me costaba creerme esa idea. No le veía tan frágil. Me costaba creer que una simple retirada como la que yo había llevado a cabo pudiera afectarle de manera profunda. Sí podía haberle impacientado o irritado, pero deprimirle, no. Era lógico por su parte pensar que, tarde o temprano, yo iba a reaparecer de alguna manera. Solo era cuestión de tiempo. Por eso me sorprendió escuchar su tono, parco y escueto. Me había hablado como un padre enfadado que no quiere dar demasiadas explicaciones a su hijo para que no se desate la ira que lleva dentro. Pero yo no era un hijo díscolo. Era su juguete, su entretenimiento.

Apagué las luces del apartamento y volví a tumbarme en el sofá. Había dormido toda la tarde y era imposible que volviera a hacerlo antes de bien entrada la noche. Me dediqué a mirar al techo y a observar las extrañas formas que hacía sobre este el reflejo de los faros de los coches que pasaban por la calle. Desde pequeño, ese había sido uno de mis pasatiempos nocturnos, acompañamiento visual a mis ensoñaciones infantiles, donde imaginaba ser esto o lo otro. De niño soñaba con ser futbolista, inventor, dueño de banco, millonario, playboy de la Costa Azul... soñaba con ser muchas cosas, pero nunca *youtuber*. Los sueños se cumplen, sí, pero deben de cumplirse esos que no recordamos, los que se desvanecen al despertar.

Tumbado en el sofá, esa noche, no soñaba. Solo observaba las formas que se dibujaban en el techo que, a veces, cuando se cruzaban dos coches que iban en dirección contraria, se yuxtaponían en un efecto que recordaba al de los caleidoscopios. No soñaba. No podía. Will me había traicionado. Eso era lo único que ocupaba mi cabeza. Desde que Connor le señaló aquella noche en mi casa, la sospecha siempre había estado ahí. Pero yo me resistía a creerlo. No era mi amigo, eso era cierto, aunque habíamos congeniado bien. No era eso lo que más dolía. Dolía verme engañado, utilizado. No podía asumir que los tentáculos de Donald hubieran llegado tan lejos, tan dentro. Había conseguido manejar mi voluntad sin que yo me diera cuenta. Y lo había hecho de la manera más fina, entrando hasta el lugar más íntimo de uno mismo: con una relación de amistad.

Saber que Donald había actuado con esa brillantez no explicaba el hecho de que Will me la hubiera jugado, en cualquier caso. No podía imaginar por qué un chaval de mi edad podía aceptar hacer algo así. ¿Dinero, chantaje? Hay que ser un vendido para participar en un plan tan perverso como ese. O estar muy desesperado. Pero, ¿qué sabía de Will como para imaginar los motivos que le habían llevado a actuar contra mí de esa manera? Nada. Las veces que nos habíamos visto solo habíamos hablado de mí. Le había contado mis problemas, mis preocupaciones, mis bajones y mis dudas. Y, a cambio, no había tenido siquiera el detalle de interesarme por él, por su vida o sus problemas. Estaba tan metido en mí mismo que no dediqué ni un segundo a mirarle. Me sentí egoísta y culpable. No solo porque si hubiera sido capaz de dedicar un poco de atención a esa persona que, parecía, se estaba preocupando por mí, a lo mejor hubiera adivinado sus intenciones; también porque delante tenía a alguien que, como yo, tendría sus problemas, sus angustias o sus desvelos personales. Y no se me había pasado por la cabeza preguntárselos. Solo era yo, yo y yo. Con Will fui tanto «yo», que, al final, se lo puse muy fácil a Donald. Mi ego había resultado ser la mejor arma para mi acosador; y Will, el canal de transmisión más eficaz. Cuando pasara todo, pensé, debía hacer un buen examen de conciencia. El cabrón de Donald, al final me estaba dando una lección. Es lo único bueno que tienen los perversos: al mostrarte la cara del mal —la suya y la de uno mismo—, te acaban enseñado algo, o mucho, de ti mismo.

De eso iba a encargarme después, cuando Donald fuera historia. O cuando lo fuera yo. Cuando el juego hubiera terminado. En esos momentos debía desprenderme de todo lo que no fuera esencial y centrarme en lo que tenía delante:

el encuentro al que Donald me había invitado para el día siguiente. El juego tenía unas normas difusas y un desarrollo imprevisible, pero sí tenía un objetivo, al menos para él: acabar conmigo. Sabía que me enfrentaba a la última ronda de la partida y que de ahí iba a salir el vencedor. Iba a ciegas, como tantas otras veces con Donald. Solo tenía el consuelo de pensar que, al menos esta vez, había llegado ahí con mis propios medios, no conducido por su mano. No era gran cosa, pero gracias a eso sentía que llegábamos en igualdad de condiciones.

Fue cuando amaneció cuando fui consciente de que en algún momento de la madrugada me había quedado dormido. No debía de haber dormido muchas horas, pero me levanté fresco y con energía. Me duché, me cambié de ropa, hice el equipaje y salí del apartamento. Lo miré por última vez antes de salir. Sabía que nunca más iba a volver ahí.

Al entrar en mi casa me sentí extraño. Había estado largos periodos de tiempo fuera, en vacaciones o por alguna gira, pero esta vez, el regreso me resultó diferente. Todo estaba como lo había dejado la última vez: el desorden, las películas apiladas, las cosas dejadas de cualquier manera, Sahara vacía... Nada nuevo. Haber estado fuera varios días no era el motivo de mi extrañeza. Era, más bien, la desconexión que había hecho en mi cabeza la que había convertido una semana en una inmensa distancia con todo lo que es mío. Fui al estudio. El ordenador estaba apagado, como lo dejé. También con eso sentí lejanía. No tuve la tentación de encenderlo, mirar mi cuenta de YouTube, cotillear por la red. Estaba fuera de todo eso. Aún no sabía si para siempre.

Sin dudar, hice lo que tenía previsto hacer. Saqué una mochilita y metí en ella una cámara y un par de baterías. Era temprano, tenía todo el día, pero quería resolver eso cuanto antes. Dejé la mochila en la entrada y me dirigí al salón. Encendí mi móvil, el de siempre. Al poco empezaron a entrarme mensajes y notificaciones de llamadas. Todas eran de los primeros días de mi exilio. A partir del segundo, nada. Bien, ya estaba conectado, solo me cabía esperar. No tuve que hacerlo mucho tiempo. Al cabo de un rato, llamó Kevin.

—He visto que estabas en línea —dijo.

—Ya veo que te alegras de verme —respondí. El aislamiento me había hecho olvidar el desencuentro que había vivido con él. El enfado había quedado atrás. Además, me había ayudado y estaba agradecido.

—¿Ya tienes las maletas preparadas?

—¿Cómo? —¿De qué narices me hablaba?

—Sales de viaje, ¿no? —Seguí sin entender nada.

—¿Dónde estás, Kevin?

—Donde siempre, con café y donuts.

—Sube, anda.

Al poco, llamó a la puerta con los nudillos. Al verme, se quedó en la puerta, mirándome con desconfianza, como si dudara de que fuera yo, Joel, quien estaba frente a él. Me aparté para dejarle pasar.

—¿De qué me estabas hablando...? —dije para romper el hielo.

—Shhh... —me reprendió señalándose las orejas y el techo mientras abría mucho los ojos con un gesto de «¿estás loco o qué?»—. Tengo que ir a ver a mi tía, ¿me acompañas?

Entró en casa y cerró la puerta tras de sí.

—Como no dejes de hablar en clave, me voy a volver loco.

—¡Que si nos vamos a hablar a la calle, joder! ¿No ves que nos puede estar escuchando? —dijo perdiendo la paciencia—. ¡Hola, Donald! —gritó a todas partes.

—Tranquilo, no hay micros ni nada. Puedes hablar tranquilo.

—¿Cómo lo sabes?

—Porque sé quién me ha traicionado —Kevin me miró con los ojos muy abiertos, esperando una respuesta—. Pensé que eras tú, pero...

—Déjate de tonterías. ¿Quién ha sido?

—Will.

—Lo sabía.

Le conté la trampa que le había tendido con Rick, cómo había picado el anzuelo y la llamada de Donald la noche anterior tras saber dónde estaba gracias a él.

—Si es que no eliges bien tus compañías.

—Lo sé, tú eres una de ellas.

Kevin sonrió. No bajaba la guardia, pero estaba deseando hablar de lo que nos había pasado. Yo era consciente de ello y estaba dilatando el momento todo lo posible para hacerle sufrir.

—¿Qué vas a hacer con tu canal? —me preguntó.

—¿Te preocupa eso o quedarte sin curro?

—Joel... —me dijo a medio camino entre un reproche y una súplica.

—Por mi parte está todo olvidado —dije. Kevin alegró un poco el gesto aunque hizo todo lo posible para que no se le notara.

—Lo siento —dijo.

—No ha sido fácil para ninguno. Yo también lo siento.

Nos quedamos en silencio unos segundos. No sabía si procedía un apretón de manos, un abrazo o nada. Éramos colegas y entre colegas rara vez se hablan las cosas. Se hace un chiste y se pasa página.

—¿Amigos? —me dijo tendiéndome la mano.

—Un abrazo, anda —dije.

—Eres un hijo de puta —me dijo al oído.

—Pero no puedes vivir sin mí —respondí. Nos separamos de inmediato. No hacía falta más para firmar la paz.

Hablamos durante un rato de la peripecia para dar con Souza-Oliveira. De mi encierro, de Rick y su voracidad, de Will, de Connor, Silvestre, Jan y Flavia, a los que, aunque no lo quisiera reconocer, había cogido cariño. Parecíamos dos viejos amigos que se reencuentran después de muchos años y tienen un montón de cosas que contarse. Volvimos a sentirnos cómodos el uno con el otro. Éramos un equipo, estaba claro. Pasara lo que pasase, lo éramos para siempre.

—¿Cuándo es? —me preguntó de forma inesperada. Aunque no venía precedido por lo que estábamos hablando, supe de inmediato de qué estaba hablando.

—Es cosa mía.

—No pensarás ir solo, que ese tío está loco.

—Lo sé, pero esto lo tengo que resolver yo. No solo porque me lo ha dicho Donald, sino porque creo que es la manera de hacerlo. Esto solo se va a terminar cuando le tenga cara a cara.

—¿Y si pasa algo?

—¡¿Más?! —dije rompiendo a reír.

No quise despedidas, ni deseos de buena suerte, ni caras de compasión. No sabía a qué me iba a enfrentar, pero insistí a Kevin en que estuviera tranquilo y que, sobre todo, no hiciera nada. No quería que la cita con Donald saliera mal por incumplir sus condiciones. Éramos él y yo, nadie más.

Un par de horas antes de la cita, me colgué la mochila con la cámara al hombro y salí de casa. Quería ir tranquilo, paseando. Cogí un par de autobuses e hice el último tramo andando. El mundo giraba como si tal cosa, ajeno a mí y a mis problemas. Me hizo sentir pequeño, una anécdota entre las millones de cosas que estaban pasando a mi alrededor. Y me gustaba verlo así. Nada iba a cambiar si dejaba de hacer mis vídeos. Nada iba a cambiar si Donald había preparado algo para humillarme más. Nada... A no ser que el desenlace fuera trágico. ¿Iba a serlo? No quería pensar en ello.

Llegué al parque casi media hora antes de las nueve. Estaba anocheciendo y tan solo se veía a algunas personas con sus perros, unos cuantos ciclistas y varias parejas tumbadas en la hierba. El lugar donde me había convocado Donald era una gran explanada libre de árboles y de cualquier elemento decorativo. Un espacio diáfano, a la vista de todos. A uno de los lados, lejos, un pequeño parking y al otro, una colina que descendía hacia un paseo que discurría junto a un lago. Comprobé en mi móvil cuál era el sitio exacto que indicaban las coordenadas. Estaba situado en el mismo centro de la explanada. Me senté en la hierba, dejé la mochila a mi lado y comprobé que, desde ahí, debido a la altura a la que estaba, no veía más que césped a mi alrededor. Una circunferencia verde y redonda a mis ojos. Mirara donde mirara, el límite era la propia explanada, punteada en sus límites por farolas situadas a una distancia regular una de la otra. A las nueve sería de noche, calculé, y la luz de las farolas no llegaba donde yo estaba. El lugar donde Donald me había citado iba a quedar en penumbra. Un lugar cotidiano y extraño. A la vista de todos, pero escondido. Con luz, pero oscuro. Escenario de cualquier acontecimiento que pudiera suceder, desde el más inofensivo —la carrera de un perro—, a la agresión más cruel. Turbador.

Como predije, cada minuto que pasaba se ensombrecía más la explanada. Las parejas que salpicaban el césped fueron levantándose, bien para irse, bien para buscar un lugar más íntimo. Los perros espaciaron sus carreras a mi alrededor, señal de que sus dueños les llamaban para atarlos a sus correas y llevárselos a casa. Cada minuto, que agotó uno a uno, lentamente, todos sus segundos, trajo un cambio, y cuando quedaban tan solo un par de ellos para las nueve en punto, la calma reinaba a mi alrededor. Donald había estudiado el lugar y sabía que, aunque estuviéramos en un parque público y abierto, no íbamos a ser más que dos sombras solitarias en mitad del césped.

En esos dos últimos minutos sentí una paz que ya no recordaba. Me sentía tranquilo, en orden, con las piezas encajadas. No temía nada y estaba dispuesto a afrontar lo que tuviera que suceder. El viaje al que me había empujado Donald desde que le hice la broma telefónica me había servido para alejarme un par de metros de mí mismo y de lo que era mi vida. Me había visto desde fuera —literalmente: los vídeos y burlas a mi costa habían circulado por la red hasta la saciedad— y gracias a eso me había conocido un poco mejor. Me había puesto al límite, haciendo y diciendo cosas que jamás hubiera imaginado que haría o diría. Sin pretenderlo, me había asomado a una parte de mí que desconocía o, mejor dicho, que sabía que tenía pero nunca me hubiera atrevido a explorar: perder los nervios, la razón, actuar sin sentido, odiar, despreciar, sentir cómo enloquecía, tener impulsos violentos... Todo aquello que uno nunca quiere ver de sí mismo y que había sido parte de mí en las últimas semanas. Pasar por ello me hacía más fuerte. Enfrentarme a las sombras que todos tenemos pero que nunca afrontamos, las alejaba de mí. Era mejor «Joel» entonces que antes de Donald. Pasara lo que pasara, ahora era invencible.

—Bien, puntual —escuché a mi espalda.

—Gracias —respondí antes de darme la vuelta. Era un «gracias» por todo lo que acababa de reflexionar sobre el efecto que la experiencia de Donald había causado en mí, pero él no podía saberlo.

—Bien, educado. Veo que vas aprendiendo la lección —respondió Donald con sorna. No imaginaba que la lección que me había dado tenía una consecuencia bien distinta de la que él pretendía. No era la sumisión tras el castigo lo que había conseguido.

Me levanté y me di la vuelta. Donald estaba algo lejos, a una distancia inexacta: lejos para mantener una conversación de tú a tú; cerca para cualquier acción física. En la oscuridad apenas podía distinguir sus rasgos. Era un hombre más bien bajo y fornido. Recortado contra las farolas que se veían al fondo de la explanada, podía distinguir unos brazos y unas manos fuertes que mantenía separadas del cuerpo. No veía su cara, tan solo que era calvo y que dos matas de pelo alborotado crecían a ambos lados de su cabeza. Me vino a la cabeza la imagen de un científico loco.

—Aquí me tienes. Tú dirás —dije. Donald se tomó un tiempo en responder. Respiraba de manera intensa y profunda. Tal vez mi tranquilidad no entraba en sus planes—. Tómate tu tiempo, no tengo prisa.

—Es muy sencillo. Todo irá bien si haces lo que te digo.

—Soy todo oídos —dije extendiendo los brazos y abriendo las palmas de mis manos hacia él en señal de estar preparado para recibir lo que fuera.

—No me gusta ese tono.

—¿Ah, no? ¿Qué tendría que hacer, suplicarte, amenazarte, atacarte? Si hemos llegado hasta aquí es porque has ganado. Lo acepto. Soy buen perdedor.

—No, no lo eres —dijo rotundo. Se pasó la mano por la boca y acarició su mentón. Debía llevar barba, supuse, pero era imposible saberlo con tan poca luz—. Eres demasiado engreído como para aceptar la derrota.

—Eso era antes. Ahora ya no tengo nada. Me lo has quitado todo.

Donald soltó el aire por la nariz para puntuar mi afirmación. Le parecía irónico, supuse. Su resistencia a aceptar mi derrota empezaba a irritarme.

—No has entendido nada —dijo con un tono altivo—. Esto no es más que una anécdota, un borrón. Mañana te levantarás y todo seguirá igual.

—No creo. He perdido mi canal, mi carrera como *youtuber*. No tengo nada —insistí.

—Sigues sin entender. No importa si haces vídeos o no. No importa si eres *youtuber* o vendedor ambulante. Lo que hagas es irrelevante. El problema eres tú.

—Así que esto ya no es una cruzada contra el mundo, vuelve a ser algo personal contra mí.

—No, amigo —hablaba desde tan lejos de mí, se creía tan por encima, que solo podía pensar en el hostión que se iba a dar cuando cayera—. Tú eres el muñeco, solo eso.

—Tanto fabricarlos te está comiendo el cerebro.

—Eres la imagen —se explicó—. El representante de un mundo detestable.

—Ya... —respondí con ironía—. Y tú estás aquí para arreglarlo.

—No —río—. No soy tan poderoso. El mundo es demasiado grande y yo demasiado pequeño. No puedo cambiar las cosas.

—Pues entonces, acéptalo. Vive y deja vivir.

Donald se quedó callado un buen rato. Pensé que si alguien nos observaba desde lejos, vería una estampa difícil de descifrar: dos hombres de pie, inmóviles, uno frente al otro, sin actuar. Nada se movía en una dirección o en otra. Era inquietante, sobre todo porque todo el mundo sabe que la materia nunca se detiene y que la pausa siempre es el preludio del movimiento. Y, tal y como estaba discurriendo la conversación, me era imposible adivinar cuál iba a ser este.

—Eso es lo que voy a hacer —dijo por fin—: dejarte vivir.

No dije nada. La cosa se ponía seria.

—Sin futuro —concluyó.

Fue el primer momento en el que moví mis piernas. Tan solo para cargar el peso en una en lugar de la otra. No sonaba bien lo que había dicho, nada bien.

—Así que vas en serio —dije con una calculada ambigüedad. No iba a ser yo quien sacara las conclusiones.

—Nunca he dejado de hacerlo.

Metió una mano en uno de los bolsillos de su abrigo y sacó de él una revólver. Di un respingo. Conociendo a Donald, podía ser uno más de sus trucos. Fabricaba muñecos, ¿por qué no iba a pensar que la pistola era falsa? Cogió el arma por el cañón y me la tendió.

—Cógela —dijo.

—Estás pirado —Me di media vuelta con la intención de irme. Era una reacción irracional: había una pistola en juego y no era ninguna broma. Sentí que el arma caía a mis pies. Me detuve.

—Cógela —insistió—. No me obligues a utilizar la mía.

Su afirmación me obligó a darme la vuelta. Donald seguía en su sitio, esta vez, tras mi ademán de alejarme, un poco más lejos de mí. Pude ver que me apuntaba con otra pistola. ¿De qué iba todo eso?

—Te dije que todo iba a salir bien si hacías lo que te decía. Cógela.

—No pienso hacerlo —respondí.

—Si no la coges, tendré que dispararte. Entonces sí que habrá terminado todo. Hazlo.

Mis opciones eran escasas. O cogía la pistola que Donald había arrojado a mis pies, o Joel Graham era historia.

—¿Y qué se supone que tengo que hacer?

—Cógela —insistió. Me agaché y cogí la pistola. Nunca había tenido una en mis manos. Nunca pensé que iba a tenerla. Era pequeña, pero pesaba. Un objeto macizo y compacto. Apenas podía controlar el temblor en mi mano—. Al principio impone, pero dentro de un par de minutos, cuando tengas que usarla, tendrás la sensación de que naciste para disparar. Le pasa a todo el mundo. Un arma da un poder que no se puede igualar con nada.

—No sé de qué va esto, pero se te está yendo la olla. Vamos a dejarnos de tonterías. No voy a usarla y tú tampoco. No creo que quieras acabar en la cárcel. Por si no lo sabías, hay hasta tres cámaras de seguridad grabando.

Señalé con la pistola hacia varios lados para indicarle los postes donde estaban las cámaras. Al llegar me había fijado en ellas. Me sorprendí al hacer ese gesto con la pistola en la mano. Donald tenía razón: muy pronto me acostumbraba a ser dueño de un arma.

—Lo sé. Y es la prueba que va a acabar contigo. Las imágenes mostrarán a Joel Graham disparando a un pobre hombre que solo se defendió de una llamada de teléfono desafortunada. Haya hecho lo que yo haya hecho, siempre apareceré como la víctima.

—¿Yo, disparándote? —pregunté perplejo.

—Si no, lo haré yo.

—Y acabarás en la cárcel —y volví a señalar las cámaras con la pistola.

—Y tú muerto.

El juego de Donald estaba llegando a un límite demasiado complejo. La elección que me proponía era irresoluble.

—Yo ya no tengo futuro —se explicó—. Tu llamada, tu actitud hacia mí me ha demostrado lo poco que valgo ya en este mundo. Que yo acabe en la cárcel es irrelevante. Igual que si muero. Eso sería, incluso, un golpe de suerte para el sistema, un estorbo menos para la sociedad: un hombre de mediana edad, sin trabajo, sin expectativas, solo molesta. En cambio tú... —Y meneó la cabeza para acentuar la ironía que veía en esa idea—. Tú eres lo que viene. Y eso es lo que importa.

—Por eso quieres matarme —afirmé.

—No, no quiero, a no ser que me obligues a hacerlo. Quiero que vivas, pero sin futuro, como un asesino. Eso es lo que quiero: despojarte de expectativas, que es lo que tú has hecho conmigo.

—Yo no he hecho nada. No soy tan poderoso.

—Eres el muñeco, Joel. Una metáfora. ¿Lo vas entendiendo?

Lo entendía a la perfección. Donald quería vengarse de un mundo que le había tratado mal, que le había utilizado en su etapa de plenitud y que, llegado el momento, le había arrojado a la cuneta. Acumulaba tal rabia contra la sociedad que mi irrupción en su vida le había servido como excusa perfecta para vengarse. No solo de mí —el muñeco, el representante casual de todo lo que odiaba—, sino de la humanidad entera.

—¿Qué eliges, tu vida o la mía?

—Las dos.

—Eso no es posible.

Donald apuntó hacia mí y, como un acto reflejo, sin pensarlo, le apunté yo a él.

—¿Lo ves? —dijo. No podía ver su rostro, pero sabía que sonreía—. La usas como si siempre hubieras tenido una.

Y era verdad. Apuntaba a su cuerpo y no era algo que hubiera premeditado. La perspectiva de morir me agarraba a la vida. Y vivir, en ese momento, implicaba apretar el gatillo de mi pistola.

—Está en tus manos. Y no tenemos toda la noche.

Frente a frente, nos apuntábamos mutuamente, como en una película de sicarios de Hong Kong. Respiraba de manera agitada y, a pesar de que el frío empezaba a caer en el parque, mi espalda sudaba. Mi cabeza intentaba resolver la ecuación con millones de operaciones a la vez. Ninguna daba exacta. No había solución. Si quería vivir, tenía que disparar.

—Eres un cerdo... —dije apretando la empuñadura de la pistola.

—Ha sido un placer —dijo Donald. Bajó el arma y abrió sus brazos para recibir el disparo.

Todo mi cuerpo temblaba. Cerré los ojos, no quería verlo. Yo, un chaval que solo se dedicaba a hacer vídeos para internet; uno cualquiera, que había dado con una tecla para divertir y entretener a la gente; yo, que quería vivir tranquilo, haciendo mi trabajo, saliendo con mis amigos, disfrutando de la vida... Yo, Joel Graham, estaba a punto de convertirme en un asesino. A punto de tirar mi vida por la borda. A punto, como quería Donald, de quedarme sin futuro. Sin abrir los ojos aún, posé el dedo sobre el gatillo. Era el último segundo antes de que mi vida fuera a cambiar para siempre.

—¿Qué pasa aquí? —Escuché. Abrí los ojos y vi a Donald agitado, mirando en todas direcciones—. ¿Les has llamado tú, imbécil?

Miré a los lados y vi un montón de sombras acercándose hacia nosotros desde todos los ángulos de la explanada. Era una legión, una masa de personas que avanzaban con paso firme hacia nosotros. Por un momento pensé que no era real, que estaba muerto, que Donald, al final, me había disparado y eso era «la muerte», el lugar donde vamos cuando dejamos de vivir y esas, las sombras que vienen a recogernos. Solo la agitación de Donald delante de mí me hizo apartar esa idea. Me miró y volvió a apuntarme.

—Solo tenías que seguir mis indicaciones —dijo con ira mientras me apuntaba de nuevo. Iba a dispararme, no tenía duda, pero esta vez no le apunté con mi pistola. La masa de gente avanzaba sin pausa y ya estaban a menos de veinte metros.

—No sé nada, Donald, ¡lo juro!

—Eres un mierda —me apuntó dispuesto a disparar.

—¡No, papá! Joel no sabe nada.

«¿Papá?». La voz había sonado a mi espalda y tanto Donald como yo, que me di la vuelta, vimos a alguien abriéndose paso entre la gente. Sabía a quién pertenecía la voz, pero no podía creerlo. La figura que se acercaba logró abrirse paso y llegar hasta nosotros.

—He sido yo —dijo Will—. Yo los he llamado.

—¿Es tu padre? —pregunté alucinado.

En ese momento la masa de gente que se acercaba llegaba a nosotros y se detenía a unos pasos formando un círculo. En primera fila pude ver a Kevin, a Connor, a Silvestre, a Jan y a Flavia que encabezaban la concentración y que, al llegar a nuestro lado, miraron desafiantes cruzando los brazos.

—¿Qué has hecho? —preguntó Donald severo a Will.

—Esto es una locura, papá —dijo Will sollozando—. Tenía que hacer algo para pararlo —Donald, incapaz de decir nada, miró a su alrededor—. Son tus seguidores, Joel. He hecho un llamamiento en la red y, ya ves, siguen de tu lado.

—Pe-pero... —Se me habían agotado las palabras. Solo sentía una inmensa bolsa de aire a punto de explotarme en el pecho.

—Will, hijo... —Donald se derrumbó y cayó de rodillas en la hierba. Will se acercó y le quitó la pistola de la mano.

—Papá... —Will le pasó la mano por el hombro—. No podías hacerlo.

—¡Dejen paso!

Harris, acompañado de varios agentes uniformados lograron llegar junto a Donald y Will. Llevaban linternas y, de pronto, el círculo que habían formado mis seguidores quedó iluminado como el escenario de una representación teatral.

—Albert Foster, queda usted detenido —dijo Harris dirigiéndose a Donald. A Albert, a quién demonios fuera ese demente.

Donald levantó la cabeza y, por fin, pude ver su cara. Era un rostro corriente, el de cualquier hombre de cincuenta años que podrías cruzarte por la calle. Era, incluso, amable. ¿Por qué se empeñó en convertirse en el héroe siniestro de una causa irrealizable? ¿Qué le habría pasado para tomar un camino tan tortuoso? Mientras dos agentes le levantaban del suelo por los hombros después de esposarlo, me miró con los ojos enrojecidos. Sentí lástima, pero no caí en la tentación de compadecerle. Había estado a punto de matarme. Había estado a punto de matarle.

—Creo que deberías darme eso, muchacho —me dijo Harris. Al mirarle, me di cuenta de que aún llevaba mi pistola en la mano. Se la di como quien se da cuenta de que lleva en la mano algo molesto y desagradable—. Tendrás que acompañarnos, creo que tienes muchas cosas que contarnos.

—Claro, inspector —dije con la tranquilidad de quien no tiene nada que temer.

—Lo siento —me dijo Will antes de irse con Harris. Un agente le llevaba cogido del brazo. No se iba a librar de dar explicaciones.

—Lo sabías todo desde el principio —le reproché.

—Era mi padre, ¿qué podía hacer?

—Lo sabías todo.

—Lo siento, Joel.

El agente tiró de él y se lo llevó. Me di cuenta de que estaba esposado.

—Vamos —me insistió Harris. Kevin nos cerró el paso.

—Mi representado exige la presencia de un abogado —dijo—. Como se ha visto, ha sido víctima de una trampa...

—Tranquilo, Kevin —le interrumpí. Levanté mi mochila del suelo—. Por si acaso, lo he grabado todo.

Al llegar a la explanada, había dispuesto la mochila de tal manera que grabara imagen y audio de todo lo que ahí iba a pasar. No podía fiarme de las cámaras de seguridad, sus imágenes podían ser equívocas. Prefería tener mi versión de los hechos.

—Gracias, chicos. Os debo una —dije a mis amigos al pasar junto a ellos.

—Da las gracias a tus seguidores —afirmó Connor—. Son ellos los que han estado a tu lado cuando los has necesitado.

Me detuve un momento antes de cruzar la masa de gente que me rodeaba a pesar de que Harris tiraba de mí con urgencia. Les miré y sonreí.

—Gracias, amigos.

Mis seguidores empezaron a aplaudir y a ovacionarme.

—No la montes, Graham, no la montes —me advirtió Harris sacándome de ahí entre el gentío que me trataba de abrazar y animar.

—¡Nos vemos en mi canal! —grité.

—¡Siete millones de visitas! —exclamó Kevin con mi *tablet* en sus manos.

—Qué pocos... —respondí simulando decepción. Nos habíamos juntado en mi casa para celebrar mi regreso y todos teníamos ganas de fiesta.

—Vas un pelín *sobrao*, ¿no? —dijo Connor—. Que es tu regreso a YouTube. Puedes darte con un canto en los dientes.

—Os estoy tomando el pelo —dije eufórico—. ¡Siete millones, qué pasada!

Había hecho un vídeo especial para volver a mi canal, una superproducción en toda regla: un musical en tono de humor donde recreaba lo que me había pasado en las últimas semanas. Quería volver a lo grande, sin dar más vueltas a lo sucedido, ni dar explicaciones, ni caer en el victimismo. Quería ofrecer una mirada divertida, reírme un poco de mí mismo —en el montaje recreaba mis grandes momentos: las humillaciones y ridículos que había hecho gracias a Donald— y decirle al mundo que sí, que me habían machacado, pero que, al final, había salido de esta y que la vida continuaba. Con risas y buen humor.

—Y solo hace tres horas que lo has colgado —dijo Kevin—. Después de esto, voy a tener que subirte mi comisión.

—Ni lo sueñes —respondí.

Habían pasado casi dos semanas desde la detención de Donald y todo había vuelto a la normalidad. Kevin seguía trabajando para mí y volvíamos a tener grandes planes para el futuro de mi canal.

—¿Creéis que lo ha visto? —preguntó Silvestre.

—En la cárcel no hay internet —aclaró Flavia.

—Qué pena. Le hubiera encantado —apuntó Connor.

—El humor es la mejor manera de combatir a gente como esta —dijo Jan.

—Sí, pero el humor no para las balas —opinó Kevin. A pesar de tener la tranquilidad de saber que todo había pasado y de que Donald estaba encerrado, pensar que todo pudo haber acabado de manera trágica aún nos provocaba angustia.

—¿Y a Will, le habrá gustado? —preguntó Connor con retintín—. Porque ese sí que era un cachondo.

—Era su padre —dije.

—Y su cómplice —añadió Kevin—. No lo olvides.

—¿Qué hubierais hecho vosotros? —pregunté—. No quiero justificarle, pero tenía una papeleta importante.

—¡Donald estuvo a punto de matarte y él participó! —dijo Kevin incrédulo.

—Por eso me salvó. Es igual de culpable, pero, al final, encontró la manera de solucionarlo. Si no llega a ser por él, ahora no estaríamos aquí.

Y era verdad. Una verdad perversa: Will había ayudado a Donald a ir contra mí y, al mismo tiempo, me había ayudado a terminar con Donald. Había hecho las dos cosas, jugado en los dos bandos. Pero al final, la victoria había sido mía. Le compadecía. Ante una situación así, testigo de la locura de tu propio padre, ¿quién sabe lo que hay que hacer? Es tu padre, no es fácil ir contra él.

—Las cosas son como son, Joel —dijo Kevin—. No puedes ser comprensivo cuando han estado a punto de acabar contigo.

—Entender las razones de tus enemigos es lo que te hace ser más fuerte en la batalla —le expliqué.

—Ahora me vas a decir que compadeces a Donald también, ¿no? —soltó Connor incrédulo.

—No, ni de coña —aclaré—. Nada justifica lo que ha hecho.

Nada. Pero cuando Harris me explicó cómo había sucedido todo, entendí un poco más por qué Donald había sido tan cruel conmigo. Hacía unos meses que le habían despedido de su empresa y de pronto, con casi cincuenta años, se vio sin futuro y sin esperanzas. Mi llamada le despertó todo el odio y resentimiento que sentía por la sociedad que le estaba apartando como un trasto viejo. Me tomó como el representante de ese mundo que le quitaba de la circulación sin motivo. Acosarme, humillarme, hundirme, amenazarme, no tenía justificación. Entenderlo, al menos, me dejaba más tranquilo.

—Es como el de *Breaking Bad* —dijo Flavia. Como era habitual, todos la miramos arqueando las cejas, esperando a entender por dónde iban los tiros—. Pero con la informática en lugar de con la metanfetamina.

—¿Alguna aclaración, o lo dejamos aquí? —preguntó Connor desconcertado.

—Es verdad —dijo Jan al rescate de su novia—. Donald es un genio de la informática. Cuando se vio fuera de su empresa, usó todo lo que sabía para ir contra Joel.

—Ya —dije lacónico. Me imaginé a Donald moviéndose por los laberintos cibernéticos como pez en el agua.

—Un perverso —sentenció Kevin.

—¿Y Sousa? —preguntó Silvestre. No quería dejar ningún cabo suelto. Sabía que los thrillers siempre acababan dando respuesta a todas las preguntas y este, aunque fuera absolutamente real, no iba a ser menos.

—Era un compañero suyo en la empresa. También le echaron —respondí. Todos recordaron la noticia sobre su despido que les llevó hasta él—. Pero está fuera del caso, nadie puede demostrar que estuvo en esa oficina.

—Siempre tiene que salvarse alguien —afirmó Silvestre—. Para hacer la segunda parte.

Todos le miramos molestos. Era un chiste, pero no el que hacía falta en ese momento.

—Pero vamos, que las segundas partes siempre son peores que las primeras. —Seguimos mirándole con cara de reproche—. Y... Vale, la he cagado.

Todos sonreímos y bajamos la mirada para perdernos en nuestros pensamientos. La presencia de Donald en nuestras vidas nos había transformado. Nos había obligado a dar lo máximo y nos había puesto en riesgo, a cada uno de una manera. Y todo, por ayudarme a mí. Durante ese silencio, miré uno a uno a mis amigos. Lo habían dejado todo para ayudarme, sin ellos, nunca lo hubiera conseguido. Tener siete millones de visitas era importante, pero sentir que a tu alrededor tienes amigos de verdad, es mucho mejor.

—Tíos... —empecé a decir. Iba a darles las gracias, pero me di cuenta de que, si lo hacía, tal cual estaba, emocionado, se iban a reír de mí hasta el fin de mis días.

—Discursito a la vista —dijo Connor. Era obvio.

—¿Qué dices? —me defendí—. Solo quería deciros que tengo hambre. —En ese momento llamaron al timbre, momento que aproveché para levantarme y que no se me viera la cara de panoli que se me había puesto—. ¡Magia!

Me levanté y fui a abrir. Era Rick, cargado de bolsas de comida del restaurante de siempre.

—Me alegro de verte, míster —me dijo.

—Y yo. —Y le di un abrazo. Rick se quedó tenso, sin devolvérmelo, cosa, por otro lado lógica ya que tenía las manos ocupadas—. Pasa, pasa... Te quedas con nosotros, ¿no?

—¡Qué va! Tengo que volver enseguida. El nuevo encargado —habían despedido a Will— es un mal parido.

—Todo lo contrario que Will, ¿no? —dije con ironía.

—Will era un *hijoeputa*, que es otra cosa.

Entramos en el salón. Mis amigos recibieron la comida con una ovación.

—Os acordáis de Rick, ¿no? —le presenté.

—Claro, tío, siéntate —le invitó Connor—. Amigos, ¿no?

—Sí, míster.

Connor y Rick se dieron la mano. Mis amigos abrían las bolsas y sacaban las tarrinas.

—¡Eh! —dijo Silvestre mirando al interior de una bolsa—. Aquí hay algo.

Me miró con cara de pánico. No podía imaginarme a qué se refería. No quería hacerlo, más bien. Silvestre me acercó la bolsa abierta para que lo viera yo mismo, pero no me atrevía a cogerla.

—¿Qué es? —pregunté, pero Silvestre se limitó a sostener la bolsa delante de mí. Todos me miraban esperando mi reacción. No tuve más remedio que cogerla y mirar en su interior. Como imaginé, dentro había una nota—. ¿Sabes algo de esto? —pregunté a Rick.

—Ni zorra —respondió angustiado.

De pronto tuve la sensación de que todo volvía a ensombrecerse, que el mal no había desparecido. Que ya no iba a tener la forma de Donald, pero que iba a seguir ahí.

Saqué la nota.

—«¡Pringado!» —leí en voz alta.

Todos estallaron en una carcajada. A pesar de que la broma me había llegado al alma, no pude más que sumarme a las risas.

—Sois unos mal paridos, *hijoeputas* —sentenció Rick.

Y mis colegas. Para siempre.

Fin